# The
# Gospel of Matthew
# according to a
# Primitive Hebrew Text

# The
# Gospel of Matthew
# according to a
# Primitive Hebrew Text

by
## GEORGE HOWARD
*Professor of Religion*
*University of Georgia*

MERCER

PEETERS

ISBN  0-86554-250-3                     MUP/H215

The paper used in this publication meets
the minimum requirements of American National Standard
for Information Sciences—Permanence of Paper
for Printed Library Materials, ANSI Z39.48-1984.

*Library of Congress Cataloging-in-Publication Data*
Bible. N.T. Matthew. Hebrew. Ibn Shapruṭ. 1987.
  The Gospel of Matthew according to a primitive Hebrew Text.
  Hebrew text of Matthew, extracted from Shem Tov ben Yitsḥak Ibn Shap-
ruṭ's Even boḥan, presented with English translation and commentary.
  Includes bibliographical references.
  1. Bible. N.T. Matthew. Hebrew. Ibn Shapruṭ—Criticism, textual.
I. Howard, George, 1935–      .
II. Ibn Shapruṭ Shem Tov, fl. 1375–1380. Even boḥan.
III. Bible. N.T. Matthew. English. 1987. IV. Title.
BS2574.H4   1987     226'.2044        87-20348
ISBN 0-86554-250-3 (alk. paper)

# Contents

# To Tere
*my wife*

# Acknowledgments

I wish to acknowledge with appreciation the British Library of London for permission to print portions of its copy of the *Even Bohan,* catalogued Add no. 26964. This manuscript serves as the base text for Matthew 1:1– 23:22 in this volume. I also acknowledge with appreciation the Ivan F. and Seema Boesky Family Library, the Jewish Theological Seminary of America of New York City, for permission to print portions of its copy of the *Even Bohan,* catalogued Ms. 2426 (Marx 16). This manuscript serves as the base text for Matthew 23:23–end in this volume. Finally, I express with appreciation the financial grant from the office of the Vice President for Research at the University of Georgia that helped make this publication possible.

University of Georgia                                                      *George Howard*
29 July 1987

# Introduction

A complete Hebrew text of Matthew appeared in the body of a four-teenth-century Jewish polemical treatise entitled *Even Bohan* (אבן בוחן, "The Touchstone"). The author, Shem-Tob ben-Isaac ben-Shaprut (sometimes called Ibn Shaprut), was born in Tudela in Castile in the middle of the fourteenth century. He later settled in Tarazona in Aragon where as a physician he practiced medicine. There he completed the *Even Bohan* about 1380, although he revised it several times—in 1385, around 1400, and even later by adding another five to the original twelve books or sections.[1] Of the original books the first deals with the principles of the Jewish faith, the next nine deal with various passages in the Bible that were disputed by Jews and Christians, the eleventh discusses certain haggadic sections in the Talmud used by Christians or proselytes to Christianity, and the twelfth contains the entire Gospel of Matthew in Hebrew along with polemical comments by Shem-Tob interspersed throughout the text.

Part one of the present volume is a publication of the Hebrew text of Matthew as found in Shem-Tob's work. A critical apparatus noting manuscript variation accompanies the text, and an English translation appears on facing pages. The polemical comments of Shem-Tob have been eliminated so that the gospel text may run continuously from beginning to end without interruption.

Part two discusses the place of Shem-Tob's Hebrew Matthew within the Hebrew-Matthew tradition as a whole. In addition it gives a literary and textual profile of the Hebrew Matthew contained in the *Even Bohan*.

---

[1]For a discussion of these later additions see Alexander Marx, "The Polemical Manuscripts in the Library of the Jewish Theological Seminary of America," in *Studies in Jewish Bibliography and Related Subjects in Memory of Abraham Solomon Freidus (1867–1923)* (New York: The Alexander Kohut Memorial Foundation, 1929) 247-78, esp. 265-70; W. Horbury, "The Revision of Shem Tob Ibn Shaprut's *Eben Bohan*," *Sefarad* 43 (1983): 221-37.

## Witnesses Used in This Edition[2]

Ms. Add. no. 26964. British Library, London. (Serves as the printed text
    for 1:1–23:22.)
A   Ms. Heb. 28. Bibliotheek der Rijksuniversiteit, Leiden.
B   Ms. Mich. 119. Bodleian Library, Oxford.
C   Ms. Opp. Add. 4° 72.Bodleian Library, Oxford.
D   Ms. 2426 (Marx 16). Library of the Jewish Theological Seminary of
    America, New York. (Serves as the printed text for 23:23–end.)
E   Ms. 2279 (Marx 18). Library of the Jewish Theological Seminary of
    America, New York.
F   Ms. 2209 (Marx 19). Library of the Jewish Theological Seminary of
    America, New York.
G   Ms. 2234 (Marx 15). Library of the Jewish Theological Seminary of
    America, New York.
H   Ms. Mich. 137. Bodleian Library, Oxford.

All the manuscripts date between the fifteenth and seventeenth centuries
and are written in various types of rabbinic script. By far the best man-
script of the lot (ms C is an exception; see below) is from the British Library, catalogued Add. 26964. Although 26964 is incomplete, covering
Matthew 1:1–23:22, the excellent quality of the text demands that it be
printed. A second manuscript of good quality, from the library of the Jewish Theological Seminary of America catalogued as #2426 (noted as #16
by Marx in "The Polemical Manuscripts in the Library of the Jewish
Theological Seminary of America," 252), serves as the basic text for Matthew 23:23–28:20. In the apparatus up to 23:23 it is noted as ms D. Ms A
from Leiden is of fair quality, but has received considerable revision in regard to improvements in grammar. Moreover, its text has been greatly assimilated to the Greek and Latin. Ms B from the Bodleian Library is of
good quality, but because of the type of pen and ink used by the scribe, the
letters often run together and are difficult to distinguish. Ms C is an almost
exact replica of the British Library manuscript including breaking off at
23:22. It is written, however, in very small letters and is sometimes difficult to read. Mss E and F are almost identical and are of mediocre quality. Ms G is the poorest in quality of all the texts, written in a sloppy hand

---

[2]For a more complete list of manuscripts see Pinchas E. Lapide, "Der 'Prüfstein' aus
Spanien," *Sefarad* 34 (1974): 230.

by a scribe who omitted and added at will. Ms H is fragmentary and contains only 1:18b-19; 2:1, 13, 16-18; 3:16; 4:1; 5:27, 28, 31-34, 38-40, 43-44; 6:5, 19-20; 7:6, 24-28; 9:10-13, 32-38; 11:11-15, 25-28; 12:1, 15-18, 22-29, 31-32, 46-47; 13:53-57; 14:28; 15:1-6, 10b-11, 20b; 16:13-20; 17:1-3; 19:16-18; 21:1-2, 18-19, 23-27; 22:23-24, 29-33; 23:16-18; 24:20, 27-28, 34-35; 26:1, 26-27, 31, 36-37; 27:15; 28:18.

## Interrelationships among the Witnesses

The manuscripts divide themselves into three groups. Group I is made up of the British Library manuscript and C. With a few exceptions the two are virtually identical. Both are carefully copied and show a minimal tendency toward scribal error and assimilation to the Greek and Latin.

Group II consists of A B H. Although they possess individual differences they clearly belong to the same family. They are characterized by careful copying with few scribal errors. They also have a definite tendency for assimilation to the Greek and Latin. B is the best of the group showing less tendency for assimilation than A. H is only fragmentary (see above).

Group III is made up of D E F G. Mss E and F are virtually identical, with D and G often reading with them. The latter two also have many individual differences. The group is characterized by some scribal error and some assimilation to the Greek and Latin. They are, however, less assimilated to the Greek and Latin than group II. D is by far the best of its group and G by far the worst.

The following stemma illustrates the broad lines of the manuscript tradition.

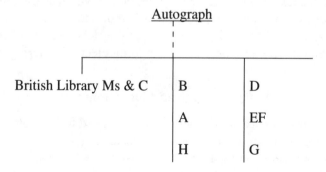

## Text and Apparatus

The present edition does not aim at producing an eclectic text. Until a more complete evaluation of the Shem-Tob Hebrew Matthew is available, plus an accumulation of more manuscripts, the printing of individual manuscripts will serve for a working text. The printed text preserves the British Library manuscript and D in their relevant sections along with their errors and inconsistencies in spelling and grammar. Periods and question marks have been added editorially to the printed Hebrew. In a few instances where the base text has a lacuna, the text of another manuscript is printed within parentheses (for example, 3:10a; 18:2b-5a).

Variants to the printed manuscripts are noted in a critical apparatus. Except for plenary and nonplenary vocalization and a few illegible scribblings the notation of all variants is complete. The limited number of manuscripts in the apparatus, of course, gives only a sampling of the kinds of variation that occur in the manuscript tradition as a whole.

## The Translation

The translation attempts to be faithful to the Hebrew without being slavishly literal. Occasionally its sense is unclear (15:5; 16:21; 17:3) because of the Hebrew. Proper names are usually given their common English spellings except where the pronunciation is clearly indicated by the Hebrew. Example: Petros 18:15 / Peter 19:27. In a number of instances a variant reading, noted in the critical apparatus, has been translated rather than the printed text. This occurs primarily when it appears necessary for the sense of the text. All such renderings are placed within parentheses. In many instances, however, the printed text is translated, in spite of difficulties, so as to preserve a disparity between the Hebrew and the Greek. In no sense is the translation a thoroughgoing electic rendering of the manuscript tradition.

## Abbreviations and Notations

( ) 1. Notes an occasional reading in the printed text supplied from another manuscript because of a lacuna.

2. Notes a variant reading in the translation where the variant is a substitution or an addition. Omissions such as in 9:18 and 10:8 are not so noted.

[ ] Notes an editorial addition in the translation.

# Part One

# Text and Translation

# The Hebrew Text

[MT 1:1-13

פרק ראשון

‏1‏אלה תולדות יש״ו בן דוד בן אברהם.

‏2‏אברהם הוליד את יצחק ויצחק הוליד את יעקב יעקב הוליד את יהודה ואחיו.

‏3‏יהודה הוליד את פרץ וזרח מתמר פרץ הוליד את חצרון חצרון הוליד את רם.

‏4‏ורם הוליד את עמינדב ועמינדב הוליד את נחשון ונחשון הוליד את שלמון.

‏5‏שלמון הוליד את בועז מרחב הזונה בועז הוליד את עובד מרות ועובד הוליד את ישי.

‏6‏ישי הוליד את דוד דוד הוליד את אשת שלמה מאשת אוריה.

‏7‏שלמה הוליד את רחבעם רחבעם הוליד את אביה אביה הוליד את אסא.

‏8‏אסא הוליד את יהושפט יהושפט הוליד את יורם יורם הוליד את עוזיה.

‏9‏עוזיה הוליד את חזקיה.

‏10‏חזקיה הוליד את מנשה מנשה הוליד את אמון אמון הוליד את יאשיה.

‏11‏יאשיה הוליד את יכניה ואחיו בגלות בבל.

‏12‏יכניה הוליד את שאלתיאל שאלתיאל הוליד את זרובבל.

‏13‏זרובב״ל הוליד את אביהוד ואביהוד הוליד את.

---

‏1:1‏ בן דוד] omit C

‏1:2‏ יהודה] יודא BEF | יצחק] ויצחק DEFG

‏1:3‏ חצרון] וחצרון EF | יהודה] יודא BDEFG

‏1:4‏ שלמון] omit A | נחשון] ונחשון ABDG | עמינדב] ועמינדב ABDG | רם] ורם ABDG

‏1:5‏ שלמון הוליד את] omit A | הזונה] omit ABDEFG | ועובד] עובד ABCDEFG

‏1:6‏ דוד] +1,2 המלך A | את אשת שלמה] את שלמה ABCDG | מאשת] מבת שבע אשת F

‏1:8‏ יהושפט] יושפט 1,2 B | יורם] ויורם EF | עוזיה] עוזיהו EF

‏1:9‏ את] +1 את הוליד אחז אחז את יותם יותם ADG

‏1:10‏ את] +1 יושיהו G | יאשיה] יאשיא A, ישיהו EF | את1] omit EF

‏1:11‏ יאשיה] יאשיא A, ישיהו EF | יכניה] יכניא A | בבל . . . ואחיו] omit EF

‏1:12‏ שאלתיאל1,2 A | יכניה] יכניא ADG | Beginning] + ואחר גלות בבל A שלתיאל

‏1:13‏ ואביהוד] את2 + ABDEFG אביהוד | אליקים הוליד את עזור + DG

# Translation

## Chapter 1

¹These are the generations of Jesus
the son of David the son of Abraham.
²Abraham begat Isaac and Isaac begat Jacob;
Jacob begat Judah and his brothers.
³Judah begat Perez and Zerah from Tamar;
Perez begat Hezron; Hezron begat Ram.
⁴Ram begat Amminadab; Amminadab begat Nahshon;
Nahshon begat Salmon.
⁵Salmon begat Boaz from Rahab the harlot;
Boaz begat Obed from Ruth and Obed begat Jesse.
⁶Jesse begat David; David begat (Solomon) from the wife of Uriah.
⁷Solomon begat Rehoboam; Rehoboam begat Abia; Abia begat Asa.
⁸Asa begat Jehoshaphat; Jehoshaphat begat Joram; Joram begat Uzziah.
⁹Uzziah begat (Jotham, Jotham begat Ahaz, Ahaz begat) Hezekiah.
¹⁰Hezekiah begat Manasseh; Manasseh begat Amon; Amon begat Josiah.
¹¹Josiah begat Jeconiah and his brothers in the Babylonian exile.
¹²(After the Babylonian exile) Jeconiah begat Shealtiel;
Shealtiel begat Zerubbabel.
¹³Zerubbabel begat Abihud; Abihud begat (Eliakim; Eliakim begat Azor.

¹⁴אקים ואקים הוליד את אליהוד.

¹⁵ואליהוד הוליד את אלעזר ואלעזר הוליד את מתן ומתן הוליד את יעקב.

¹⁶ויעקב הוליד את יוסף. הוא יוסף איש מר״ים הנקרא משיח ובלעז קריס״טוס.

¹⁷(וכל תולדות מאברהם עד דוד תולדות י״ד ומדוד עד גלות בבל תולדות י״ד ומגלות בבל עד יש״ו תולדות י״ד.

## פרק שני

¹⁸ולידת מיש״ו היה בזה האופן) ויהי כאשר היתה אמו ארוסה ליוסף קודם שידע אותה נמצאת מעוברת מרוח הקדש.

¹⁹ויוסף איש צדיק היה ולא רצה לישב עמה ולא לגלותה להביאה לבושה ולא לאוסרה למות אבל היה רוצה לכסות עליה.

²⁰ובחשבו בזה הדבר בלבו והנה מלאך נראה אליו בחלום ואמר יוסף בן דוד אל תירא לקחת אשתך מר״ים שמרוח הקדוש היא מעוברת.

²¹ותלד בן ותקרא שמו ישו״ע כי הוא יושיע את עמי מעונותם.

²²כל זה לגמור מת שנכתב מאת הנביא על פי ה׳.

²³הנה העלמה הרה ותלד בן וקראת שמו עמנואל שר״ל עמנו אלקים.

²⁴ויקץ יוסף משנתו ויעש ככל אשר צוה אותו מלאך ה״ ויקח את אשתו.

²⁵ולא ידע אותה עד שילדה בנה הבכור ויקרא את שמו ישו״ע.

## פרק שלישי

¹ויהי כאשר נולד יש״ו בבית לחם יהודה בימי הורודוס המלך והנה חוזים בכוכבים באים ממזרח לירושלם.

²לאמר איה מלך היהודים הנולד. ראינו סבבו במזרח ובמתנות חשובות באו להשתחוות לו.

---

1:14 at [את, omit E, ABDEFG | אקים [ואקים DG | עזור הוליד את צדיק צדוק הוליד את DG + [Beginning 1:14
עזור עזור + A (supralinear)

1:15 מתן ומתן ABDEFG | מתן [ומתן ABDEFG | אלעזר [ואלעזר ABDEFG | אליהוד [ואליהוד ABDEFG

1:16 קריסטוס [קריס״טוס DEFG | בלעז A, לעז [ובלעז ABCDEFG | אם ישו + [מרים ABDEFG | יעקב [ויעקב
E קרישטוש ABDFG, קרישטוס

1:17 Vs. 17 found only in mss DG

1:18 מאורסה [ארוסה G | ישו [מישו G | found only in mss DG . . . [ולידת A האופן

1:19 אישה [איש ABDEFGH | 2 1 AH [צדיק היה

1:20 הנה [והנה ABEFG | אליו [omit A | ואמר [לאמור BCDEFG

1:21 מעונותיו [מעונותם A | עמו [עמי A

1:22 השם [ה״ G ◦ | על פי הנביא [הנביא על פי ה״ AB | ה׳ G ◦

1:23 אלים [אלקים A

1:24 אלוהים [ה״ G ◦ F | המלאך [מלאך ה״ | יוסף [omit G

1:25 את [omit BDEFG

2:1 מאגוש [מאגוש A | והנה [והנה BDEFG + | יודא [יהודה BDEFG

2:2 כוכבו [D | כוכבו BCDFG, כוכב A, ככבים[סבבו G | אשר + [הנולד 2:2
A ובאנו במתנות חשובות [ובמתנות חשובות באו

[14]Azor begat Zadok; Zadok begat) Achim;
Achim begat Elihud.

[15]Elihud begat Eleazar; Eleazar begat Mattan; Mattan begat Jacob.

[16]Jacob begat Joseph. This Joseph was the husband of Mary (the mother of Jesus) . . . who is called the Messiah, that is, Christ.

[17](So all the generations from Abraham unto David were fourteen generations and from David unto the Babylonian exile were fourteen generations and from the Babylonian exile unto Jesus were fourteen generations.

[18]The birth of Jesus was in this way:) It came to pass when his mother was betrothed to Joseph, before he knew her, she was found pregnant by the Holy Spirit.

[19]Joseph was a righteous man and did not wish to dwell with her or to expose her by bringing her to shame or binding her over to death. He rather wished to conceal her.

[20]While he thought on this matter in his heart, behold an angel appeared unto him in a dream and said: Joseph son of David do not fear to take your wife Mary because she is pregnant by the Holy Spirit.

[21]She will bear a son and you will call his name Jesus because he will save my people from their sins.

[22]All this was to complete what was written by the prophet according to the Lord:

[23]Behold the young woman will conceive and bear a son and you will call his name Emmanuel, that is, God with us.

[24]Then Joseph awoke from his sleep, did according to all which the angel of the Lord commanded him and took his wife.

[25]But he did not know her until she bore her firstborn son and he called his name Jesus.

## Chapter 2

[1]It came to pass when Jesus was born in Bethlehem of Judah in the days of Herod the king, behold astrologers came from the East to Jerusalem
[2]saying: Where is the king of the Jews who has been born. We have seen (his star) in the East and (we) have come with important gifts to worship him.

[MT 2:3-14

³וישמע הורודוס המלך ויבהל וכל יושבי ירושלם עמו.

⁴ויקבוץ כל גדוליו ויבקש מהם אם היו יודעים באיזה מקום נולד המשיח.

⁵ויענו אליו בבית לחם יהודה ככתיב על פי הנביא

⁶ואתה בית לחם יהודה אפרתה ארץ יהודה הן אתה צעיר באלפי יהודה ממך לי יצא להיות מושל בישראל.

⁷אז קרא המלך הורודוס לקוסמים בסתר וישאל מהם היטב זמן ראית הכוכב להם.

⁸וישלחם לבית לחם ויאמר אליהם לכו ושאלו היטב בעד הילד ובמוצאכם אותו הגידו לי וגם אני אבא אליו להשתחוות.

⁹וישמעו אל המלך וילכו והנה הכוכב אשר ראו במזרח הולך לפניהם עד בואם אל המקום. וכאשר באו בית לחם עמד נגד המקום אשר שם הילד.

¹⁰ויהי כאשר ראו את הכוכב שמחו שמחה גדולה עד מאד.

¹¹ויביאו אל הבית וימצאהו ואת מר״ים אמו ויכרעו לפניו וישתחוו לו ויפתחו את אמתחותיהם ויביאו אליו מנחת זהב ולבונה ומור בלעז מי״רא.

¹²ויצוו בחלום לבלתי שוב אל הורודוס מהמלאך אמר להם ויפנו דרך ארצם בדרך אחרת.

## פרק רביעי

¹³המה הולכים והנה מלאך ה״ נראה אל יוסף קום וקח את הנער ואת אמו וברח למצרים ושם תעמוד עד אמרי אליך כי הורודוס יבקש את הנער להרוג.

¹⁴ויקח את הנער ואת אמו.

---

²:³ A וישמע [וישמע

²:⁴ B, גדלים וחכמים וסופרים A, גדולי החכמים הכהנים והסופרים [גדוליו | G omit [כל
F, גדוליהם החכמים והסופרים D, גדולי החכמים והסופרים E, גדוליהם החכמים
G החכמים והסופרים | נולד [ילד ABDEF, ישו ילד G

²:⁵ BCDEFG דכתיב A, דכתיב דכתב [ככתיב | BDEFG יודא [יהודה

²:⁶ D omit [להיות | ABDEFG אין [הן | BDEFG יודא [יהודה²,³ | DEFG(marg) יודא AB, omit [¹יהודה | EF omit

²:⁷ EF omit [המלך הורודוס | EF 1 2 [מהם היטב | A מהם הטיב D ראית [ראית | read נראה D [להם

²:⁸ A אלי [לי | F הילד [הנולד | A הטב [היטב | AF להם [אליהם | F יודא + [לבית לחם | G להשתחווות לו [אליו להשתחוות

²:⁹ F לו E, או אליו [אל המלך | B אליו [אליו | B לפניו [לפניו

²:¹¹ C ומיצוהו [לו | ABDEFG וימצאוהו [וימצאהו | BCG ויבואו [ויבאו | ADEF, ויבאו ויביא | EF omit [בלעז מירא | ABDG לעז [בלעז | EF לו

²:¹² ABDEFG מהמלאך לבילתי שוב אל הורודוס [לבלתי . . . להם | ABDEFG ויפנו דרך אחרת ללכת אל ארצם [ויפנו . . . אחרת

²:¹³ DG לפי שעתיד + [אליך | DGH לאמר + [יוסף | EF ליוסף [אל יוסף | DGH בחלום + [נראה | ABCDEF 1 2 3 להרוג את ישו הנער [את הנער להרוג | G להרוג להרוג

²:¹⁴ A, בלילה וילך למצרים D, בלילה וירד מצרימה + [אמו | G D(marg) ויקם + [Beginning | DG

³Herod the king heard and was dismayed
and all the inhabitants of Jerusalem with him.
⁴So he gathered all his nobles and inquired from them if they knew
where the Messiah would be born.
⁵They answered him: In Bethlehem Judah, as it is written according to
the prophet:
⁶You Bethlehem Judah, Ephrathah, land of Judah, behold you are insignificant among the clans of Judah; from you there shall come forth to
me one to be ruler in Israel.
⁷Then King Herod called the magicians in secret and asked them well
concerning the time the star (appeared) to them.
⁸He sent them to Bethlehem and said unto them: Go and inquire well
concerning the child and when you find him inform me. I also will go
to him to worship.
⁹They harkened unto the king and went and behold the star which they
saw in the East was going before them until they came to the place.
When they entered Bethlehem it stood before the place where the child
was.
¹⁰When they saw the star they rejoiced with exceedingly great joy.
¹¹They (came) into the house, found him and his mother Mary, knelt before him, worshiped him, opened their sacks, and brought to him gifts
of gold, frankincense, and myrrh, that is, mira.
¹²Then they were commanded in a dream by the angel who spoke to
them not to return to Herod; so they returned to their land by another
route.
¹³As they were going, behold the angel of the Lord appeared unto Joseph
(saying:) Arise, take the boy and his mother, flee to Egypt and stay
there until I tell you, because Herod will seek the boy to kill him.
¹⁴So he took the boy and his mother

[MT 2:15-3:4]

15וֵיהי שם עד מת הורוד״וס לגמור מה שנאמר על פי הנביא וממצרים קראתי לבני.

## פרק חמישי

16אז ראה הורודוס שראו אותו הקוסמים וירע אליו מאד ויתעצב אל לבו ויצו וישלח לכל שריו להרוג לכל הילדים אשר בבית לחם וגבוליה הנולדים מזמן אשר אמרו לו הקוסמים שנולד הנער.
17אז נשלם הדבר מה שאמר ירמיה הנביא
18קול ברמה נשמע נהי בכי תמרורים רחל מבכה על בניה וכו.
19ויהי כאשר מת הורוד״וס המלך ומלאך ה״ נראה בחלום אל יוסף במצרים.
20לאמר קוס קח את הנער ואת אמו ולך אל א״י כי מתו המבקשים את הנער להמית.
21ויקם ויקח את הנער ואת אמו וישובו אל א״י.
22וישמע כי הורקנוס שמו ארגי״לאס מלך ביהודה תחת הורודוס אביו. וירא ללכת שם ויזרזהו המלאך בחלום ויפן אל ארץ הגלגל.
23ויבא וישכון בעיר הנקראת נאזרית לקיים מה שאמר הנביא נאזרת יקרא.

## פרק ששי

1בימים ההם בא יוחנן המטביל דורש במדבר יהודה.
2ואמר חזרו בתשובה שמלכות שמים קרובה לבא.
3לקיים מה שנאמר ע״י ישעיהו הנביא קול קורא במדבר פנו דרך ה״ ישרו בערבה מסילה לאלקינו.
4והנה יוחנן היה לבוש מצמר הגמלים ועור שחור אזור במתניו ומזונו הארבה ודבש היערים.

---

2:15 ויהי [ וישב D | פי [ יד G
2:16 שראו [ שלעגו DGH | ויצו וישלח [ ADEFG 1 2 | ללכל [2 את כל D | G משני שנים ולמטה הנולדים +, DH משני שנים ולמטה כפי הזמן [מזמן
2:17 הנביא [ omit FH | מה [ omit ABDEFGH
2:18 נהי [ omit G | רחל . . . בניה [ omit F | בניה [ + מאנה להנחם על בניה כי איננו A
2:19 המלך [ omit ABDEFG
2:20 להרוג את הנער [את הנער להמית A, 3 2 1 BDG, 3 1 EF
2:21 לא״י [אל א״י ABDEFG
2:22 המלאך [ G ויאר [וירא BF, omit D | ביהודה [ביודא B בלעז A, לעז [שמו DG | ונשמע [וישמע B הגליל [הגלגל A לאמר [ + בחלום A | ומזורו מהמלאך +
2:23 נזרות A, נזארת [נאזרת A | כי [ + הנביא [ CDG נאזרת EF, נזראת B, נזרות A, נזארת [נאזרית B, נזראת EF
3:1 יודא [יהודה BCDEFG
3:3 ישרו [ omit G | לאלקינו . . . ישרו [ omit ABEFG | הנביא [ מא׳ [מה שנאמר ע״י A
3:4 הגמלים [ G צמר גמלים [מצמר הגמלים ABDG | מלבוש [לבוש EF | והיה יוחנן [והנה יוחנן היה +, ABDEF ואזור +, ABDEF על בשרו ואזור [ G

<sup>15</sup>and was there until Herod died, to fulfill what
  was spoken by the prophet: Out of Egypt I called my son.
<sup>16</sup>Then Herod saw that the magicians had (mocked) him and was very
  displeased. Being grieved at heart, he commanded that word be sent to
  all his princes to kill all the male children who were in Bethlehem and
  its borders who had been born from the time when the magicians spoke
  to him concerning the birth of the boy.
<sup>17</sup>Then was fulfilled that which Jeremiah the prophet spoke:
<sup>18</sup>A voice was heard in Rama, lamentation and bitter weeping, Rachel
  weeping for her children, etc.
<sup>19</sup>It came to pass when King Herod died the angel of the Lord appeared
  in a dream to Joseph in Egypt
<sup>20</sup>saying: Arise, take the boy and his mother and go to the land of Israel
  because those who were seeking the boy to kill him are dead.
<sup>21</sup>So he arose, took the boy and his mother, and they returned to the land
  of Israel.
<sup>22</sup>Then he heard that Horcanus, his name is Argelaus, reigned in Judah
  in the place of Herod his father, and he feared to go there. So the angel
  urged him in a dream that he should turn unto the land of Gilgal.
<sup>23</sup>He came and dwelt in a city called Nazarith in order to fulfill what the
  prophet said: He shall be called Nazareth.

## Chapter 3

<sup>1</sup>In those days came John the Baptizer preaching in the wilderness of Ju-
  dah.
<sup>2</sup>He said: Turn in repentance, for the kingdom of heaven is about to
  come,
<sup>3</sup>to fulfill what was said by Isaiah the prophet: A voice of one crying in
  the desert, prepare the way of the Lord, make straight in the wilderness
  a path for our God.
<sup>4</sup>Behold John was clothed with the hair of camels and black leather
  girded his loins and his food was locust and the honey of the forest.

⁵אז יצאו אליו מירושלם ומכל יהודה ומכל המלכות סביבות הירדן
⁶ואז מתודים חטאתם וטובלים בירדן על מאמרו.

## פרק שביעי

⁷וירא כי רבים מהפרושים בלעז פָארִיזֵיאַי ומן הפרושים באו
לטבילתו ויאמר להם לברוח מן הקצף לעתיד לבא מהאל.
⁸עשו פרי תשובה השלמה.
⁹ואל תאמרו בלבבכם אבינו אברהם. אמן אני אומר לכם שיוכל
אלקים להקים את בנו אברהם מן האבנים האלה.
¹⁰(וכבר הגיע הגרזן לשרש העץ אשר לא יעשה פרי טוב יכרת
ובאש ישרף. וישאלו לו החבורות א״כ מה נעשה. ויען להם יוחנן
מי שיש לו שתי כתנות יתן הא׳ למי שאין לו. ויבאו העם
להטביל.) וישאלוהו רבים מה נעשה ויען להם תצטערו לשום
איש ולא תענשום ותשמחו בחלקיכם. וכל העם היו חושבים
ומדמים בלבם נמול יוחנן הוא יש״ו.
¹¹וויוחנן ענה לכולם באמת הנני מטביל אתכם בימי תשובה ואחר יבא
חזק ממני שאיני ראוי להתיר שרוך נעלו. והוא יטביל אתכם באש
רוח הקדוש.
¹²אשר בידו מזרה לזרות את גרנו ויאסוף הדגן לאוצרו והתבן ע״כ.

## פרק שמיני

¹³אז בא יש״ו מהגליל את הירדן להטביל מיוחנן.
¹⁴ויוחנן היה מספק להטבילו ויאמר אני ראוי להטביל מידך ואתה
בא אלי.
¹⁵ויען יש״ו ויאמר לו הנח שכן אנו חייבים להשלים כל צדקה ואז
הטבילוהו.

---

³:⁵ FG מלכות A, הממלכות [המלכות | BDG יודא [יהודה | EF מיהודה ומירושלם [מירושלם ומכל יהודה
³:⁶ B פי + [על | G ומתדים [מתודים | omit ABDEFG [ואז
³:⁷ ABDEFG | הצדיקים [הפרושים | ADEFG פאריישאוש [פארִיזֵיאַי | ADEFG לעז [בלעז
DG, אלהם זרע תנינים מי למד לכם A, אלהם שרש פתנים מי הורה לכם [להם
G מן האל [מהאל | ABDEFG העתיד [לעתיד | EF אלהם שרש פתנים מידם
³:⁸ ABDEFG שלמה [השלמה | DG זאת + [עשו
³:⁹ BDEFG האלקים A, אלקים [אלקים
³:¹⁰ כרתי + [לא | DG ושרש [לשרש | וכבר . . . להטבל] omit Brit. Lib. ms & C, Text = ABDEFG
יוחנן + [להם | EFG רבינו [רבים | omit AB, רביני [רבים | omit A [העם | D פנונת [כתנות | B שני [שתי | A
ABDEFG | בחלקכם [בחלקיכם | G ותר + [תענשום | A תצערו [תצטערו | BDEFG יוחנן לא A, לא
ABDEFG אם באולי יוחנן הוא ישו [יוחנן . . . ישו | omit ABDEF [נמול
³:¹¹ ABCDEFG הוא [והוא | EF והוא | ABDG, + אתד | EF אחרי + [ביא | DEF במי [בימי | EF אמר [ענה
ABDEFG ישרוף באש אשר לא תכבה + [והתבן | D ביד [בידו
³:¹² ABDEFG
³:¹³ B אל [את
³:¹⁴ A על ידיך [מידך | EF להטבל [להטביל
³:¹⁵ BC יוחנן + ,ADEFG הטבילהו יוחנן [הטבילוהו | ABDEFG אליו [לו

⁵Then they came out to him from Jerusalem, from
all Judah and from all the kingdom round about the Jordan,
⁶and at that time were confessing their sin and were baptizing in the Jordan because of his word.
⁷He saw that many of the Pharisees, that is, Pharizei, and (Sadducees)
came to his baptism and he said to them: (Offspring of serpents who
taught you) to flee from the wrath to come from God.
⁸Produce the fruit of repentance.
⁹Do not say in your heart: Abraham is our father. Truly I say to you that
God is able to raise up his son Abraham from these stones.
¹⁰(Already the axe has reached the root of the tree; he who does not produce good fruit will be cut down and burned in the fire. The crowds
asked him: if so what shall we do. John answered them: He who has
two shirts let him give one to him who has none. So they came to be
baptized.) Many asked him: What shall we do. And he answered them:
Be anxious for (no) man and do not chastise them, and be pleased with
your lot. And all the people were thinking and reckoning in their circumcised heart: John is Jesus.
¹¹John answered all of them: Behold I truly baptize you in the days of repentance, but another comes (after me) mightier than I, the thong of
whose sandal I am not worthy to unfasten. He will baptize you with the
fire of the Holy Spirit.
¹²His winnowing fork is in his hand to fan his threshing floor and he will
gather the grain into his granary and the straw (he will burn with fire
which is not quenched).
¹³Then came Jesus from Galilee (to) the Jordan to be baptized by John.
¹⁴But John was doubtful about baptizing him and said: I should be baptized by you, and you come to me.
¹⁵Jesus answered and said to him: Permit it, because we are obliged to
fulfill all righteousness; then (John baptized him).

<sup>16</sup>ומיד שעלה מן המים נפתחו לו השמים וירא רוח אלקים יורדת
כיונה ושרתה עליו.

<sup>17</sup>והנה קול מן השמים אומר זה בני אהובי מאד מאד נאהב וחפצי בו.

## פרק תשיעי

<sup>1</sup>אז לוקח יש״ו ברוח הקדוש למדבר להתנסות מהשטן.

<sup>2</sup>ויצום מ״ יום וארבעים לילה ואח״כ נרעב.

<sup>3</sup>מקרב המנסה ואמר לו אם בן אלקים אתה אמור שהאבנים האלה
ישובו לחם.

<sup>4</sup>ויען יש״ו ויאמר לו כתוב כי לא על הלחם לבדו וגו׳.

<sup>5</sup>אז לקח אותו השטן בעיר הקדוש ויעמידהו על מקום היותר גבוה
שבכל המקדש

<sup>6</sup>ואמר אליו אם אלקים אתה דלג למטה וכ׳ כי מלאכיו יצוה לך
לשמרך בכל דרכיך וגו.

<sup>7</sup>ויען אליו יש״ו שנית לא תנסה את ה׳ אלקיך.

<sup>8</sup>וישא אותו השטן בהר גבוה מאד ויראהו כל ממלכות הארץ וכבודם

<sup>9</sup>ויאמר לו כל אלה אתן לך אם תפרע אלי.

<sup>10</sup>אז ענה לו יש״ו לך השטן בלעז שָׁאטָאנָאס שכן כתיב את ה״
אתפלל ואותו לבדו תעבוד.

<sup>11</sup>אז עזב אותו השטן והנה מלאכים קרבו אליו וישרפוהו.

## פרק עשירי

<sup>12</sup>ויהי בימים ההם וישמע יש״ו כי נמסר יוחנן במאסר וילך אל
הגלגל.

<sup>13</sup>ויעבור את נאזראל וישכון בכפר נחום ראיתה לעז מַארִיטְמָה בקצה
ארץ זבולון

<sup>3:16</sup>A אלים [אלקים | G דמות + [ויאר | G מהשמים [מן השמים | EF עלה [שעלה
<sup>3:17</sup>G מאהב [נאהב | ABDEFG מהשמים [מן השמים
<sup>4:1</sup>B הקדוש [הקדוש
<sup>4:3</sup>A האלו [האלה | G אלוה ,A אלהים [אלקים | omit DEF לו | ABDEFG ויקרב [מקרב
ABEFG, יחיה האדם + [לבדו | ABCDEF הוא + [כתוב | omit G לו כתוב | A לך [לו<sup>4:4</sup>
D יחיה האדם כי על כל מוצא פי ה
<sup>4:5</sup>G שבבית [שבבל
<sup>4:6</sup>אליו] לו EF אלקים] אלים בן אלוה ABDEF, בן אלוה G [וכ׳ | דרכיך . . . [לשמרך ABDEFG
BDEF על כפים ישאונך וכו׳ A על כפים ישאונך פן תיגף באבן רגליך + [דבריך omit G
<sup>4:7</sup>A אלהיך [אלקיך BEF שם + [את | BDEFG ג״כ כתיב + ,A כן כתיב + [שנית | G ויאמר [ויען
<sup>4:8</sup>את + G [ויראהו
<sup>4:9</sup>BDEFG תכרע A, תכרע ותשתחוו [תפרע
<sup>4:10</sup>ADEFG התפלל [אתפלל | שאטאנאס AC, שאטאנש B, שטאנש DFG [בלעז | לעז ADEFG שאטאנאש
<sup>4:11</sup>ABCDEFG וישרתוהו [וישרפוהו
<sup>4:12</sup>B הגליל [אל הגלגל | omit A, המלך F [במאסר
<sup>4:13</sup>G | נאזרתאל F, בנזארת C, בנזארת F, נאזראל BD, נאזראל A, נזראל [נאזראל omit F [את
BG, omit D | בלעז [לעז FG, רמתה D, מתה C, מרתה B, ראתה A, ברמתה A, ראיתה [ראיתה A ויבא וישכן [וישכון
G ראמטה מראאטאנה F מרטימה C, מארטמה B, מאראטימה AD, מרא טימא [מאריטמה

¹⁶Immediately when he came up from the water
the heavens were opened to him and he saw the Spirit of God coming
down like a dove and it dwelt upon him.
¹⁷Then behold a voice from heaven was saying: This is my son, my beloved, he is loved very very much and my pleasure is in him.

## Chapter 4

¹Then Jesus was taken by the Holy Spirit into the wilderness to be
tempted by Satan.
²He fasted forty days and forty nights and afterwards was hungry.
³The tempter drew near and said to him: if you are the Son of God say
that these stones should turn into bread.
⁴Jesus answered and said to him: It is written: not by bread alone, etc.
⁵Then Satan took him to the holy city, placed him on the highest point
in all the temple
⁶and said to him: If you are God, jump down, for it is written: he has
commanded his angels in regard to you to keep you in all your ways,
etc.
⁷Jesus answered him again: You shall not tempt the Lord your God.
⁸ So Satan took him to an exceedingly high mountain, showed him all
the kingdoms of the earth and their glory
⁹ and said to him: All these things I will give to you if you bare your
head to me.
¹⁰Then Jesus answered him: Go Satan, that is, Satanas, for it is written: I
will pray to the Lord and him only you will serve.
¹¹Then Satan left him and behold angels drew near to him and (ministered) to him.
¹²It came to pass in those days Jesus heard that John had been delivered
up into prison, so he went into Gilgal.
¹³He passed by Nazeral and dwelt in Capernaum-Raithah, that is, Mari-
tima, on the outskirts of the Land of Zebulun,

14לקיים מה שאמר ישעיהו הנביא

15ארצה זבולון וארצה נפתלי דרך הים עבר את הירדן גליל הגוים.

16העם ההולכים בחושך ראו אור גדול יושבי בארץ צלמות אור נגה עליהם.

## פרק י"א

17מכאן ואילך התחיל יש"ו לדרוש ולדבר חזרו בתשובה שמלכות שמים קרובה.

18וילך יש"ו על שפת הים הגליל וירא שני אחים שמעון שיקרא סימ"ון ונקרא פֵּייטְ"רוֹס וְאַנְדִירְ"יאָה אחיו משליכים מכמרותיהם בים שהיו דייגים.

19ויאמר להם לכו אחרי ואעשה אתכם מדייגים אנשים.

20ויעזבו מכמרותיהם באותה שעה וילכו אחריו.

21ויט משם וירא שני אחים אחרים יעקב ויוחנן אחים בני זבדיאל בלעז זָבָאדְ"אוֹ וְזָאבְ"אדָה ואביהם באניה מכינים מכמרותיהם ויקרא אותם.

22וימהרו ויניחו מכמרותיהם ואת אביהם וילכו אחריו.

## פרק י"ב

23ויסב יש"ו אל ארץ הגליל ללמד קהלותם ומבשר להם זבד טוב לעז מַאוְונְגַ"יֵילְייוֹ ממלכות שמים ומרפא כל חולים וכל מדוה בעם.

24וילך שמועתו בכל ארץ סור"יא וישאו אליו כל החולים מכל מיני חלאים משונים אחוזים השדים והנבעתים מרוח רעה והמתרעשים וירפא אותם.

25וילכו אחריו רבות מַקפ"ולי והג"ליל מירו"שלם ויוד"א ועבר היר"דן.

---

את] omit AEF4:15

שימון A, omit ]סימון CDEFG | שנקרא B, הנקרא ]שיקרא omit A, הים] ADEFG | BG
מכמרותיהם] BCDEFG ואנדריאה A, ואנדריאש ]ואנדיריאה BDEFG פיטרוש A, פאטרוש ]פייטרום
מכמרותיהם BDG

מאנשים AG, שמונים ]אנשים | מהאנשים ADEFG דייגים ]מדייגים | A אלהם ]להם4:19 BDEF

וזאבאדה EF זבאדו BC, זבדאו A, זבדאו ]זבאדאו DG לעז או ACEF, לעז ]בלעז omit G ]בני4:21
עמהם + ]באניה EF אביה B, וזבדיא C רזבדיא ]ואביהם ABDG, אביהה עמהם ABDG, וזבדיאל ADEFG, ובדאל
ABDG

וינחוהו וינחוהו וינוהו + ]וימהרו4:22 G

לעז ]לעז AB, omit EF דבר ]להם זבד | omit DG להם] AB קהלותם ]קהלותם DG על A, כל ]אל4:23
חולי AEF, חלי ]חולים F | אואנגיליזאר DEG אוונגיליזאר A אואנגילונטאר ]מאוונגיילייו BG בלעז
BDG

וירפאו B, ]וירפא | מכל ]וכל4:24

מירושלם G | הגליל A, ומהגליל ]והגליל | A מקאפולי A מקאפולי ]מקפולי ABCDEFG חרבות ]אחריו +4:25
A ומעבר ]ועבר | EFG ויהודה A, ויהודה ]ויוד"א | וירדא G ומיהודה AB וירושלם ומירושלם

[14]in order to fulfill that which Isaiah the Prophet said:

[15]Land of Zebulun and land of Naphtali, the way of the Sea, beyond the Jordan, Galilee of the gentiles.

[16]The people who walked in darkness have seen a great light; those who sat in the land of deep darkness a light has shined upon them.

[17]Henceforth Jesus began to preach and to say: Repent for the kingdom of heaven is near.

[18]Jesus went along the shore of the sea of Galilee and saw two brothers, Shimon, who is called Simon, also called Petros, and Andrea his brother casting their nets into the sea because they were fishermen.

[19]He said to them come after me and I will make you fish for men.

[20]So they left their nets in that hour and went after him.

[21]He turned from there and saw two other brothers, James and John, brothers who were sons of Zebedeel, that is, Zabadao and Zabadah, and their father in a boat setting up their nets and he called them.

[22]They hastened and left their nets and their father and followed after him.

[23]Then Jesus went around the land of Galilee teaching their assemblies and was preaching to them the good gift, that is, mavangeleo, of the kingdom of heaven and was healing all the sick and every disease among the people.

[24]So a report about him went into all the land Syria and they brought unto him those who were sick from various kinds of diseases, those possessed by demons, those who were terrified by an evil spirit and those who shook, and he healed them.

[25]Many followed him from Kapoli and Galilee, from Jerusalem, Juda, and across the Jordan.

## פרק י״ג

‏¹ויהי אחרי זה בעת ההיא וירא החבורות ויעל ההר וישב. ויקריבו לו תלמידיו

‏²ויפתח פיו וידבר אליהם לאמר.

‏³(אשרי שפלי רוח שלהם מלכות שמים.)

‏⁴אשרי החוכים שינוחמו.

‏⁵(אשרי הענוים שהם ירשו ארץ.)

‏⁸אשרי זכי הלב והמה יראו אלקים.

‏⁹אשרי רודפי שלום שבני אלקים יקראו.

‏¹⁰אשרי הנרדפים לצדק שלהם מלכות שמים.

‏¹¹אשריכם כאשר ירדפו ויגדפו אתכם ויאמרו אליכם כל רע בעדי ויכזבו.

‏¹²שישו ושמחו ששכרכם רב מאד בשמים שכן רדפו הנביאים

## פרק י״ד.

‏¹³בעת ההיא אמר יש״ו לתלמידיו מלח אתם בעולם אם המלח יבטל טעמו במה יומלח ואינו שוה כלום אלא שיושלך בחוץ להיות מרמס רגלים.

‏¹⁴מאור אתם בעולם. עיר בנויה על ההר לא תוכל להסתר.

‏¹⁵לא ידליקו נר להשים אותו במקום נסתר שלא תאיר רק משימים אותו על המנורה להאיר לכל בני הבית.

‏¹⁶כן יאיר מאורכם לפני כל אדם להראותם מעשיכם הטובים המשובחות ומכבדות לאביכם שבשמים.

‏¹⁷בעת ההיא אמר יש״ו לתלמידיו אל תחשבו שבאתי להפר תורה אלא להשלים.

‏¹⁸באמת אני אומר לכם כי עד שמים וארץ אות אחת ונקודה אחת לא תבטל מהתורה או מהנביאים שהכל יתקיים.

---

⁵:¹ ABDEFG ויקרבו [ויקריבו

⁵:² omit EF [לאמר

⁵:³ Whole vs] omit Brit. Lib. ms BCDEFG; text = A

⁵:⁴ vs 4] omit G; placed after vs 5 A | הברכים [החוכים A

⁵:⁵ vs 5] omit Brit. Lib. ms BCDEFG; text = A

⁵:⁶ vs 6] omit all mss

⁵:⁷ vs 7] omit all mss

⁵:⁸ vs 8] omit G | אלים [אלקים A

⁵:⁹ אלים [אלקים A | השלום [שלום G

⁵:¹² שלפנכם + [הנביאים | omit EFG | רב [רב G | ששכר בחרב EF, ששכרכם [ששכרכם G | כי שכרכם EF, ושאחו [ושמחו A

⁵:¹³ לרגלים [רגלים ABDEF; omit G | לחוץ [בחוץ A | שיושלח [שיושלך AEF | יולחו [יומלח A

⁵:¹⁵ כל [לכל B | לשים [להשים DEFG

⁵:¹⁷ והנביאים לא באתי להפר + A | התורה או הנביאים לא באתי להפר [תורה | omit EF [שבאתי D

⁵:¹⁸ מהתורה [מהתורה A | תתבטל [תבטל A | יוד [אות BCDEFG שממושו [שמושו A; + עוד שימושו [עד | omit D [כי

A הנביאים [מהנביאים B | ומן הנביאים [או מהנביאים B | מן התורה

## **Chapter 5**

¹ It came to pass after this when he saw the crowds that he went upon the mountain and sat down. Then his disciples (came to) him

² and he opened his mouth and spoke to them saying:

³ (Blessed are the humble of spirit for theirs is the kingdom of heaven.)

⁴ Blessed are those who wait for they shall be comforted.

⁵ (Blessed are the meek for they shall inherit the earth.)

⁸ Blessed are the innocent of heart for they shall see God.

⁹ Blessed are those who pursue peace for they shall be called sons of God.

¹⁰Blessed are those who are persecuted for righteousness for theirs is the kingdom of heaven.

¹¹Blessed are you when they persecute and revile you and say against you all kinds of evil for my sake, but speak falsely.

¹²Rejoice and be glad for your reward is very great in heaven for thus they persecuted the prophets.

¹³At that time Jesus said to his disciples: You are salt in the world. If the salt is neutralized in regard to its taste with what will it be salted? It is fit for nothing but to be cast outside to be trampled under foot.

¹⁴You are light in the world. A city built upon a hill cannot be hidden.

¹⁵They do not light a lamp to place it in a hidden place where it cannot shine; but they place it upon a lampstand so that it might shine for all in the house.

¹⁶Thus let your light shine before every man to show them your good deeds which are praised and glorified before your father who is in heaven.

¹⁷At that time Jesus said to his disciples: Do not think that I came to annul the Torah, but to fulfill it.

¹⁸Truly I say to you that until heaven and earth (depart) not one letter or dot shall be abolished from the Torah or the Prophets, because all will be fulfilled.

[MT 5:19-30

<sup>19</sup>ואשר יעבור מאמר א″ מהמצוות אלו אשר אלמד אחרים בן הבל יקרא מלכות שמים והמקיים והמלמד גדול יקרא במלכות שמים.

## פרק ט″ו

<sup>20</sup>בעת ההיא אמר יש″ו לתלמידיו באמת אני אומר לכם אם לא תגדל צדקתכם יותר מהפרושים והחכמים לא תבואו במלכות שמים.

<sup>21</sup>הלא שמעתם מה שנאמר לקדמונים לא תרצח ואשר ירצח חייב הוא משפט מות.

<sup>22</sup>ואני אומר לכם שהמכעיס לחבירו חייב הוא למשפט ואשר יקרא לאחיו פחות יחייב במשפט בהקהל ואשר יקראוהו שוטה חייב לאש גהינם.

<sup>23</sup>ואם תקריב קרבנך למזבח ותזכיר שהיה לך עם חברך דין והוא מתרעם ממך מאיזה דבר

<sup>24</sup>הנח קרבניך שם לפני המזבח ולך לרצותו קודם ואחר כך הקרב קרבניך.

## פרק ט″ז

<sup>25</sup>אז אמר יש″ו לתלמידיו ראה שתמהר לרצות שונאך בלכתך עמו בדרך פן ימסור אותך לשופט וזה השופט ימסורך לעבד לתת אותך לבית הסוהר.

<sup>26</sup>באמת אני אומר לך לא תצא משם עד תנתן פרוטה אחרונה.

## פרק יז

<sup>27</sup>עוד אמר להם שמעתם מה שנאמר לקדמונים לא תנאף.

<sup>28</sup>ואני אומר לכם שכל הרואה אשה ויחמוד אותה כבר נאף עמה בלבה.

<sup>29</sup>ואם יסיתך עיניך הימין נקר אותה ותשליכה ממך.

<sup>30</sup>וכן אם יסיתך ידך חתוך אותה. טוב לך שתפסיד אחד מאבריך מכל גופך בגהינם.

---

D כן קטן ]בן הבל | ABDEFG וילמד ]אשר אלמד | ABCDEFG ממצוות ]מהמצוות | A קטן + ]וא[ 5:19
]במלכות | ABDEFG במלכות ]מלכות |

למשפט ]במשפט | BEF חייב הוא ADG חייב ]יחייב | A במשפט ]למשפט | EF את חברו ]לחבירו 5:22
ABEF | ABCEFG יקראהו

EF הקרבת ]הקרב | omit ABDEFG ]כך | A 2 1 ]לרצותו קודם | ABDEFG קרבנך ]קרבניך[1.2] 5:24
5:23 ABDEFG 2 1 3 ]עם חברך דין | ABDEFG ותזכיר ]ותזכיר

A לשונאך ]שונאך | B ויאות ADEFG יאות ]ראה 5:25
G האחרונה ]אחרונה | EF שתנן ABDG, תתן ]תנתן 5:26

omit D ]לקדמונים 5:27
BDEFGH בלבו ]בלבה | ABDEFG לאשה ]אשה | EF אני ]ואני 5:28
B ותשליכו A, וישליכהו ]ותשליכה | AB אותו ]אותה | AD עינך ]עיניך | EF הסיתך ]יסיתך 5:29
C כל ABDEFG, כל ]מכל | CEF מאיברך B, מאיברך ]מאבריך | ABDEFG משיאבד כל ]שתפסיד 5:30

[19]He who shall transgress one word of these commandments
(and shall teach) others, shall be called a vain person (in the) kingdom
of heaven; but whoever upholds and teaches [them] shall be called
great in the kingdom of heaven.

[20]At that time Jesus said to his disciples: Truly I say to you if your righteousness is not greater than the Pharisees and the sages you shall not
enter into the kingdom of heaven.

[21]Have you not heard what was said to those of old: you shall not murder
and whoever murders is guilty of a judgment of death.

[22]But I say to you, he who angers his companion is guilty of judgment;
he who calls his brother inferior shall be guilty of judgment before the
congregation; (he) who calls him a fool is guilty of the fire of Gehenna.

[23]If you should offer your gift at the altar and remember that you have a
quarrel with your companion and he is complaining about you because
of this matter,

[24]leave your gifts there before the altar and go to appease him first and
afterwards offer your gifts.

[25]Then Jesus said to his disciples: See that you hasten to appease your
enemy while you are walking with him in the way lest he deliver you
to the judge and this judge delivers you to the servant to put you into
the prison.

[26]Truly I say to you, you will not come out from there until the last piece
of money is given.

[27]Again he said to them: You have heard what was said to those of long
ago, you shall not commit adultery.

[28]But I say to you that everyone who sees a woman and covets her has
already committed adultery with her in (his) heart.

[29]If your right (eye) seduces you put it out and cast it from you.

[30]Also if your hand thus seduces you cut it off. It is better for you to suffer the loss of one of your limbs than all your body in Gehenna.

## פרק י״ח

31עוד אמר יש״ו לתלמידיו שמעתם מה שנאמר לקדמונים שכל העוזב אשתו ושלח לתת לה גט כריתות ובלעז ליבֵי״ל רִיפּוּדְיּוֹ.
32ואני אומר לכם שכל העוזב אשתו יש לו לתת לה גט כריתות כי אם על דבר נאוף הוא הנואף והלוקח אותה ינאף.

## פרק י״ט

33עוד שמעתם מה שנאמר לקדמונים לא תשבעו בשמי לשקר ותשיב לה״/ שבועתך.
34ואני אומר לכם לבלתי השבע בשום עניין לשוא לא בשמים שכסא אלקים היא.
35ולא בארץ שהדום רגליו הוא לא בשמים שעיר אלקים היא.
36ולא בראשך שלא תוכל לעשות שער א״/ לבן או שחור.
37אבל יהיו דבריכם הן הן וגם לא לא. כל הנוסף על זה הוא רע.
38ועוד שמעתם מה שנאמר בתורה עין תחת עין שן תחת שן.
39ואני אומר לכם לבלתי שלם רע תחת רע אבל המכה בלחיך הימין הכן לו השמאל.
40ואשר ירצה לחלוק עמך במשפט ולגזול כתניך עזוב אליו מעילך.
41ואשר ישאל אותך לילך עמו אלף פסיעות לך עמו אלפיים.
42השואל ממך תן לו והרוצה ללות ממך אל תמנע.

## פרק כ׳

43עוד אמר יש״ו לתלמידיו שמעתם מה שנאמר לקדמונים ואהבת לאוהבך ותשנא לשונאך.
44ואני אומר לכם אהבו אויביכם ועשו טובה לשונאכם ומכעיסכם והתפללו בשביל רודפיכם ולוחציכם

---

5:31 לה] omit A | לקדמונים] לקדמים DEFG | ושלח] ישלח CDG | לתת] omit DG | יש לו AEFH, שלח ושלח DEFG | לקדמונים] BE | ובלעז] לעז ADG, בלעז] כריתות] vs 31 vs 32 (hap) F | . . . vs 31 ]כריתות vs 32 vs 31 E ריפודאויו A, די ריפוג׳ ]ריפודיייו | ריפודיו׳] omit H ]ובלעז . . . ריפודייו

5:32 כריתות . . . ]יש] omit A | אם] omit כל ]שכל GH | כריתות . . . ]ואני] omit F (hap. see vs 31) | DGH

5:33 עוד] אמר B ולא ]ולא EF | שבועתך] שבועתכם EF

5:34 אלקים] אלים A, אלהים G | היא] היא ABDEFGH הם ]אלקים

5:35 אלהים ]אלקים ABEFG | בשמים] בירושלם ABEFG | היא] היא BDEFG | הוא] הוא BD לא ]שהדום A | בשמים] . . . הוא A | omit (hap) D

5:36 ולא] לא ABEFG; omit (hap. see vs 35) D | שלא] כי לא G

5:37 Beginning] + היא אלקים שעיר בירושלים לא ]דבריכם A ADEF, omit BG או ]וגם D הזה ]זה BEF לאו לאו ]או לא לא D

5:38 ועוד] עוד H שן תחת ]omit (hap) EF

5:39 הכן] תן G רע תחת ]רע ABDEFGH | המכה] למכה D

5:40 אותה B, לו ]אליו | כתנתך CDGH, כתנך B, כתנך A, כותנך] אם C ]ואשר | ואם H

5:41 ישאל] יאנוס ABDEFG | לילך] ללכת ABDG

5:44 לשונאכם] טוב A טובה ]ועשו . . . omit BDEFG | ולוחצכם ]לאויביכם A לאויבכם ]אויביכם B אני ]ואני A ולוחצכם ]ולוחציכם A רודפכם ]רודפיכם A בעד ]בשביל H לשונאיכם

[31]Again Jesus said to his disciples:

You have heard what was said to those of long ago that everyone who leaves his wife and divorces [her] is to give her a bill of divorce, that is, libela repudio.

[32]And I say to you that everyone who leaves his wife is to give her a bill of divorce. But concerning adultery he is the one who commits adultery and he who takes her commits adultery.

[33]Again you have heard what was said to those of long ago: You shall not swear by my name falsely, but you shall return to the Lord your oath.

[34]But I say to you not to swear in vain in any matter, neither by heaven because it is the throne of God,

[35]nor by earth because it is the footstool of his feet, nor by (Jerusalem) because it is the city of God,

[36]nor by your head for you are not able to make one hair white or black.

[37]But let your words be yes yes or no no. Everything in addition to this is evil.

[38]Again you have heard what is said in the Torah: an eye for an eye, a tooth for a tooth.

[39]But I say to you, do not repay evil for evil; but he who smites your right cheek provide for him the left.

[40]He who wishes to oppose you in judgment and to rob your shirt, leave to him your garment.

[41]He who asks you to go with him a thousand steps, go with him two thousand.

[42]To him who asks from you give and from him who wishes to borrow from you do not hold back.

[43]Again Jesus said to his disciples: You have heard what was said to those of long ago that you shall love the one who loves you and hate the one who hates you.

[44]But I say to you, love your enemies and do good to the one who hates you and vexes you and pray for those who persecute you and oppress you,

[MT 5:45-6:8

⁴⁵למען תהיו בני אביכם שבשמים שמזריח שמשו על טובים ורעים
וממטיר על רשעים וצדיקים.
⁴⁶אם תאהבו אוהביכם איזה שכר לכם?
הלא עזי פנים אוהבים אוהביהם?
⁴⁸היו אתם תמימים כאשר תם אביכם.
¹השמרו פן תעשו צדקתכם לפני האדם להלל אתכם ואם תעשו
לא יהיה לכם שכר מאת אביכם שבשמים.

## פרק כ"א

²עוד אמר להם יש"ו כאשר תעשו צדקה לא תרצו להעביר כרוז
וחצוצרות לפניכם כמו החנפים בלעז איפוקְרָאטֶיס
שעושים צדקתם ברחובות ובשווקים בעד שיראו אותם בני
אדם. אמן אני אומר לכם שכבר קבלו שכרם.
³ואתם כאשר תעשה צדקה אל ידע שמאלך מה יעשה ימינך
⁴להיות מתנך בסתר ואביך הרואה הנסתרות ישלם לך.

## פרק כ"ב

⁵בעת ההיא אמר יש"ו לתלמידיו בשעה שתתפללו אל תרימו קול
ואל תהיו כחנפים העצבים האוהבים להתפלל בבתי כנסיות
ובמקצוע חצרות ומתפללים בגבוהות שישמעו וישבחו בני אדם.
אמן אני אומר לכם שכבר קבלו שכרם.
⁶ואתה בהתפללך בא למשכבך וסגור דלתיך בעדך והתפלל לאביך
בסתר ואביך הרואה בסתר ישלם לך.
⁷ואתם כאשר תתפללו אל תרבו דברים כמו שהמינים חושבים
שברוב דברים ישמעום.
⁸ואתם אל תראו שאביכם שבשמים יודע דבריכם קודם שתשאלו ממנו?

---

5:45 Beginning] + למען תהיו בני אביכם שבשמים ועשו טוב
| BDEFG (Dit) לשונאיכם ומכעיסכם והתפללו בשביל רודפיכם ולוחציכם
A הממטיר [וממטיר | G הרעים ועל הטובים [טובים ורעים
5:46 A אוהבהם [אוהביהם | G את | + [אוהבים | A יהיה | + [שכר | AC אוהבכם [אוהביכם
5:47 vs 47] omit all mss
5:48 ABCDEFG תמימים [תמיהים
6:1 B על פני A, לעיני [לפני
6:2 איפוקריטיש A, איפוקריטאש [איפוקראטיס | A לעז [בלעז | G ואתם שמעתם ABDEF, ואתם [ישו
BDG, איפוקרט EF | שיראו [שיראו | ABC(?)DEFG [אדם | G האדם [אדם
6:4 ABDEFG מתנתך [מתנך
6:5 שיראו אותם [שישמעו וישבחו | ABD ובמקצוע [ובמקצוע | omit C [העצבים | EF יהושע [ישו
ABEF, ושיראו אותו DG | [אדם DG האדם
6:6 G שבשמים | + [לאביך | omit A [בעדך | B דלתך [דלתיך | B למשכב [למשכבך
6:7 A ישמיעון [ישמעום
6:8 [שתשאלו | EF שהתפללו | + [קודם | A דבריכם [דבריכם | DG תראו להם AB(?)EF, תדמו להם [תראו
EF ותשאלו

[45]in order that you might be sons of your father
who is in heaven who causes his sun to shine on the good and evil and
causes it to rain on the bad and the just.

[46]If you love those who love you what is your reward? Do not the impu-
dent love those who love them?

[48]Be you (perfect) as your father is perfect.

## Chapter 6

[1] Beware lest you do your righteousness before men that they might
praise you; if you do you will not have a reward from your father who
is in heaven.

[2] Again Jesus said to them: When you do righteousness do not wish to
make a proclamation or [sound] trumpets before you as the hypocrites,
that is, ipocrates, who do their righteousness in the streets and in the
marketplaces in order that men might see them. Truly I say to you they
have received their reward already.

[3] But you when you do righteousness let not your left hand know what
your right hand is doing,

[4] in order that your gift might be in secret and your father who sees hidden things will reward you.

[5] At that time Jesus said to his disciples: When you pray do not raise
your voice and do not be like the sad hypocrites who love to pray in the
synagogues and in the corner of the courtyards and pray with haughty
speech that men might hear and praise them. Truly I say to you they
have received their reward already.

[6] But you when you pray go to your couch, close your doors upon you
and pray to your father in secret and your father who sees in secret will
reward you.

[7] So you when you pray do not make many words as the heretics who
think that by the multitude of words they will make them heard.

[8] Do you not see that your father who is in heaven knows your words before you ask him?

⁹וכן תתפללו אבינו יתקדש שמך
¹⁰ויתברך מלכותך רצונך יהיה עשוי בשמים ובארץ.
¹¹ותתן לחמנו תמידית.
¹²ומחול לנו חטאתינו כאשר אנחנו מוחלים לחוטאים לנו
¹³ואל תביאנו לידי נסיון ושמרינו מכל רע אמן.
¹⁴אם תמחול לבני אדם עונותיהם ימחול אביכם שבשמים עונותיכם.
¹⁵ואם לא תמחלו להם לא ימחול לכם עונותיכם לכם.

## פרק כ"ג

¹⁶עוד אמר להם וכאשר תצומו אל תהיו כחנפים העצבים שמראים
עצמם עצבים ומשנים פניהם להראות צמותם לבני אדם אמן אני
אומר לכם שכבר קבלו שכרם.
¹⁷ואתם בצומכם רחצו ראשיכם
¹⁸שלא תראו מתענים לבני אדם אלא אלא אביך שהוא בסתר ואביך שהוא
בסתר ישלם לך.

## פרק כ"ד

¹⁹עוד אמר להם אל תרבו לצבור אוצרות בארץ כדי שיאכלנו רקב
ותולעה או יחפרו הגנבים ויגנבום.
²⁰עשו לכם אוצרות בשמים במקום שרימה ותולעה לא יאכלם
ובמקום שהגנבים לא יחפרו ויגנבו.
²¹באותו מקום שיהיה אוצרך שם.
²²וניר גופך עיניך אם עיניך לנוכח יביטו בל גופך יחשוך.
²³ואם האור שבך מחשיך כל דרכיך יהיו חשוכים.

6:9 EF התקדש [יתקדש | omit DG [שמך | A שמך [שבשמים + [אבינו
6:10 D [עשויה [עשוי
6:11 B, לחמינו תמידית תן היום לנו A, לחמנו תמידי תן היום לנו [ותתן . . . תמידית |
omit G [ותתן | EF לחמנו תמידית תן היום לנו D, לחמינו תמידי תן היום לנו
G היום לנו + [תמידית | C לחמינו [לחמנו
6:12 omit ABDEFG [לנו¹]
6:13 ADE ושמרנו [ושמרינו | B תביאנו [תביאנו
6:14 G לכם [אביכם | . . . עונותיכם | ABDEFG תמחול [תמחול
6:15 omit G [להם | omit G [לכם² | ABD, omit EF את [את¹ | אונותיכם לכם [עונותיכם
6:16 צומותם [צמותם | D ולמשנים [ומשנים | B עצבים [עצבים | EF כאשר [וכאשר | omit A [אמר
A את + [קבלו | DE צומתם ABFG,
6:17 C בצומכם [בצומכם
6:18 F הוא [שהוא² | A הוא + [הוא¹ | ABDEFG לאביך [אביך² | בסתר²] + A הוא
6:20 omit H [לכם
6:21 BDEFG יהיה לבך A, יהא ליבך [יהיה לבך | A [שם | מקום [המקום
6:22 ABCDEFG כל גופך יזהיר [בל . . . יחשוך | G ועיניך [עיניך | A, omit EF, עינך [עיניך¹ | AB וניר [וניר
6:23 מחשיך [מחשיך | C + [Beginning] ABDEFG, + ואם עיניך כהו כל גופך יחשיך +[יחשיך גופך כל לאו ואם C
ABCDEFG מחשכים יהיו כל דרכיך [כל . . . חשוכים | ABCDEFG חשוכים [יחשיך

[9] But thus you shall pray: Our father, may your name be sanctified;

[10]may your kingdom be blessed; may your will be done in heaven and on earth.

[11]Give our bread continually.

[12]Forgive us our sins as we forgive those who sin against us,

[13]and do not lead us into the power of temptation but keep us from all evil, amen.

[14]If you forgive men their sins your father who is in heaven will forgive your sins.

[15]But if you do not forgive them he will not forgive you your sins.

[16]Again he said to them: When you fast do not be as the sad hypocrites who make themselves appear sad and who change their faces to show their fastings before men; truly I say to you they have received their reward already.

[17]But you when you fast wash your heads

[18]that you might not appear to men to be fasting, but (to) your father who is in secret, and your father who is in secret will reward you.

[19]Again he said to them: Do not keep on heaping up treasures on earth so that decay and the grub devour it or thieves dig through and steal them.

[20]Make for yourselves treasures in heaven where the worm and the grub do not devour them and where thieves do not dig through and steal.

[21]In the place where your treasure is (there will your heart be).

[22]The lamp of the body is your eyes. If your eyes look straight ahead your body shall not be dark.

[23](If your eyes grow dim your whole body will become dark;) and if the light which is in you becomes dark, all your ways will be dark.

## פרק כ"ה

24בעת ההיא אמר יש"ו לתלמידיו לא יוכל איש לעבוד לשני
אדונים כי אם האחד ישנא והא" יאהב או לאחד יכבד ולאחד
יבזה לא תוכלו לעבוד האל והעולם.

25לכן אני אומר לכם שלא תדאגו למאכל לנפשותיכם ולא במלבוש
לגופכם שהנפש יקרה מהמזון והגוף מהמלבוש.

26הסתכלו בעוף השמים אשר לא יזרועו ולא יקצורו ולא יאספו
אוצרות ואביכם העליון מכלכל אתכם הלא אתם יקרים מהם?

27מי בכם מהדואגים שיוכל להוסיף בקומתו אמה אחת?

28א"כ על מה תדאגו בלבוש ראו חבצלת השרון לעז גיל"יון החומש.

29ואני אומר לכם שהמלך שלמה בכל כבודו לא היה מלובש כמוהו.

30ואם תבן הנשאר בקמות לעז פֵּי"נָן אשר היום לחה ומחר יבשה
ושמים אותה בתנור האל מלביש אותה כ"ש אנחנו מקטני אמנה.

31וא"כ שהאל יחשוב מכם אל תדאגו לומר מה נאכל ומה נשתה

32שכל אלה הגופים מבקשים. ויודע אביכם שכל אלה אתם צריכים.

33בקשו קודם מלכות אלקים וצדקתו וכל אלה הדברים ינתנו לכם.

34אל תדאגו ליום מחר שיום מחר ידאגו ממנו די לו ליום בצרתו.

## פרק כ"ו

1אל תדינו פן תדונו.

2באיזה דין תדונו ובאיזה מדה תמודו ימודד לכם.

3ולמה תראו קש בעין זולתך ולא תראה קורה שבעיניך?

4ואיך תאמר לזולתך כתר לי זעיר ואוציא קש מעיניך הנה
הקרה בעיניך.

5החנף תוציא קודם הקורה מעיניך ואח"כ תוציא הקש
מעין זולתך.

---

6:24 G באל A, את + [האל B | לא + [לא B | או לאחד A | [ולאחד A + את + [2לעבוד 6:24
[מהמלבוש EF | לגופותיכם omit B, לגופכם | A בלבוש [במלבוש A | לא [שלא EF | באמת [לכן 6:25
A מהלבוש
ABDEFG אואם [אתכם G באוצרות ABDEF, לאוצרות [אוצרות DG | יחסה [יאספו 6:26
G אחד [ואחד EF | על קומתו [בקומתו EF | בהם [בכם 6:27
ABDFG בהגדלה אינה טווה ואורגת [החומש A, גילין BC, גיליין DG, omit EF | ליריו [ליריו G | וגילין 6:28
ADEFG כמוה [כמוהו B | ואני [ואני 6:29
[אנחנו B | ומשימין [ומשימים A | ולמחר [ומחר A | ליחה [לחה B | בלעז [לעז EF | במוץ [בקמות 6:30
אתם ABDEFG | קטני [מקטני ABDEFG
G אלהים A, אלים [אלקים DG | בקיימו [בקשו 6:33
B דואג ADEF, ידאג [ידאגו ABDEFG לכן + [Beginning] 6:34
DG תדונו [תדינו 7:1
ABCDEFG ימודו [ימודד E באיזה [ובאיזה omit B (hap) . . . [באיזה 7:2
C קודם [קורה BEF | תראה [תראו 7:3
ABDEFG והנה [הנה EF | לרעך [לזולתך 7:4
DEFG ואחר [ואח"כ DEFG | שבעיניך [מעיניך EFG | הוציא AD, הוצא [תוציא 7:5
G מזולתך [זולתך omit G | הקש מעין

²⁴At that time Jesus said to his disciples:

No one is able to serve two masters except he hates the one and loves the other, or he honors the one and despises the other; you cannot serve God and the world.

²⁵Therefore I say to you: do not be anxious for the food for your souls nor for the clothing for your body because the soul is more precious than food and the body than clothing.

²⁶Behold the birds of the sky which sow not nor reap nor gather into barns, but your exalted Father feeds (them). Are you not more precious than they?

²⁷Who among you of those who are anxious is able to add to his height one cubit?

²⁸If this is the case, why are you anxious for clothes? Behold the lilies of Sharon, that is, "Gilyon," (in growing they neither spin nor weave).

²⁹But I say to you that King Solomon in all his glory was not clothed like these.

³⁰If God clothes the straw which is left in the standing grain, that is, penon, which is fresh today and tomorrow is dried up and is placed into the oven, so much the more [will he clothe] (you) who are little of faith.

³¹If God so thinks of you, do not be anxious saying what shall we eat and what shall we drink,

³²because all these things the bodies seek. But your Father knows that you need all these things.

³³Seek first the kingdom of God and his righteousness and all these things will be given to you.

³⁴Do not be anxious for tomorrow because tomorrow will be anxious for itself. Sufficient for itself is today with its trouble.

## Chapter 7

¹Judge not lest you be judged.

²With what judgment you judge and with what measure you measure it will be measured to you.

³Why do you see the straw in the eye of the other person but you do not see the beam in your own eyes?

⁴How is it that you say to the other person: wait for me a while and I will cast the straw out of your eyes, (and) behold the beam is in your own eyes.

⁵Hypocrite, first cast the beam out of your eyes and afterwards you will cast the straw out of the eye of your fellowman.

## פרק כ"ז

⁶עוד אמר להם אל תתנו בשר קדש לכלבים ואל תשימו פניכם לפני חזיר פן יכרסמנו אותה לעיניכם ויחזרו אותה לקרוע אתכם.
⁷שאלו מהאל וינתן לכם בקשו ותמצאו דפקו ויפתחו לכם.
⁸כל השואל יקבל ולאשר יבקש ימצא ולקורא יפתח.
⁹מי בכם שיבקש בנו ממנו לפרוס לחם ויתן לו אבן?
¹⁰או אם יבקש דג ויתן נחש?
¹¹ואם אתם עם היותכם רעים תבואו לתת מתנות טובות לפניכם כ״ש אביכם שבשמים שיתן רוחו הטוב למבקשיו.
¹²וכל מה שתרצו שיעשו לכם בני אדם עשו להם זאת התירה ודברי הנביאים.

## פרק כ"ח

¹³בזמן ההוא אמר יש"ו לתלמידו באו בשער הצר ששער האבדון רחב ומצולה ורבים הולכים בה.
¹⁴כמה השער צר וכבד הדרך המשייר לחיים ומעטים המוצאים אותה.

## פרק כ"ט

¹⁵עוד אמר להם הזהרו מנביאי השקר הבאים לכם במלבושי צמר דומים לצאן שמתוכם זאבים טורפים.
¹⁶ובמעשיהם תכירום הילקוט אדם מן הקוצים ענבים ומן הברקונים תאנים?
¹⁷שכל עץ טוב יעשה פרי טוב וכל עץ רע יעשה פרי רע.
¹⁸ועץ הטוב לא יוכל לעשות פרי רע ועץ רע לא יוכל לעשות פרי טוב.

---

7:6 להם] + ישו A | קדש] קודש BD | פניכם] פנינכם AEF, פנינכם BDGH |
¹אותה] omit EF, אותם H | חזיר] חזירים A, החזירים H | יכרסמנו] יכרסמו ADGH, יכרסמנה EF | אותה] + H |
²אותה] omit ADEFG | לעיניכם] ברגלהם A, לעיינכם C |
7:7 וינתן] ויתן A
7:8 יקבל] יקבלו G | ולקורא] ולקרוא B
7:9 לפרוס] + ABDEFG | לו] + A
7:10 ויתן] + A
7:11 הטוב] הטובה ABDEFG | לבניכם] לבנכם A, לבניכם BDEFG | תביאו] תבאו AEF, תביאו DG | תבואו] +
7:12 ודברי] וספרי EF
7:13 באו] בואו G | הצר] הזה EF | ומצולה] ומסילה A, מצלה DEFG | ורבים] והבית EF
7:14 אותה] אותו ABDEFG | וכבד] וכמה כבד ABDEFG | המשייר] המשיר AG, המיישר BDEF | צר השער] ABDEFG 1 2
7:15 שמתוכם] שבתוכם ABDEFG | צמר] הצמר ABDEFG
7:16 מן] בין G
7:17 פרי רע] omit D
7:18 רע . . . הטוב ועץ] omit C (hap) | ועץ] ועץ¹ | והעץ EF | רע¹˒²] הרע G

⁶Again he said to them:
Do not give holy flesh to dogs nor place your (pearls) before swine lest (they) chew them before you and turn to rend you.

⁷Ask from God and it will be given to you, seek and you will find, knock and it will be opened to you.

⁸Everyone who asks will receive, by the one who seeks it will be found, and to the one who calls it will be opened.

⁹Who is there among you whose son asks him for a piece of bread and he gives him a stone?

¹⁰Or if he should ask for a fish, he gives (him) a snake?

¹¹But if you being evil come to place good gifts before you so much the more your father who is in heaven will give his good spirit to those who seek him.

¹²Everything you wish that men should do to you do to them; this is the Torah and the words of the prophets.

¹³At that time Jesus said to his disciples: Enter in the narrow gate because the gate of destruction is wide and deep and many are going through it.

¹⁴How narrow is the gate and grievous the way (that leads straight) to life and few are those who find it.

¹⁵Again he said to them: Beware of false prophets who come to you in wool clothing like sheep, but inside are tearing wolves.

¹⁶By their deeds you will know them. Does a man gather grapes from thorns or figs from briars?

¹⁷Every good tree makes good fruit and every bad tree makes bad fruit.

¹⁸The good tree cannot make bad fruit nor can the bad tree make good fruit.

וכל עץ אשר לא יעשה פרי טוב כאשר ישרף.¹⁹

לכן כפריים ר״ל במעשיהם תכירום.²⁰

שכל האומר אלי אדוני לא יבא במלכות שמים אבל העושה רצון²¹
אבי שבשמים יכנס במלכות שמים.

רבים אומרים אלי ביום ההוא אדוני אדוני הלא בשמך נבאנו²²
ובשמך שדים הוצאתנו ואותות רבות על שמך עשינו?

ואז אמר להם מעולם לא ידעתי אתכם סורו ממני כל פועלי און.²³

## פרק שלשים

עוד אמר להם כל השומע דברים אלו ועושה אותם דומה לאיש²⁴
חכם שבנה בית בסלע.

וירד הגשם עליו והרוחות מקישות אותו ולא יפול לפי שיסודו אבן.²⁵

וכל השומע דברי אלה ולא יעשם דומה לאיש שוטה אשר בנה²⁶
ביתו על החול.

וירדו גשמים ויבואו זרמים ויפילוהו נופל מפלה גדולה.²⁷

ובעוד שיש״ו היה מדבר דברים אלו כל העם היו תמהים מרוב²⁸
טוב הנהגתו

לפי שהיה דורש להם בכח גדול שלא כשאר החכמים.²⁹

## פרק ל״א

ויהי כאשר ירד יש״ו מן ההר וחבורות רבות אחריו.¹

והנה מצורע אחד בא וישתחוה לו לאמר אדו׳ אם תוכל לרפאת אלי.²

ויט יש״ו את ידו ויגע בו לאמר רוצה אני שתטהר ובאותה³
שעה נטהר המצורע מצרעתו.

---

7:19 ישרף BD | ישרף [ישרוף | BDEFG באש | omit A, כאשר]

7:20 כפריים] ינכרום בפרים A

7:21 אבי + | G | [²במלכות | DEFG כל + | אבל] omit B (hap) | שמים . . . אבל] האומר] אומר G | שמים שבשמים G שמים²] omit A, שמים

7:22 אומרים] יאמרו ABDEFG | אלי] לי EF | נבאנו] נבחרו EF | שדים] omit C | הוצאתנו] הוצאנו
ABDEFG

7:23 אמר] אומר ABDEFG

7:24 בית] ביתו ABCDEFGH

7:25 בו] אותו AH

7:26 יעשם] יעשה EF

7:27 נופל] ונפל ABCDEFG, H | ויפילוהו] ויפילוה | omit H | זרמים ויבואו] ACDEFG | ויבואו] ויבאו
omit H

7:28 האלו] האלו BD, AH | אלה] אלו האלה AH | דברים] דברים EF | שהיה מדבר ישו] שישו היה מדבר
ABCDEFGH גדול] מגדול | מרוב] omit C | העם היו] 3 1 2 H | כל העם היו

7:29 לפי] + שהוא ABDEFG | דורש להם] 1 2 A

8:1 מן ההר] מהר G | הנוצרי] A | ישו] + וישו G

8:2 לרפאת] לרפאות B | אם] + ותרצה A | וישתחוה] וישתחות D | אדו] omit B אדני]

8:3 אני] omit G | באותה] ובאותה | המצורע] DEF ונטהר + A, ממנו ונטהר BDEFG

¹⁹Every tree which does not make good fruit
(is burned in the fire).

²⁰Therefore it is according to fruits, that is, by their deeds, you will
know them.

²¹Because not everyone who says unto me, Lord, will enter the kingdom
of heaven but the one who does the will of my Father who is in heaven
will enter the kingdom of heaven.

²²Many will say to me in that day, Lord, Lord, did we not prophesy in
your name and in your name cast out demons and do many signs in
your name.

²³Then I will say to them: I never knew you. Depart from me all you
workers of iniquity.

²⁴Again he said to them: Everyone who hears these words and does them
is like a wise man who built (his) house on a rock.

²⁵The rain came down against it and the winds beat it and it did not fall
because its foundation was a rock.

²⁶Everyone who hears these my words and does not do them is like a
foolish man who built his house upon the sand.

²⁷The rains came down, the floods came and fell against it (and it fell)
with a great fall.

²⁸While Jesus was speaking these words all the people were greatly as-
tonished at his conduct

²⁹because he was preaching to them with great power, not as the rest of
the sages.

## Chapter 8

¹It came to pass when Jesus came down from the mountain that a great
crowd [came] after him.

²Then behold a leper came and worshipped him saying: Lord, are you
able to heal me.

³Jesus stretched forth his hand and touched him saying: I wish that you
be cleansed, and in that hour the leper was cleansed from his leprosy.

[MT 8:4-16

⁴ויאמר אליו יש״ו השמר לך פן תגיד לאדם ולך לכהן להקריב
קרבניך כאשר צוה משה בתורתכם.

## פרק ל״ב

⁵ויהי כבואו בכפר נחום המרתה ויבא אליו שר המאות ויתחנן לו
⁶לאמר אדוני בני שוכב בביתי מחולי הכווץ בלעז פִּירַא׳/לְשִׁיזָה
ומתחלחל מהמחלה.

⁷ויאמר אלי יש״ו אני אלך וארפאהו.

⁸ויען שר המאות ויאמר לו אדו׳ אינך ראוי שתבא תחת גגי אלא
שתגזור אומר וירפא.

⁹ואני אדם חוטא ויש לי ממשלת תחת ידי פירושים ופרשים ורוכבים
ואומר אני לא״ מהם לך וילך בא ויבא ולעבדי עשו זה ויעשו.

¹⁰וישמע יש״ו ויתמה ולבאים אחריו אמר אמן אני אומר לכם לא
מצאתי אמונה גדולה בישראל.

¹¹כי האומר אני לכם שיבואו רבים ממזרח וממערב וינוחו
עם אברהם ועם יצחק ועם יעקב במלכות שמים

¹²ובני המלכות יש לנו במחשכי גהינם ושם יהיה בֶּכִי וְתִחְזַק שָׁנַיִם.

¹³ויאמר יש״ו לשר המאות לך וכאשר האמנת יעשה לך.
ונרפא הנער בעת ההיא.

## פרק ל״ג

¹⁴בעת ההיא בא יש״ו לבית פיטיירוס והנה חותנתו שוכבת מקדחת.
¹⁵ויגע לידה ויעזבה הקדחת. ותקם ותשרתהו.
¹⁶ויהי לעת הערב ויבאו אליו אחוזי השדים וירפאום במאמרו
לבד וכל החולי ריפא

---

8:4 ABDEFG והקרב [להקריב | ABDEFG קרבנך [קרבניך | ABDEFG

8:5 AEF הרמתה [המרתה | ACDG בבואו [כבואו

8:6 פראלשיאה A, פרלאטיקו [פיראלשיזה | ACDEFG לעז [בלעז | A הכיווץ [הכווץ | G הֹמֹ + [מחולי
B, ה פיראלשיאה | DG⁽⁷⁾ פיראלאשינו | EF

8:7 ABCDEFG אליו [אלי

8:8 ABDEFG איני [אינך | G אליו | G לו | omit G [ויען

8:9 omit A [מהם | ABDEF פרשים [פירושים . . . ורוכבים | ABDEF ותחת [תחת
וילך + ABD, ולאחד EF [זה | omit BEF [ולאחד

8:10 omit AG [גדולה | A 2 1 [אמן אני | omit G [אמן | omit EF [אמר אמן | G ויאמר [ישו ויתמה |
ABDEFG כמו בזה + [בישראל

8:11 EFG עם יעקב [ועם יעקב | DEFG עם יצחק [ועם יצחק | A, ויצחק [ועם יצחק | ABDEFG אומר [כי האומר |
omit EF [במלכות שמים

8:12 ABDEFG וחירוק [ותחזק | B יהי [יהיה | EF גהנם | BDG, גיהנם [גהינם | ABDEFG יושלכו [יש לנו

8:13 G הילד [הנער | G וירפא [ונרפא | G עלך [לך | B והאמנת [האמנה | B כאשר אמרת [וכאשר

8:14 ABDEFG פיטו [פיטרוס | A אמר [בא

8:15 ADEFG ותשרתם [ותשרתהו | EF ויניחנה [ויעזבה

8:16 ABDEFG החולים [החולי | AEFG וירפאם [וירפאום | A רבים + [השדים | A לו [אליו | G ויהיה [ויהי
omit EF [ריפא

[4]Then Jesus said to him:

Be careful lest you tell any man, but go to the priest to offer your gifts as Moses commanded in your law.

[5]It came to pass when he entered into Capernaum-hamartha that a captain of hundreds came to him and implored him,

[6]saying, Lord, my son lies in my house with the sickness of contraction, that is, (paralatiko) and he is weak with the illness.

[7]Jesus said to (him): I will go and heal him.

[8]The captain of hundreds answered and said to him: Lord (I) am not worthy that you should come under my roof; only make the decision that he might be healed.

[9]I am a sinful man and I have authority under the Pharisees and [I have] horses and riders and I say to one of them go and he goes, come and he comes, and to my servants do this and they do it.

[10]Jesus heard and was amazed and said to those who were following him: verily I say to you and I have not found a great faith in Israel (like this).

[11](I say) to you that many will come from the East and from the West and will rest with Abraham, Isaac and Jacob in the kingdom of heaven;

[12]but, the sons of the kingdom (will be cast) into the darkness of Gehenna; there will be weeping and (gnashing) of teeth.

[13]Then Jesus said to the captain of hundreds: Go; as you have believed, it will be done to you. So the lad was healed at that time.

[14]At that time Jesus went into the house of Peter and behold his mother-in-law was lying sick with a fever.

[15]He touched her hand and the fever left her. Then she arose and ministered to him.

[16]At the time of evening they brought to him those seized by demons and (he) healed them by his word alone and he healed every sickness,

[MT 8:17-28]

<sup>17</sup>לגמור מה שנאמר ע״י ישעיה הנביא ז״ל אכן חליינו הוא נשא ומכאובינו הוא סבלם.

## פרק ל״ד

<sup>18</sup>ויהי אחרי זאת וירא יש״ו חבורות רבות סביבותיו ויצוה ללכת עבר הים.

<sup>19</sup>ויקרב חכם א״ ויאמר לו אדו׳ אלך אחריך בכל מקום שתלך.

<sup>20</sup>ויען אליו יש״ו לשועלים חורים ולעוף קנים ולבן אדם בן הבתולה אין מקום להכניס ראשו.

<sup>21</sup>וא׳ מתלמדיו אמר לו עזוב אותי שאלך ואקבור את אבי.

<sup>22</sup>ויאמר לו יש״ו בא אחרי ועזוב המתים לקבור מתיהם.

## פרק ל״ה

<sup>23</sup>ויהי כאשר באו יש״ו באניה ויבואו תלמידיו אחריו.

<sup>24</sup>ויהי סער גדול בים והגלים הולכים מאד והאניה חשבה להשבר.

<sup>25</sup>ויקרבו אליו תלמידיו ויבקשו ממנו לאמר אדונינו הושיענו פן נאבד.

<sup>26</sup>ויאמר אליהם למה תתראו מקטני אמנה. ויקם ויצו לים ולרוחות שינוחו ומיד נחו.

<sup>27</sup>והאנשים אשר שם שראו תמהו ויאמרו מי הוא זה שהרוחות והים עושה רצונו.

## פרק ל״ו

<sup>28</sup>ויהי כאשר עבר הים ויעבור עבר הים במלכות גַּארְגְיזָאנִי נקראים בלעז גְיֵינְיטְרַ״ארוֹס ויפגעו בו שנים אחוזי שדים יוצאים מהקברים משתגעים עד שלא יוכל איש לעבור בדרך ההיא.

---

8:17 ע״/י] על פי ABDEFG | חליינו] omit A | הנביא ז״ל] חילונו C

8:19 ויקרב חכם] ויקרא אדם EF

8:20 ולעוף] ולעופות G

8:21 מתלמדיו] מתלמידיו ABDEF | שאלך] omit A

8:22 ואמר לו] א״ל G ועזוב] + את A | מתיהם] המתים B

8:23 באו] בא ABCDEFG

8:24 והאניה] והוא G | הולכים] נכנסים באניה ABDEFG | מאד] omit EF בים]

8:25 ויבקשו] ויקיצוהו ABDEFG

8:26 אליהם] להם A | תתראו] תראו ABDEFG | מקטני] קטני ABDEFG | ויקם] omit A

8:27 עושה] אשר הים והרוחות G ABDEFG | ואמרו] ויאמרו A | שהרוחות והים] שהרוחות והרוחות ,A

8:28 נקראים] נקרא BE, omit גַארגיזאני] גדרי ABCDEFG | לים] היֵם[2] EF מעבר[2] עבר] גיניטראדוס A, גינטרארוס B, גיניטראריש C, גיניטרמריט EF, גיניטרארוס] גייניטרארוס G בלעז] לעז A | שנים] שני AEF אחוזי] אחוזים EFG | שדים] מהשדים G | איש] ההיא] ההוא BG omit C

¹⁷to complete what was said by Isaiah the prophet,
of blessed memory: surely our sicknesses he bore and our pains he suffered.

¹⁸It came to pass after this Jesus saw many crowds around him and he
commanded to go across the sea.

¹⁹Then there came to him a sage and he said to him: Master I will follow
you wherever you go.

²⁰Jesus answered him: the foxes have holes and the birds have nests, but
the Son of Man, the son of the virgin, has no place to enter his head.

²¹Then one of the disciples said to him: allow me to go and bury my father.

²²Jesus said to him: Follow me and let the dead bury their dead.

²³It came to pass when Jesus entered a boat his disciples followed him.

²⁴Then there came a great storm on the sea and the waves were coming
on excessively and the boat was thought to be breaking up.

²⁵Then his disciples came to him and begged him saying: O our master
save us lest we perish.

²⁶He said to them: Why do you look at one another, O you little of faith.
Then he arose and commanded the sea and the winds that they should
be quiet and immediately they became quiet.

²⁷When the men who were there saw they marveled and said: Who is this
that the winds and the sea do his will.

²⁸It came to pass when he crossed over the sea and passed by the region
beyond the sea into the realm of the (Gaderi), that is, Ginitraros, there
met him two demon-possessed men coming out of the tombs, raging
until when no man could pass by that way.

[MT 8:29-9:8

29ויצעקו אליו לאמר מה לך עמנו יש״ו בן אלקים באת קודם הזמן
לצערנו וגם להשמידנו? ויש״ו אמר להם צאו משם מחנות רעות.
30ושם קרוב מהם עדרי חזירים רבים רועים.
31ויפגעו בן השדים יען יש לנו לצאת מכאן תן לנו רשות לבא באלו
החזירים.
32ויאמר להם לכו. ויצאו השדים מהאנשים ויבאו בחזירים וילכו כל
העדר בבהלה ונשמטו בים ומתו במים.
33ויפחדו הרועים ויברחו ויגידו בעיר הכל. ותהום כל העיר.
34ויצאו לקראת יש״ו. ויראו אותם ויחלו פניו לבלתי עבור בגבולם.

פרק ל״ז

1ואז יש״ו בא באניה וישוטו וישובו לעירו.
2ויקרבו לפניו חולה א״ מכווץ בלעז פָארָא׳לְטיקו וישכב על מטתו.
יש״ו אמונתם ויאמר לחולה תתחזק בני. באמונת האל כי נמחלו
וירא
עונותיך.
3וקצת החכמים אומרים בלבם זהו מגדף.
4וירא יש״ו מחשבותם ויאמר אליהם למה תחשבו רעה בלבבכם.
5זהו קל לאמר נמחל עוניך או קום לך?
6רק להודיעכם שבן אדם יכול למחול עונות בארץ אז אמר לחולה
קום וקח מיטתך ולך.
7ויקם וילך אל ביתו.
8ויראו החבורות ויראו מאד ויהללו לאל אשר נתן יכולת לבני
אדם לעשות כאלה.

---

8:29אליו] + השדים A | אלקים] אלים A | וגם להשמידנו] ולהשמידנו ADEF, לצערנו] B
לצערינו] B עמנו] omit EF להשמידנו ולצערנו] לצערנו וגם להשמידנו G
8:30מהם] להם G | עדרי] עדר A, מחני G
8:31מכאן] מכנן G | לבא] מבני אדם D, להכנס G
8:32השדים מהאנשים] השדים האלו מבני אדם B, מהאנשים השדים G | ויאמר] omit (hap) EF . . . בחזירים G
וילכו] וילך ABCD, והלך EF
8:33ותהום] ותהם ABDG
8:34אותם] אותו ABDEFG
9:1בא] + בא A | וישב] וישובו A | וישוטו] וישומו CD
9:2חולה] חולי B | מכווץ] מכיווץ A, מקמץ B | בלעז] לעז ADEFG | פארלטיקו] פראלטיקו A,
פראליטיקו C, פליטיקו DG, פליטיקו EF | וישכב] מושכב ABDEFG | תתחזק] התחזק ABDEFG
9:3החכמים] מהחכמים A, חכמים G | זהו] זה BEF
9:4בלבבכם] omit D
9:5זהו] איזהו EF זה A, | קל] קלל G | נחמל] נחמלו ABG | לך] ולך ABDEFG
9:6יכול] + אדם BDEFG | אמר] + ישו EF | ולך] וילך B
ABDEFG 2 1 3 | למחול עונות בארץ] מחול עונות בארץ
9:7ויקם . . . ביתו] וילך החולה לביתו G
9:8האדם] B

²⁹They cried out to him saying:

What is between you and us, Jesus son of God. Have you come before the time to grieve us and to destroy us? Then Jesus said to them: Come out from there evil host.

³⁰There near them were herds of many swine feeding.

³¹So the demons entreated him: Since we have to go out from here, grant us authority to go into these swine.

³²Then he said to them: Go. The demons went out from the men and entered the swine and all the herd went in sudden haste, slipped off into the sea and died in the water.

³³Those who were feeding [them] feared, fled and told everything in the city. So the whole city was frightened.

³⁴Then they went out to meet Jesus. They saw them and entreated him not to pass over into their border.

## Chapter 9

¹Then Jesus entered a boat; they set sail and returned to his city.

²They brought to him one who was sick with contractions, that is, paralitico, lying upon his bed. Jesus saw their faith and said to the sick man: have courage my son. It is by the faith of God that your sins have been forgiven.

³Some of the sages were saying in their heart: This one blasphemes.

⁴Jesus saw their thoughts and said to them: Why do you think evil in your heart.

⁵(Which) is easier to say: your sins are forgiven, or, rise walk?

⁶But to inform you that the Son of Man is able to forgive sins on earth, then he said to the sick man: Arise and take your bed and walk.

⁷He arose and went to his house.

⁸The crowds saw, feared exceedingly and praised God who had given power to men to do such things.

## פרק ל"ח

⁹ויהי כאשר עבר יש"ו משם וירא איש אחד יושב על שלחן החלוף מתתיה שמו בלעז מָאט׳׳יאו ויאמר לו לך אחרי ויקם וילך אחריו.
¹⁰ויוליכוהו לביתו לאכול. ויהי בעת אכלו והנה פריצים רבים ורשעים בשלחן והנה סועדים עם יש"ו ותלמידיו.
¹¹ויראו הפרושים ויאמרו לתלמידיו למה רבכם יושב ואוכל עם הפריצים והרשעים.
¹²וישמע יש"ו ויאמר בבריאים אינם צריכים רפואה כי אם החולה.
¹³לכו ולמדו הכתוב כי חסד חפצתי ולא זבח ולא באתי להשיב הצדיקים כי אם הרשעים.

## פרק ל"ט

¹⁴אז קרבו אליו תלמידי יוחנן ויאמרו לו למה אנו והפרושים מתענים הרבה פעמים ותלמידך אינם מתענים.
¹⁵ויען להם יש"ו ויאמר לא יוכלו חבירי החתן לְבְכּוֹת ולהתענות בהיותו עמהם. יבואו ימים וילקח מהם החתן ויצומו.
¹⁶לא יאבד איש חתיכת מלבוש חדש במלבוש ישן לחוזק החתיכה משוך מהמלבוש הבלויה ויקרע יותר.
¹⁷ולא ישימו יין חדש בכלים ישנים פן ישברו הכלים וישפוך היין והכלים יאבדו. רק חדש בכלי חדש ושניהם ישמרו.

## פרק ארבעים

¹⁸ויהי בדברו אליהם ויקרב שר אחד וישתחוה לו לאמר אדו' בתי אתה עתה מתה. בא נא ושים ידך עליה והחיה.
¹⁹ויקם יש"ו וילך הוא ותלמידיו עמו.
²⁰והנה אשה אחת שופעת דם שתים עשרה שנה בא אחריו ותגע בציצית בגדו.

---

9:9 ⁹ישו משם[ 2 1 ABDEFG | מתתיה[מתתיא A | מתתיא A | לעז[בלעז | לעז ADEFG | מאטיאו[מאטיאו A מטיב, BDEF,
G מאטי C, מאטיו
9:10 omit H ויוליכוהו[ויוליכהו ABDEFG | וסועדים[והנה סועדים ABDEFGH | ותלמידיו
G הפרושים[ + ופריצים 9:11
ABCDEFG החולים[החולה | רפואה[לרפואה A, לרפוא BDGH | ABDEFGH הבריאים[בבריאים 9:12
A לא[²ולא A 9:13
A ותלמידיך[ותלמידד | omit B פעמים[ omit G | והפרושים[ G והפרושים + | יוחנן[יוחנן 9:14
G יבא[יבואו B של[ + | חבירי[חבירי 9:15
ABDEFG ימשוך[משוך | ABDEFG החדשה[ + החתיכה[החתיכה | A חבר[יחבר | שחוזק[לחוזק ABDEFG
A אות[יותר | A, הישן G | הבלויה[הבלויה EF, במלבוש G | המלבוש[מהמלבוש
AEF בכלים חדשים[בכלי חדש | ABDEFG יין[ + רק[רק 9:17
9:18 שר[שר | EF אלף[ + adu[אדו omit B | אתה[עתה מתה omit ADEFG | 2 1 ADE,
G אותה[ + החיה[החיה | omit C מתה[מתה G | מתה ועתה F, מתה אתה שתה B, מה עתה
9:20 אחת[omit A | בא[באה AD בציצית[בציצית ADEF

⁹It came to pass when Jesus passed on from there
he saw a man sitting at the table of exchange, Matthew was his name,
that is, Matyeo, and he said to him: Follow me. So he arose and followed him.

¹⁰Then (he) brought him to his house to eat. It came to pass while he was
eating that behold many violent and evil men were at the table and behold they were dining with Jesus and his disciples.

¹¹The Pharisees saw [this] and said to his disciples: Why does your
teacher sit and eat with violent and evil men.

¹²Jesus heard [this] and said: The healthy have no need (for) healing, but
the sick.

¹³Go and learn that which is written: I desire kindness and not sacrifice; I
have not come to restore the righteous but the wicked.

¹⁴Then the disciples of John came to him and said to him: Why do we
and the Pharisees fast often but your disciple(s) do not fast.

¹⁵Jesus answered them and said: The friends of the bridegroom cannot
weep and fast while he is with them. The days will come when the
bridegroom will be taken from them; then they will fast.

¹⁶No man wastes a piece of new garment on an old garment (because)
the force of the piece (stretches) the worn out garment and it tears
more.

¹⁷Nor do they put new wine into old vessels lest the vessels break and the
wine spills out and the vessels perish. But new (wine) is for new vessels and both of them are preserved.

¹⁸It came to pass when he had spoken to them a captain approached and
bowed down to him saying: Master my daughter has just died. Please
come and place your hand upon her and restore her to life.

¹⁹Jesus arose and went, he and his disciples with him.

²⁰Then behold a woman with a flow of blood for twelve years came behind him and touched the fringe of his garment.

‏²¹ואומרת בלבבה אם אגע בלבושו לבד ארפא מיד.
‏²²וישב פניו ויאמר אליה התחזקי בתי בש״ית שאמונתך רפאך.
‏באותה שעה נרפאת
‏²³ויהי בבואו בית השר וירא אנשים רבים בוכים.
‏²⁴ויאמר אליהם צאו כולכם חוצה ואל תבכו שהנערה ישנה ולא
‏מתה. ויהי כמצחק בעיניהם. ואומרים הלא אנו רואים שהיא מתה.
‏²⁵ובההוציאם אותם החוצה בא אליה יש״ו ויגע בידה ותקם הנערה.
‏²⁶ותצא שמועה זאת בכל הארץ ההיא.

‏פרק מ״א

‏²⁷ויעבור משם יש״ו והנה שני עורים רצים אחריו וצועקים
‏אליו חנינו בן דוד.
‏²⁸ויהי הבית ויקרבו אליו העורים. ויאמר
‏²⁹אמונתכם תרפא אתכם.
‏³⁰ותפקחנה עיני שניהם מיד ויראו. ויצום לאמר השמרו
‏פן יודע הדבר.
‏³¹והם יצאו ויגלוהו בכל הארץ ההיא.

‏פרק מ״ב

‏³²ויצא משם יש״ו ויביאו לפניו איש אלם והשד בתוכו.
‏³³ויוציא את השד וידבר האלם. ויפלאו החבורות ויאמרו
‏לא נראה כזה בישראל.
‏³⁴ויאמרו הפרושים באמת בשם השדים מוציא השדים.
‏³⁵ויסב כל הערים והמגדלים מלמד בבתי כנסיות
‏ומבשר בשורות ומרפא כל חילי וכל מדוה.

‏9:21 ואומרת] אומרת ABDEFG | בלבבה] בליבה A, בלבה EF | לבד] בלעד B
‏9:22 וישב] ויסב ABDEFG | פניו] omit G | אליה] + בתי EF | התחזקי] התחזקו E | בתי בשית
‏בשית] בשית G | שאמונתך] שאמונך F | באל בש A, BDEF | באותה] ובתאותה | ABCDEFG
‏נרפאת] נתרפאת F
‏9:23 בבואו] כבוא G | בית] בבית A | אנשים] + ונשים G
‏9:24 שאומרים ABDEF, אורים G | ואומרים] והיה G | ויהי] והיה G | אליהם] להם ABDEF, omit G
‏9:25 בידה] בה EF
‏9:26 שמועה] השמועה G | זאת] הזאת G
‏9:27 חנינו] חוננו A, BDEF חננו G
‏9:28 ויהי] + בבואו AB, + כבואו DEFG
‏9:30 עיני שניהם] ענהם A | לאמר] לומר A | השמרו] + לכם EF
‏9:31 ההיא . . . בכל] omit B
‏9:32 לפניו] אליו A
‏9:33 את] omit G | כזה] omit EF
‏9:34 באמת] omit A
‏9:35 חולי] חלים A, + אל G, + את ABDEFH

[21]She was saying in her heart:
If only I touch his garment I will immediately be healed.

[22]He turned and said to her: Courage my daughter. May you have a long life; your healing is because of your faith. In that very hour she was healed.

[23]It came to pass when he entered the house of the captain he saw many people weeping.

[24]He said to them: Go outside all of you and stop weeping because the girl is asleep and not dead. But in their eyes he was as one who jests. They were saying: Have we not seen that she is dead.

[25]When he had put them outside Jesus went to her, touched her hand and the girl arose.

[26]This report went out in all that land.

[27]Jesus passed on from there and behold two blind men were running after him and crying out to him: Have mercy on us, Son of David.

[28]He came to the house and the blind men drew near to him. He said:

[29]Your faith will heal you.

[30]The eyes of the two men were immediately opened and they saw. He commanded them saying: Be careful lest the matter be made known.

[31]As for them, they went out and made him known in all that land.

[32]Jesus went out from there and they brought before him a dumb man who was demon possessed.

[33]He cast out the demon so that the dumb man spoke. The crowds were amazed and said: We have not seen it like this in Israel.

[34]The Pharisees said: Truly in the name of demons he casts out demons.

[35]He went around all the cities and towers teaching in the synagogues and preaching the good tidings and healing every illness and every sickness.

[MT 9:36-10:9

<sup>36</sup>וירא יש״ו החבורות ויחמול עליהם שהיו יגיעים
ושוכבים כצאן אשר אין להם רועה.
<sup>37</sup>אז אמר לתלמידיו הקמה מרובה והקוצרים מעטים.
<sup>38</sup>חלו נא פני בעל הקמה וישלח הקוצרים רבים לקצור קומתו.

## פרק מ״ג

<sup>1</sup>אז קרא יש״ו לי״ב תלמידיו ויתן להם יכולת על כל רוח טומאה
להוציא מהאדם ולרפאת כל חולי וכל נגע.
<sup>2</sup>ואלה שמות י״ב השלוחים נקראו אפוסְט״וֹלוֹס סִימ״וֹן
נקרא פִּיְיטֶר״וֹס וְאַנְדְרֶ״יְאָה אחיו
<sup>3</sup>פִילִיפ״וֹס ובורטולָאֲמֵיאוֹס יעקב נקרא גאי״מי ויוחנן
אחיו בני זבדיאל טוֹמָא״ס ומתתיה הוא מָאטַ״יְאוֹ מלוה בריבית
בפרסום ויעקב אַלוּפֵיאֵי וְטַרֵיַא״וֹס
<sup>4</sup>שמעון כנעני לעז סִימ״וֹן קַאֲנָאַ״נָאיוֹס וְיוּדַ״א אַסְקַאר״יְוֹטָה
אשר אחר זה מסרהו.
<sup>5</sup>אלה שנים עשר שלח יש״ו ויצו אליהם לאמר בארצות הגוים
אל תלכו ובערי השמרונים אל תבואו.
<sup>6</sup>לכו לצאן אשר נדחו מבית ישראל.
<sup>7</sup>ובשרו להם שתתקיים מלכות שמים.
<sup>8</sup>רפאו החולים והחיו המתים והנה טהרתם המצורעים והוציאו
השדים מבני אדם. ואל תקבלו שכר. חנם קבלתם ובחנם תתנו.
<sup>9</sup>אל תצברו כסף וזהב ולא ממון בכיסכם

<sup>9:36</sup> יגיעים [יגעים ADEFGH
<sup>9:37</sup> מעטים [מועטים A
<sup>9:38</sup> קומתו [קמתו A | הרבה [רבים G | קוצרים [הקוצרים A | שישלח [וישלח G | אל [בעל הקמה AEFH
<sup>10:1</sup> מהאדם [מאדם G
<sup>10:2</sup> אפוסטולוס [אפושטואלאש A, אפוסטוליס B, אפוסטולים D, אפוסטולוש G |
שימון [סימון ABDG | פיטרוס [פייטרוס A, פטרוס B, פיטרוש DG | פיטרוש [פיטרוס A,
ואנדריאש [ואנדריאה B | אחיו . . . נקראו [omit EF | אחיו] + (marg of Brit. Lib. ms)
יָקוֹפוֹס דִי זֶיבְּידֵיְיאוֹ גִיוְוָאנֵי הוא אחו שלוֹ
<sup>10:3</sup> ובירטולומיאוש [ובורטולאמיאוס A, פיליפוש [פילילפוש . . . נקרא] omit EF | פיליפוס [פיליפוש ADG |
גיאימי [גאימי G | וברטאלומיאוש D, ובירטולומיאוש C, ובורטולמיאוס B, ובורטולומיאוש EF |
מאטי [מאטיאו C | מאטיו ABDEF, זאבדל G | זבדאל [זבדיאל DEF, מאטיב [מאטיו AEG |
וטדיוש G | וטאדיאוש BDEF, וטאדיאוש A, וטדיאוש [וטריאוס DEFG | ברבית [בריבית
<sup>10:4</sup> קאנאניאוס EF, קאנאניוס BCD | קאנאניוס [קאנאנאיוס A, קנאניאוש [קנאנאיוס ABEFG | שימון [סימון B | לעז [בלעז
אסכריוטא B, איסכורייוטו [איסכריוטא A, אסקאריוטה [אסכריוטה EF , וידא [ויהודה A, וידא [וידא G | כנאניאוס
B מסרהו [מסרהו B | זה [אסכריואטי EF, אסכריאטי G | זה] omit B | איסכריוטא D, אסכריוטי C,
<sup>10:5</sup> אלה [+ שנים שנים A | תבואו [+ אלה G | ישו] + לכן G
<sup>10:6</sup> לכן] omit G
<sup>10:7</sup> שתתקרב [שתתקיים ABDEFG
<sup>10:8</sup> תתנו [תקבל G | תקבלו [תקבל ABDEFG | וטהרו [והנה טהרתם A | מתים [המתים A | חולים [החולים
הלמדו EF
<sup>10:9</sup> בכסכם [בכיסכם G | ואל [אל A

<sup>36</sup>Jesus saw the crowds and had pity on them because they
were weary and lying [around] like sheep without a shepherd.

<sup>37</sup>Then he said to his disciples: The standing grain is much but the reap-
ers are few.

<sup>38</sup>Entreat now the Lord of the standing grain that he send many reapers to
harvest his grain.

## Chapter 10

<sup>1</sup>Then Jesus called his twelve disciples and gave them power over every
unclean spirit to cast them out from man and to heal every sickness and
every plague.

<sup>2</sup>These are the names of the twelve apostles, called Apostolos: Simon,
called Petros, and Andrea his brother,

<sup>3</sup>Philipos, and Bortolameos, and James, called Jimi, and John his
brother, sons of Zebedeel, Tomas and Matthew, that is Matio, why by
reputation was a lender of [money] for interest, James Aluphei and Ter-
eos,

<sup>4</sup>Simon the Canaanite, that is, Simon Cananayos, and Juda Ascareyo-
tah, who after this betrayed him.

<sup>5</sup>These twelve Jesus sent; he commanded them saying: To the lands of
the Gentiles do not go and into the cities of the Samaritans do not enter.

<sup>6</sup>Go to the sheep who have strayed from the house of Israel.

<sup>7</sup>Preach to them that the kingdom of heaven will be fulfilled.

<sup>8</sup>Heal the sick, restore life to the dead, (cleanse) the lepers and cast out
demons from men. Do not take wages. Freely you received, freely you
shall give.

<sup>9</sup>Do not heap up silver and gold; nor [have] wealth in your purse,

[MT 10:10-22

‏10ולא חליפות שמלות ולא מנעלים ולא מקל בידכם. ראוי הפועל לקבל די אכילתו.

‏11ובכל עיר ובכל מגדל אשר תבואו מי האיש הטוב שבתוכם ושם תנוחו עד שתצאו.

‏12ובבואכם אל הבית תנו להם שלום לאמר שלום בזאת הבית שלום לכל היושבים בתוכה.

‏13ואם תהיה הבית ההיא ראויה תבא שלומכם עליה ואם לא תהיה ראויה תשוב שלומכם לכם.

‏14ואשר לא יקבל אתכם ואשר לא ישמע אליכם תצאו מן הבית ההיא והעתקם רגליכם מן העפר.

‏15אמן אני דובר אליכם יותר טוב יהיה אל סדום ואל עמורה ביום ההוא מן העיר ההיא.

פרק מ״ד

‏16הנני שולח אתכם כצאן בין הזאבים תהיו ערומים כנחשים וענים כיונים.

‏17הזהרו בבני אדם. לא ימסרו אתכם בקהלותם ובבתי כנסיותם

‏18ולפָחות וְלַמלָכים. תוכלון בעדי להעיד להם ולגוים.

‏19כאשר יתפשו אתכם אם תחשבו מה שתאמרו שבשעה שתצטרכו יבא לכם מענה.

‏20אינכם המדברים כי אם רוח קדשו של אבי הוא הדובר בכם.

‏21ימסור האח את אחיו למות והאב לבנו ויקומו הבנים על האבות ויובילו אותם עד למות.

‏22ותהיו ללעג וזעוה לכל העמים על שמי אכן מי שיסבול עד עת קץ יושע.

‏10:10 לקבל] לקבלהו DG | די] omit DEFG
‏10:11 omit G | ושם] G שאלו | שאלו +] שאלו את ABDEF, | תבואו] G ועיר ובכל מקום ומקום + | עיר] omit G
‏10:12 להם] לה ABDEFG
‏10:13 ואם] והיה | G ההיא] omit A | ואם לא תהיה ראויה] וא״ל G
‏10:14 אתכם] אליכם ABDEF | תצאו +] חוצה A | מן הבית ההיא] מן העיר או מהבית ההיא | G ההיא] מהעפר] מן העפר | G ותעורו] ונערו ABDEF, | והעתקם] ADEF או העיר ההיא + | G
‏10:15 אליכם] לכם AG | ביום ההוא מן העיר היא] 3 4 5 1 2 G
‏10:16 הנני] הנה EF | אתכם] לכם EF | כצאן] כמו הצאן ABDEFG | בין] בקרב ABDEFG הזאבים] | וענים] וענוים ABDEFG | כיונים A זאבים
‏10:17 בקהלותם] בקהלותם A | לא] שלא G
‏10:18 ולפחות ולמלכים] 2 1 EF ולמלכים] ולמלאכים C | תוכלון] תוכלו EG
‏10:19 יתפשו] תתפשו G אם] ואם ABDEFG | שתצטרכו] שתצרכו AG
‏10:20 המדברים] מדברים EFG | קדשו] הקדש EF
‏10:21 האח] באח G | ויקומו] יקומו G האבות] אבותם C הבנים] ABDEFG, | ויובילו] יובילו G
‏10:22 שמי] omit G

according to a Primitive Hebrew Text                                      45

[10]or changes of clothes, or shoes, or a staff in your hand.
The workman is worthy to receive enough for his food.

[11]In every city and in every tower that you enter (ask) who is the good
man among them and there remain until you go out.

[12]When you enter into the house give to them a shalom saying: shalom to
this house; shalom to all who dwell in it.

[13]If that house should be worthy your shalom will come upon it, but if it
is not worthy your shalom will return to you.

[14][When] one does not receive you or listen to you, you shall go out
from that house and (shake off) your feet from the dust.

[15]Truly I say unto you, it will be better for Sodom and Gomorrah in that
day than for that city.

[16]Behold I send you like sheep in the midst of wolves. Be as crafty as
serpents and humble as doves.

[17]Beware of men. They will not deliver you up in their congregations
and houses of assembly,

[18]but to governors and kings. You will be able to bear witness on my be-
half to them and to the Gentiles.

[19]When they seize you do not consider what you will say because in the
hour that you are in need an answer will come to you.

[20]It will not be you who speak but the Holy Spirit of my Father will
speak through you.

[21]Brother will deliver up brother to death and a father his son; the sons
will rise up against (their) fathers and lead them unto death.

[22]You will become a derision and a fright to all the nations because of
my name. Whoever endures, however, until the time of the end will be
saved.

## פרק מ"ה

23עוד אמר יש"ו לתלמידיו כאשר ירדפו אתכם בעיר הזאת ברחו לאחרת אמן אני אומר לכם לא תשלימו לכם ערי ישראל עד כי יבא בן אדם.

24אין תלמיד גדול מרבו ולא העבד גדול מאדוניו.

25די לתלמיד להיות כרבו ולעבד כאדוניו. אם לבעל הבית יקראו בעל זבוב כ"ש לבני ביתו.

26אל תראו מהם שאין דבר שלא יראה ולא נעלם.

27אני אומר לכם בחשך אמרו אותו באור.

28ואל תפחדו מהורגי שאין בידם להרוג הנפשות רק פחדו לאשר יכולת בידו לאבד הנפש והגוף בגהינם.

29הלא שני צפורים אבדו בפרוטה אחת ולא תפול אחת מהם על הארץ כי אם ברצון אביכם שבשמים?

30הלא שערות ראשיכם כלם ספורים?

31אל תראו שטובים מצפורים אדם.

32המשבח אותי בפני אדם אשבחנו לפני אבי שבשמים.

## פרק מ"ו

34באותה שעה אמר יש"ו לתלמידיו אל תחשבו שבאתי לשים בארץ אלא חרב.

35באתי להפריד האדם הבן מאביו והבת מאמה.

36והאויבים להיות אהובים.

37האוהב אביו ואמו יותר ממני איני ראוי לו.

39האוהב את נפשו יאבדיה האובד אותי בשבילי ימצאנה.

---

10:23 ABDEF האדם [אדם | ABDEF omit [כי | ABDEFG לסבוב [²לכם | G לכם + [ברחו

10:24 ABDEFG התלמיד [תלמיד

10:25 G קראו [יקראו

10:26 [נעלם + ידע שלא ABDEF, + ידע G

(+) אותו G) + לאוזן ספרו אותו (omit G אותו) בשער + [באור | ABDEFG אשר + [Beginning 10:27 ABDEFG ואשר (אשר DG) תשמעו

10:28 BDG בגיהנם [בגהינם F וגוף [והגוף DG הגויות [הגויות BEF, הגויות A, הגוות + [מהורגי |

(?) EF האל ית + [ברצון | EF לארץ [על הארץ G לא [ולא | ABDEFG ימכרו [אבדו | G (?) [אביכם שבשמים

10:30 A ראשכם [ראשיכם E שער [שערות

10:31 ABCDEFG אתם [אדם | BCDEFG מצרים [מצפרים A, מצפרים [מצפורים D שמונים [שטובים

10:32 G בפני [לפני C לפני [לפני A, בני + [בפני

10:33 All mss omit vs 33 except A which reads:
ואשר יכחש בי לפני בני אדם אכחש בו לפני אבי שבשמים

10:34 ABD, + לשום שלום [לשים EFG שלום + ABD

10:36 ABDEFG אהובים [אהובים DG שהיו [להיות

10:37 AD אינו ראוי לי [איני ראוי לו

10:38 All mss omit vs 38

10:39 omit G בשבילי ימצאנה [בשבילי ימצאנה AEF אותה [אותי ABDEFG יאבדיה [יאבדיה DG האב והבן [האוהב

²³Again Jesus said to his disciples:
When they persue you in this city flee to another; truly I say to you,
you will not have completed for yourselves all the cities of Israel before the Son of Man comes.

²⁴No disciple is greater than his teacher nor is the servant greater than his
master.

²⁵It is sufficient for the disciple to be like his teacher and for the servant
to be like his master. If they call the master of the house Baalzebub so
much the more the sons of his house.

²⁶Do not fear them because there is nothing which will not be seen nor
hidden (which will not be made known).

²⁷(That which) I say to you in darkness say it in the light; (that which
you hear by the ear tell it in the gate).

²⁸Do not fear those who kill (bodies) who have no power to kill souls;
but fear the one who has power to destroy the soul and the body in
Gehenna.

²⁹Are not two sparrows (sold) for a small coin and not one of them will
fall to the earth except by the will of your Father who is heaven?

³⁰Are not all the hairs of your head numbered?

³¹Do not fear because (you) are better than the sparrows.

³²He who praises me before man I will praise before my Father who is in
heaven.

³⁴In that hour Jesus said to his disciples: Do not think I have come to put
(peace) on the earth, but a sword.

³⁵I have come to separate mankind, the son from his father and the
daughter from her mother.

³⁶The enemy is to be loved ones.

³⁷He who loves his father and his mother more than me, I am not suitable for him.

³⁹He who loves his life will lose it, he who loses (it) for my sake will
find it.

⁴⁰המקבל אתכם יקבל אותי והמקבל אותי יקבל את אשר שלחני.

⁴¹המקבל נביא לשם נביא יקבל שכר הנביא והמקבל צדיק לשם
צדיק יקבל שכר הצדיק.

⁴²והנותן כלי א׳ של מים קרים לאחד מתלמידי הקטנים לשם
תלמידי אמן אני אומר לכם שלא יאבד שכרו.

## פרק מ״ז

¹ויהי בכלות יש״ו לצוות לשנים עשר תלמידיו ויעבור משם
ויצום ללמד ולהוכיח בעריהם.

²וישמע יוחנן בהיותו תפוס מעשה יש״ו וישלח שנים מתלמידיו

³לאמר לו האתה הוא מי שעתיד לבא או נקוה אחר.

⁴ויען להם יש״ו לכו והגידו ליוחנן את אשר ראיתם ואשר שמעתם

⁵העורים רואים ופסחים הולכים והמצורעים נטהרים
והחרשים שומעים והחיים מתים והענוים מתפשרים.

⁶ואשרי אשר לא יהיה נבוך בי.

⁷ויהי המה הולכים ויחל יש״ו לדבר אל החבורות מיוחנן.
לראות מה יצאתם במדבר קנה מושלכת ברוח?

⁸או מה יצאתם לראות? התחשבו שיוחנן אדם לבוש בגדים רבים?
הנה לובשי הבגדים רבים בבתי המלכים.

⁹א׳כ מה יצאתם לראות נביא? באמת אני אומר לכם שזה גדול
מנביא.

¹⁰זהו שנכתב בעדו הנני שולח מלאכי ופנה דרך לפני.

## פרק מ״ח

¹¹עוד אמר יש״ו לתלמידיו באמת אני דובר לכם בכל ילדי
הנשים לא קם גדול מיוחנן המטביל.

¹²מימיו עד עתה מלכות שמים עשוקה קורעים אותה.

---

10:40[המקבל . . . ²אותי[ omit G

10:42[שלא[ לא A

11:1[ויצום[ ויצא D

11:2[שנים[ + עשר EF (?)

11:3[האתה[ אתה A

11:4[ואת[ omit A

11:5[והמתים חיים ABDEF | והחיים מתים[ EF | מטהרים[ נטהרים F | הפסחים BDE, והפסחים[ מתבשרים EF
ופסחים[ מתפשרים EF

11:6[ואשר . . . בי[ ואשר לא יהיה נכון בי EFG (?)

11:7[ויהי המה הולכים[ omit A | אל[ את A | מיוחנן[ ביוחנן B | יצאתם[ + לראות A

11:8[אדם[ omit D | לבוש[ לובש ADEFG | ²רבים[הרבים A, omit G

11:10[לפני[ omit G | שולח[ + לכם AE | לפני . . . מלאכי[ הנביא (?) את E, omit F

11:11[אומר[ דובר AH

11:12[ועד[ עד G | שמים[ omit G | עשוקה[ + והנבלים A, והנבלים BDEFGH

⁴⁰He who receives you receives me
and he who receives me receives the one who sent me.
⁴¹He who receives a prophet in the name of a prophet will receive the reward of the prophet; he who receives a righteous one in the name of a
righteous one will receive the reward of the righteous one.
⁴²He who gives a vessel of cold water to one of my little disciples in the
name of my disciple truly I say to you that he will not lose his reward.

## Chapter 11

¹It came to pass when Jesus finished commanding his twelve disciples
that he passed on from there and commanded them to teach and reprove
in their [own] cities.
²John, when he was in captivity, heard of the work of Jesus and sent
two of his disciples
³saying to him: Are you the one who is to come or should we expect another.
⁴Jesus answered them: Go and tell John that which you have seen and
that which you have heard:
⁵the blind see, the lame walk, the lepers are cleansed, the deaf hear, the
dead are revived and the poor are acquitted.
⁶Blessed is he who is not perplexed in me.
⁷It came to pass as they were going that Jesus began to speak to the
crowds about John: You went out into the wilderness to see what? A
reed cast about by the wind?
⁸Or what did you go out to see? Do you think that John was a man
clothed in noble garments? Behold those who wear noble garments are
in king's houses.
⁹If so, what did you go out to see, a prophet? Truly I say to you that this
one is greater than a prophet.
¹⁰This is he about whom it is written: behold I am sending my messenger
and he will make the way clear before me.
¹¹Again Jesus said to his disciples: Truly I say to you, among all those
born of women none has arisen greater than John the Baptizer.
¹²From his days until now the kingdom of heaven has been oppressed
(and senseless persons) have been rending it.

The Gospel of Matthew

<sup>13</sup>שכל הנביאים והתורה דברו על יוחנן.
<sup>14</sup>ואם תרצו לקבלו הוא אליה העתיד לבא.
<sup>15</sup>למי אזנים לשמוע ישמע.

פרק מ"ט

<sup>16</sup>עוד אמר יש"ו זה הדור אדמהו לנערים היושבים בשוק קוראים זה לזה
<sup>17</sup>ואומרים שדנו ולא דקדקתם ספרנו לכם ולא בכיתם.
<sup>18</sup>כי בא יוחנן ואינו אוכל ושותה ואומרים עליו שהוא אחוז משדים.
<sup>19</sup>ובן האדם בא לאכול ולשתות ואומר עליו שהוא זולל וסובא ואוהב לפריצים וחוטאים והסכלים שופטים לחכמים.

פרק חמשים

<sup>20</sup>אז התחיל יש"ו לקלל הנערים שנעשו מאותותיו ולא חזרו בתשובה.
<sup>21</sup>אי לך בורוזואים ואי לך בית שידה שאם בצור וסדום לעז טיראו דֵיטֵיר אוֹ סָדוֹמָה נעשו האותות שנעשו בכם היו חוזרות בתשובה בזמן ההוא בשק ואפר.
<sup>22</sup>אמן אני אומר לכם יותר קל יהיה לצור וסדים אכן.
<sup>23</sup>ואתה כפר נחום אם לשמים תעלה? משם תורד. שאם בסדום נעשו מאותות שנעשו בך אולי תשאר. עד שאול תורד.
<sup>24</sup>אמן אני אומר לך שיותר קל יהיה לארץ סדום ליום הדין ממך.

פרק נ"א

<sup>25</sup>בעת ההיא נתרומם יש"ו ואומר אני ישתבח אני בורא שמים והארץ שהסתרת דברים אלה מהחכמים והנבונים וגלית אותם לענים.

---

<sup>11:13</sup>שכל] לכל DGH | והתורה] + כולה A | דברי] דברו D, דוברים H
<sup>11:14</sup>לקבלו] + מלכות שמים B (?) | אליה] אליהו ABDG
<sup>11:16</sup>אדמהו] אדמה DEFG
<sup>11:17</sup>ספדנו] ספרנו ABCDEF | דקדקתם] רקדתם ABEFG, מדתם D | שרנו לכם] שדנו ABDEFG
<sup>11:18</sup>משדים] מהשדים A, השדים EF
<sup>11:19</sup>ואומר] ואומרים AG | אדם] האדם ABEFG
<sup>11:20</sup>התחיל] אתחיל G | הנערים] הערים ABCDEFG | + בהן A, + בהם BDEFG
<sup>11:21</sup>בורוזואים] בורוזואים A, כורזואים BEF, כורוזואים D, כורזואים G | בית] בת DG | שידה] שׂידָה A, טיראו וסדומה] טיראו . . . סדומה B | לעז] בלעז G | וצדון EF | וסדום] בפור ADG | בצור טיר או שדומה BDG, טיר או שדומה EF
<sup>11:22</sup>וסדום] ולסדום AB | אכן] מכם ADG, מכאן B, מכך EF
<sup>11:23</sup>משם] תורד A | תורד'] תוריד B | שאול תורד] היום הזה A
<sup>11:24</sup>קל] omit E, להיות F | יהיה] . . . קדום ABDG | תהיה] omit G
<sup>11:25</sup>ישו'] omit ABCDEFG אני] G ברוח הקדש ABDE, + ברוח + אני'] ישתבח] ישתבך A אני'[ אני + מהחכמים] מן החכמים A | וגלית אותם] וגילתם FG וארץ] והארץ ABCDEF | השמים] שמים AEF ולענים] לענים ABCDEFG וגליתו] B לענים

[13]For all the prophets and the law spoke concerning John.

[14]If you wish to receive it, he is Elijah who is going to come.

[15]He who has ears to hear, let him hear.

[16]Again Jesus said: I will liken this generation to lads who sit in the market place calling to one another

[17]saying: (We sang to you) and you did not (dance; we wailed) to you and you did not weep.

[18]Because John came neither eating or drinking they say concerning him, he is possessed of demons.

[19]But the Son of Man came eating and drinking and one says concerning him: he is a glutton, a drunkard and a friend to violent men and sinners; so fools judge the wise.

[20]Then Jesus began to curse (the cities in which) his signs were done for they did not turn in repentance.

[21]Woe to you (Corozim) and woe to you Beth Saida, for if in Tyre and Sodom, that is, Tirao deter or Sidomah, the signs had been done which were done in you they would have turned in repentance at that time in sack cloth and ashes.

[22]Truly I say to you it shall be easier for Tyre and Sodom (than for you).

[23]You Capernaum, if you ascend to heaven from there you will be brought down. Because if in Sodom the signs which were done in you had been done perhaps she would have remained. Unto Sheol you will be brought down.

[24]Truly I say to you that it shall be easier for the land of Sodom in the day of judgment than for you.

[25]At that time Jesus raised himself up and said: Be praised (my Father) creator of heaven and earth, because you have hidden these words from the wise and prudent and have revealed them to the humble.

<sup>26</sup>אמנם כי כן ישר לפניך אבי.

<sup>27</sup>הכל נתון לי מאת אבי. ואין מכיר את הבן אלא האב בלבד ולאב
אין מכיר אלא הבן ולאשר ירצה הבן לגלותו.

<sup>28</sup>בואו אליו כל היגעים ונושאי העמל ואני אעזור אתכם לשאת
עולכם.

<sup>29</sup>צאו עולי עולכם ולמדו ממני ותכירו כי עני אני וטוב ובר
הלבב ותמצאו מרגוע לנפשותיכם

<sup>30</sup>רק ומשאי קל.

## פרק נ"ב

<sup>1</sup>בעת ההיא עבר יש"ו בקמות ביום השבת ותלמידיו רעבים
התחילו לעקור השבולים ולפרוך אותם בין ידיהם ולאכול אותם.

<sup>2</sup>ויראו הפרושים ויאמרו אליו הנה תלמידך עושים דבר שאינו
נכון לעשות ביום השבת.

<sup>3</sup>ויען להם יש"ו ולא קראתם מה שעשה דוד כשהיה רעב ואנשיו

<sup>4</sup>בבית האלקים שאכלו מלחם הפנים בלעז פא"ן סאג"רה שאינו
נאכל אלא לכהנים בלבד.

<sup>5</sup>וגם בתורה לא קראתם שהכהנים בבית המקדש מחללים לפעמים
השבתות ואין להם חטא?

<sup>6</sup>אמן אני אומר לכם שמקדש גדול ממנו הוא.

<sup>7</sup>אילו ידעתם מהו חסד חפצתי ולא זבה לא הייתם מחייבים
התמימים.

<sup>8</sup>שבן אדם אדון השבת.

## פרק נ"ג

<sup>9</sup>ויהי לקצת הימים ויעבור משם יש"ו ויבא בבתי כנסיותם.

<sup>11:26</sup>אמנם] + אבי ABDEFGH [ישר] רצוי A, יש H [אבי] omit ABDEFGH
<sup>11:27</sup>אם כי] <sup>1</sup>אלה] omit GH [את] G מאת + [מאת] H מאבי [מאת אבי] B נתן [נתון] H כל [הכל] H
ולמי שירצה [ולאשר ירצה] omit EF [ירצה] H כי אם] <sup>2</sup>אלה] C, omit H [בלבד] לבד H
<sup>11:28</sup>לשנות [לשאת] AB אלי [אליו] H לכו [בואו] DG
<sup>11:29</sup>הלבב [לבב] BDEFG עליכם A, עלכם [עולכם] צאו] omit C (hap) [צאו . . . עולכם] שאו AB
A לנפשותכם [לנפשותיכם] B
<sup>11:30</sup>רק] רק BDEFG שעולי] + ושעולי A, + Beginning]
C התחילו [התחיל] B תלמידיו [ותלמידיו] <sup>12:1</sup>
<sup>12:2</sup>ויראו] + אותם F הפרושין [הפרושים] F הנה] omit A נכון [הנון] F, omit G
<sup>12:3</sup>ולא] B לא [שעשה] ABDG עשה [רעב] + הוא A
<sup>12:4</sup>האלקים] A בלעז [בלעז] לעז ABDEF פאן סאגרה [סאגרה] omit G סאגרה [שאגרט] A שאגראט B
EF שגראש D שאגראטו
<sup>12:5</sup>השבתות [השבת] EF
<sup>12:6</sup>הוא] + זה A, omit G
<sup>12:7</sup>מהו] G כי מהוא B, זבה [זבח] ABDEFG
<sup>12:8</sup>אדם [האדם] EF השבת [השמים] EF
<sup>12:9</sup>כנסיותם] כנסיותיהם A, כנסיותהם D

²⁶Truly this is because it was upright before you, my Father.

²⁷All has been given to me from my Father. There is none who knows
the son but the Father alone and the Father no one knows but the son
and to whomever the son wishes to reveal him.

²⁸Come unto me all you who are weary and who are enduring labor and I
will help you to bear your yoke.

²⁹(Take) my yoke as your yoke and learn of me and know that I am humble and good and pure of heart and you shall find rest for your souls,

³⁰(because my yoke is soft) and my burden light.

## Chapter 12

¹At that time Jesus passed through the standing grain on the Sabbath day
and his disciples being hungry began to pluck the ears and to crush
them between their hands and to eat them.

²The Pharisees saw it and said to him: Behold your disciples are doing
that which is not proper to do on the Sabbath day.

³Jesus answered them: Have you not read what David did when he was
hungry and his men

⁴in the house of God when they ate from the bread of the Presence, that
is, paan sagrah, which is not to be eaten except by the priests alone.

⁵Also in the Torah have you not read that the priests in the Temple
sometimes profane the Sabbaths and are without sin?

⁶Truly I say to you that the temple is greater than this.

⁷If you had known what this is: I desire kindness and not (sacrifice), you
would not have convicted the innocent.

⁸For the Son of Man is lord of the Sabbath.

⁹It came to pass at the end of the days that Jesus passed on from there
and entered into their Synagogues.

[MT 12:10-25

<sup>10</sup>ושם אדם וידו יבשה וישאלוהו לאמר אם מותר בשבת לרפאתו.

<sup>11</sup>ויאמר להם מי בכם מי שיש לו צאן אחת ותפול בשוחה ביום השבת ולא יקימנה.

<sup>12</sup>כ״ש האדם שהוא טוב ממנה. לפיכך מותר לעשות ויש לאדם לעשות יותר טוב בשבת.

<sup>13</sup>אז אמר לאיש נטה ידך. ויט ידו ותשב כמו האחרת.

<sup>14</sup>ואז נוסדו הפרושים וינכלו אליו להמיתו.

## פרק נ״ד

<sup>15</sup>ויהי אחרי זאת וידע יש״ו ויט משם וילכו אחריו חולים רבים וירפא את כולם.

<sup>16</sup>ויצום לאמר לבל יגלוהו

<sup>17</sup>לקיים מה שנאמר ע״י ישעה

<sup>18</sup>הן נערי אשר בחרתי בחירי רצתה נפשי אתן רוחי עליו ומשפט לגוים יגיד.

<sup>19</sup>ולא ירהה ולא ירוץ ולא ישמע אחד בחוץ.

<sup>20</sup>קנה רצוץ לא ישבור ופשתה כהה לא יכבנה עד ישים לנצח משפט

<sup>21</sup>ולשמו גוים ייחלו.

## פרק נ״ה

<sup>22</sup>אז הובא לפניו אדם אחד עור ואלם והשד בתוכו וירפא אותו. וראו

<sup>23</sup>ונפלאו החבורות ויאמרו הלא זה בן דוד.

<sup>24</sup>וישכימו הפירושים וישמעו ויאמרו זה אינו מוציא השדים אלא בבעל זבוב בעל השדים.

<sup>25</sup>וידע מחשבותם יש״ו ויאמר אליהם במשל כל מלכות שביניכם מחלוקת תשומם וכן כל עיר ובית שתפול מחלוקת בתוכם לא יתקיים.

---

<sup>12:10</sup>וישאלוהו] A, וישאלוה EF

<sup>12:13</sup>ותשב] EF וישב

<sup>12:14</sup>וינכלו] EF ויתנכלו | אליו] omit D

<sup>12:15</sup>זאת] כן EF | וידע ישו] H 1 2 | ויט] ועבר H | וירפא] רפא והוא H

<sup>12:16</sup>לאמר] omit H | לבל] לבלתי H | שלא G, לא EF, | יגלוהו] יגלהו DG, יפרסמוהו H

<sup>12:17</sup>לקים] שיתקיים בעבור H | ישעה] ישעיה AB, ישעיה CDEFGH

<sup>12:18</sup>נערי] עבדי DEFH | ומשפט] משפט EF

<sup>12:19</sup>ירהה] ירהא A, יכבה G | בחוץ] + קולו ABCDEF

<sup>12:20</sup>ישים] ישליך ABDEFG | לנצח] ישים C 1 2

<sup>12:22</sup>לפניו] לפני ישו G | אחד] omit H | וראו] וראה ABDEFGH

<sup>12:24</sup>השדים] שדים BG | בעל] שר AB-DEFG | וישמעו] omit ABDEFGH | וישכימו] וישמעו ABDEFGH

<sup>12:25</sup>מחלוקת<sup>1</sup>] 2 1 ABDEFGH | שביניכם] שבנהם A, שביניהם DEFGH | ובית] או בית A | בתוכם] בנהם A | מחלוקת<sup>2</sup>] מחלוקתם F, מחלוקתם E

[10]A man was there with a withered hand; so they asked him
saying: Is it permissible to heal him on the Sabbath.

[11]He said to them: Who among you has a sheep that falls into a pit on the
Sabbath day and does not raise it up.

[12]So much the more is man better than that. Therefore it is permissible
and [necessary] for man to do better on the Sabbath.

[13]Then he said to the man: Stretch out your hand. He stretched out his
hand and it returned as the other.

[14]Then the Pharisees took counsel and plotted to put him to death.

[15]It came to pass after this that Jesus knew it; so he turned aside from
there. Many sick followed him and he healed all of them.

[16]Then he commanded them saying not to reveal him,

[17]in order to establish what was spoken by Isaiah:

[18]behold my servant whom I have selected, my chosen one with whom
my soul is pleased; I will put my spirit upon him and he will declare
justice to the nations.

[19]He will not fear nor will he run nor shall one hear (his voice) in the
street.

[20]A crushed reed he will not break and a dim wick he will not quench
until he establishes justice forever,

[21]and in his name the Gentiles hope.

[22]Then there was brought to him a blind and dumb man who was demon
possessed; he healed him. The crowds saw [it]

[23]and marveled and said: Is this not the Son of David?

[24]The Pharisees were quick to hear [this] and said: This one does not cast
out demons except by Beelzebub the lord of demons.

[25]Jesus knew their thoughts and said to them in a parable: Every kingdom among you divided shall be made desolate, and so every city or
house in which division shall fall shall not stand.

[MT 12:26-38

²⁶ואת השטן מוציא שטן אחר מחלוקת ביניכם איך תעמוד מלכותו?

²⁷ואם אני מוציא השדים בבעל זבוב בנים שלכם למה לא הוציאם ולזה יהיו הם שופטיכם.

²⁸ואם אני מוציא השדים ברוח אלקים באמת בא קץ מלכות.

²⁹ואיך יוכל איש לבא בבית גבור לקחת את כליו אם לא יקשור אותו תחילה? ואח״כ ישלול בביתו.

## פרק נ״ו

³⁰מי שאינו עמדי לנגדי. הוא מה שלא יתחבר עמי יכפור בפועל.

³¹כן אני אומר לכם שכל חטא וגדוף ימחל לבני אדם וגדוף הרוח לא ימחל.

³²וכל האומר דבר נגד בן האדם ימחל לו. וכל האומר דבר נגד רוח הקדוש לא ימחל לו לא בעה״ז ולא בעה״ב.

³³עשו עץ טוב כפרי טוב או עץ רע כפרי רע שהאמת מן הפרי יודע העץ.

³⁴משפחת פתנים אוך תוכלו לדבר טובות בהיותכם רעים? והלא הפה מתעוררת הלב מדברת.

³⁵אדם טוב מאוצר לב טוב יוציא טוב ואדם רע מאוצר לב רע ויציא רע.

³⁶אומר אני לכם שמכל הדברים אשר ידבר האדם חייב לתת חשבון ליום הדין.

³⁷על פי דבריך תהיה נשפט ועל פי מעשיך תתחייב.

## פרק נ״ז

³⁸בעת ההיא בא ליש״ו קצת פירושים וחכמים לאמר נרצה לראות אות מהשמים בעבורך.

---

¹²:²⁶ ואת] שטן C | ביניכם] בנהם A, ביניהם BDEFGH | השטן C | ואם A

¹²:²⁷ בנים] בנים GH omit | F omit | הוציאם] הוציאום ADEFH, תוציאום G

¹²:²⁸ אלקים] באמת מלכות שמים G | אלקים . . . ברוח] omit EF | אלקים] אלים A | מלכות . . . אלקים] EF | + אלקים] omit D | קץ] + באמת . . . מלכות | H אלקים באמת מלכותו B אלקים ומלכותו A, אלים + מלכות] B

¹²:²⁹ בביתו] ביתו ABDEFGH | ואחר] ואח״כ ABDGH

¹²:³⁰ בפועל] בי DG, במעל ABEF | יתחבר] מתחבר EF | שלא] שאינו EF | מי AEF, ומי] מה BDG

¹²:³¹ כן] על כן ABEF | ימחל²] ימחל B | ימחל¹&²] ימחל DG

¹²:³² האדם] אדם H | רוח הקדוש] הדוח EF | הקדוש] הקדש ABD

¹²:³³ עץ²] על D

¹²:³⁴ ואתם] מדבר B | מתעוררת] מההתעוררות A | מדברת] מדבר B | ואתם] A

¹²:³⁵ לב] + EF, ABDG אדם] ואדם

¹²:³⁶ ידבר] דבר C

¹²:³⁸ ההיא] ההוא D | בא] באו ABDEFG | קצת] מקצת A | פירושים] הפרושים A | וחכמים] והחכמים נרצה] נרצו B | מהשמים] משמים F | בעבורך ADEF

26(If) Satan casts out another satan, there will be division
among (them); how will his kingdom stand?

27If I cast out demons by Beelzebub why do your sons not cast them out?
Therefore they will be your judges.

28But if I cast out demons by the Spirit of God truly the end of [his] kingdom has come.

29How shall a man be able to enter the house of the strong man to take
his goods unless he bind him first? Then he shall plunder his house.

30Whoever is not with me is against me. (Whoever) does not join himself
to me denies (me).

31(Therefore) I say to you that every sin and blasphemy will be forgiven
the sons of men, but blasphemy of the Spirit shall not be forgiven.

32Everyone who says a word against the Son of Man it shall be forgiven
him. But everyone who says a word against the Holy Spirit it shall not
be forgiven him either in this world or in the world to come.

33Make the true good according to good fruit or the tree bad according to
bad fruit; because the truth is: from the fruit the tree will be known.

34Family of vipers, how can you speak good things when you are evil?
Surely the mouth awakens, the heart speaks.

35A good man from the treasure of a good heart brings forth good; an
evil man from the treasure of an evil heart brings forth evil.

36I say to you that for all the words which a man shall speak he will be
obliged to give an account on the day of judgment.

37According to your words you will be judged and according to your
deeds you will be convicted.

38At that time there came to Jesus some of the Pharisees and sages saying: We wish to see a sign from heaven by you.

[MT 12:39-13:1

39וַיאמר להם דור רע וחנף מבקש אות ואות לא ינתן לו אלא האות
של יונה.

40שכאשר היה במעי הדגה ג׳ ימים וג׳ לילות כן יהיה בן אדם
בבטן הארץ ג׳ ימים וג׳ לילות בקבר.

41אנשי ננוה יקומו למשפט עם זה הדור וירשיעו אותו כי חזרו
בתשובה לדברי יונה ואני גדול מיונה.

42מלכת שבא בלעז רֵיזִינָה ״דִי אִישְׁטְרִיאָה תקום למשפט עם זה הדור
ותרשיעם שבאה מקצות הארץ לשמוע חכמת שלמה והנני גדול
משלמה.

43וכיוצא רוח טומאה מהאדם הולך בציות מבקש מנוח ולא ימצא.

44אז אומר אשיב לביתי אשר יצאתי ממנו ובא ומוצא אותו ריק
בטוח ונכון.

45אז יקח שבעה רוחות יותר רעים ממנו ובאים עמו ויושבים
שם ויהיה אחרית האדם רע מראשיתו. כן יהיה לדור הרע הזה.

## פרק נ״ח

46עודנו מדבר על כל החבורות והנה אמו ואחיו עומדים בחוץ
מבקשים ממנו לדבר עמו.

47ויאמר לו אדם אחד הנה אמך ואחיך מבקשים לראותך.

48ויען למגיד מי אחי ומי אמי.

49ויפרוש כפיו על תלמידיו ויאמרו אלו הם אמי ואחי.

50כל העושה רצון אבי שבשמים הוא אחי ואחיותי ואמי.

## פרק נ״ט

1ביום ההוא יצא יש״ו מהבית וישב על שפת הים.

12:39 הנביא + A | ]יונה G לך | EF, לך [להם A | ]לו
12:40 נקבר [בקבר F | ]ימים E, + ימים [2ימים | לילות BDEG | האדם A, האדמה [אדם G | כשהיה [שכאשר היה
ABCDEFG
12:41 לדבר [לדברי A | הרע EF + | הדור [נ]ננוה [ננוה A
12:42 ראינה דאישטריאה A, רֵיינה די אישטוריאש [רֵיזִינה די אישטריאה ADEFG | לעז [בלעז B,
EF הרע + | הדור [G | ראינה די אישטריאה EF, ראינה די אישטריטה D, ראינה די אשטריאה
12:43 מאדם F | מהאדם [מהאדם BEF | הטומאה [טומאה AE | וכשיוצא [וכיוצא
EF לבקש [מבקש A | לעז פירליליוקאש שיקאש + [בציות
12:44 אשוב [אשיב A | אומרת [אומר ABDEFG
12:45 ויהי [ויהיה A | יושבים F יושבים DG, והולכים [ויושבים
12:46 עם [על ABDEFGH | אחיו EF | אמו ואחיו [ממנו . . . עמו ]omit D (hap)
12:47 מבקשים . . . ויאמר [omit D
12:48 אחי [ואחי A 1 2 | אמי . . . ABDEFG אליו + [למגיד
BEF אליהם [אלו הם ABCDEFG ויאמר [ויאמרו
12:49 G אמי ואחי ואחיתי [אחי ואחיותי
13:1 EF בעת ההיא [ביום ההוא

[39]He said to them: An evil and wicked generation seeks a sign,
but no sign will be given to it except the sign of Jonah.

[40]For as he was in the bowels of the fish three days and three nights, so
will the Son of Man be in the belly of the earth, (buried) for three days
and three nights.

[41]The men of Nineveh will rise up in judgment with this generation and
shall condemn it because they turned in repentance at the words of
Jonah and I am greater than Jonah.

[42]The queen of Sheba, that is, Rezinah de Isteriah, will rise up in judgment with this generation and shall condemn it because she came from
the ends of the earth to hear the wisdom of Solomon and behold I am
greater than Solomon.

[43]When the unclean spirit goes out from the man he goes through water-
less places seeking rest, but does not find it.

[44]Then he says: I will return to my house from which I came out, and he
goes and finds it empty, safe, and ready.

[45]Then he takes seven spirits more evil than himself and they go with
him and dwell there and the latter state of the man is worse than his
first. Thus it will be to this evil generation.

[46]While he was speaking to all the crowds behold his mother and his
brothers were standing outside seeking him to speak with him.

[47]A man said to him: Behold your mother and your brothers are seeking
to see you.

[48]He answered the one who spoke (to him): Who are my brothers and
who is my mother.

[49]He stretched out his hands to his disciples and said: These are my
mother and brothers.

[50]Everyone who does the will of my Father who is in heaven is my
brothers, my sisters and my mother.

# Chapter 13

[1]On that day Jesus went out of the house and sat on the shore of the sea.

[MT 13:2-18

2ויתחברו אליו חבורות עד שנצטרך לבא באניה וכל החבורה
עומדת בחוץ.

3וידבר להם דברים רבים במשלים ויאמר להם איש יוצא מביתו
בבוקר לזרוע את זרעו.

4ובזרעו נפל ממנו בדרך ואכל אותו העוף.

5וממנה נפלה באבן שאין שם עובי עפר ובצמחו נתייבש לפי
שאין שם עפר לרוב.

6ובחום השמש עליו נשרף ונתייבש שאין לו שורש.

7וממנו נפל בין הקוצים ויגדלוהו הקוצים ויעמדוהו.

8וממנו נפל בארץ טובה ויעשה פרי ותבואה האחד מאה והשני
ששים והשלישי שלשים.

9למי אזנים לשמוע ישמע.

10ויקרבו אליו תלמידיו ואמרו לו תלמידיו למה תדבר במשלים.

11ויאמר שלכם נתן מלכות שמים להכיר ולא להם.

12למי שיש לו ינתן עוד ולמי שאין לו מה שהוא חושב
ילקח ממנו.

13לזה אני מדבר במשלים שהם רואים ואינם רואים שומעים
ואינם שומעים

14לגמור מה שנאמר ע″י ישעיה הנביא לך ואמרת לעם הזה
שמעו שמוע ואל תדעו וראו ראה ואל וכו'.

15השמן לב העם הזה ואזניו הכבד ועיניו השע פן יראה
בעיניו וכו'.

16ואשרי עיניכם שרואות ואזניכם ששומעות.

17אמן אני דובר לכם שנביאים רבים וצדיקים התאוו לראות מה
שאתם רואים ולא ראו ולשמוע מה שאתם שומעים ולא שמעו.

18ואתם שמעו משל הזורע.

---

13:2 מבחוץ [בחוץ A, בחוף B
13:3 omit F [את | G לבקר [בבוקר | omit EFG [רבים
13:5 = D(marg) [לפי . . . לרוב | C שם + | שם [שם | DG ממנו נפלה, AEF וממנו נפל [וממנה נפלה
13:6 וֻבחום . . . וֻנתייבש = D(marg), ms G unclear
13:7 ויגדלו הקוצים ויעממוהו A, ויעממֹוהו ויגדלו הקוצים [ויגדלוהו | ויעמדוהו EF . . . ויעמדוהו [נפל
B, ויעממוהו DG, ויגדלו הקוצים ויעממהו C, ויגדל הקוצים ויעמדוהו EF (hap)
13:8 תבואה [ותבואה | EF וישו [ויעשה EF
13:10 C אתה + [תדבר | omit ABDEFG [²תלמידיו
13:11 השמים [שמים G
13:12 שיש לו [יש לו + ABDEFG | חושב [חשב + | לו [ינתן ABDG
13:14 ראו [ראה AEF | תבינו [תדעו G omit | לעם [העם A אל העם [הנביא . . . ²ואל | EF לקיים [לגמור
D תבינו + ABEF, ²ואל [ואל + תדעו A
13:15 בעיניו [בעיניו G omit | ואזניו . . . G omit AF [בעיניו
13:17 התאוו [ידאגו EF

²Crowds joined themselves to him until when
he needed to enter a boat; the whole crowd was standing (on the shore).
³He spoke to them many things in parables and said to them: A man
went forth from his house in the morning to sow his seed.
⁴In his sowing some of it fell on the road and the birds ate it.
⁵Some of it fell among rocks where there was no density of soil and
when it sprang up it withered because there was not much soil there.
⁶When the sun above it became warm; it was burned and dried up because it had no root.
⁷Some of it fell among the thorns and the thorns (grew and darkened it).
⁸Some of it fell on good ground and it made fruit, the first brought forth
a hundred, the second sixty and the third thirty.
⁹Whoever has ears to hear let him hear.
¹⁰Then his disciples drew near to him and his disciples said to him: Why
do you speak in parables.
¹¹He said: To you it has been given to know the kingdom of heaven but
not to them.
¹²Whoever has, it will be given (to him) again, but whoever has nothing,
that which he thinks (he has) will be taken from him.
¹³For this [reason] I speak in parables because they see but do not see,
hear but do not hear,
¹⁴in order to fulfill what was said through Isaiah the Prophet: Go and say
to this people, hear but do not know, see but do not (understand).
¹⁵Make the heart of this people fat and make their ears heavy and blind
their eyes, lest they should see with their eyes.
¹⁶Blessed are your eyes that see and your ears that hear.
¹⁷Truly I say to you that many prophets and righteous men desired to see
what you see but did not see it, and to hear what you hear but did not
hear it.
¹⁸But hear you the parable of the sower.

[MT 13:19-30

¹⁹הזורע הוא בן אדם והזרע שנפל בדרך כל השומע מלכות שמים ולא יבין. יבא השטן ויחתוף מלבו כל מה שנזרע בו. וזהו הזרע שנפל על הדרך.

²⁰ואשר נפל על האבן הוא השומע דבר האל וקבלנו מיד בשמחה.

²¹והוא בלא שורש ומבוכה ובבא מעט צער וצרה להם השטן משכחו מלבם.

²²ואשר נפל בקוצים זה השומע את הדבר ובחמדתו לאסוף עושר השטן משכחו דבר האל ולא יעשה פרי.

²³ואשר נפל בארץ הטובה הוא השומע את הדבר ומבין ועושה פרי ר״ל ממעשים טובים. ויוציא מן הא״ מאה ומן השני ששים ומן השלישי שלשים. הא״ מאה זהו מטהרת הלב וקדושת הגוף. ומהאחד ששים זהו מפרישות האשה. ומהשלישי שלשים זהו מקדושה בזיווג בגוף ובלב.

## פרק ששים

²⁴וישם לפניהם משל אחר. מלכות שמים דומה לאיש הזורע כשזרעו זרע טוב.

²⁵ויהי כאשר בני אדם ישנים בא שונאו ויזרע על החטים זון בלעז בריא״גה וילך.

²⁶ויהי כאשר גדלה העשב לעשות פרי וראה הזון.

²⁷ויקרבו עבדי בעל השדה אליו ויאמרו לו אדונינו הלא זרע טוב זרעת. ומאין היה הזון?

²⁸אמר להם שונאי עשו זה ויאמרו לו עבדיו נעקור הזון.

²⁹ויאמר להם לא פן תעקרו החטה.

³⁰אלא הניהו זה וזה ויגדל עד הקציר ובעת הקציר אמר לקוצרים לקטו הזון ראשונה וקשרו אותה חבילות חבילות לשרוף והחטה תנו באוצר.

---

¹³:¹⁹שזרע [שנזרע EFG | ויחתוף [ויחתוף G | omit [שמים | ADEF האדם [אדם | B משל + [Beginning]
זה A, זהו [וזהו G | EF

¹³:²⁰ABDEFG ויקבלנו [וקבלנו ABCDEFG את + [השומע G | אבן [האבן

¹³:²¹EF צרה וצער [צער וצרה EF | ומכוסה ABDG, ומבוכה [ומבוכה

¹³:²²האל [אלהים EF | מלבם + EF, omit G [משכחו | אל [את A | זהו [זה EF | אל הקוצים [בקוצים ABCDEFG

¹³:²³C, ומה״ב [ומהאחד G | השלישי [שלישי omit ABDEFG | ר״ל [ר״ל omit AG | את] זה וזהו A | והוא omit B [בזיווג EFG | מקדושה [מקדושה BDG, ומא EF | ומא והמאחד A, ומהא ומהשלישי EF והא

¹³:²⁴ABDEFG בשדהו [כשזרעו A (?) | ציאלאים [לאיש BEFG | והוא + [שמים

¹³:²⁵AEFG, ויראאגה [בריאגה ADEFG | לעז [בלעז A | החטה [החטים AD | האדם [אדם A | ויהיא [ויהי A | ויראאגא C, בריאגא D [ויך | omit AEF

¹³:²⁶G נראה B, (?) ונתראה [וראה

¹³:²⁷A זרעתה [זרעת

¹³:²⁸G כן [זה ABDEFG עשה [עשו

¹³:²⁹A, omit G לו [לא FG לה [להם

¹³:³⁰ABDEFG את + [לקטו G | אמור [אמר C בעת [ובעת B עת + [עד D | יגדל [ויגדל A אותה + [תנו A omit [²חבילות ABDEFG אותו [אותה EFG תחלה [ראשונה

[19]The Sower is the Son of Man
and the seed which fell on the road is every one who hears the kingdom of heaven and does not understand it. Satan comes and snatches away from his heart everything which was sown in it. This is the seed which fell on the road.

[20]That which fell upon the rocks is the one who hears the word of God and receives it immediately with joy.

[21]But he is without root and is (in) confusion and when a little trouble and distress come to them Satan causes [them] to forget from their heart.

[22]That which fell among the thorns, this is the one who hears the word and in his desire to gather wealth, Satan causes him to forget the word of God that he should make no fruit.

[23]That which fell into the good earth is the one who hears the word and understands it and makes fruit, that is, from good works. He brings forth from the first a hundred, from the second sixty and from the third thirty. As for the hundred, this is the one purified of heart and sanctified of body. As for the sixty this is the one separated from women. As for the thirty, this is the one sanctified in matrimony, in body and in heart.

[24]He set before them another parable. The kingdom of heaven is like a man who sows good seed (in his field).

[25]It came to pass when the men were sleeping, his enemy came and sowed tares over the wheat, that is, beriyagah, and he went away.

[26]It came to pass when the herb grew up to make fruit he saw the tares.

[27]The servants of the master of the field drew near to him and said to him: Master did you not sow good seed. Then whence came the tares?

[28]He said to them: My enemy (did) this. His servants said to him: We will uproot the tares.

[29]He said to them: No, lest you uproot the wheat.

[30]But let them remain together and grow up until the harvest and in the time of the harvest I will say to the reapers: gather the tares first and bind them into individual bundles for burning and the wheat put into the granary.

## פרק ס"א

³¹וישם לפניהם משל אחר. מלכות שמים דומה לגרגיר חרדל שיקח אותו אדם ויזרעהו בשדה.

³²והוא דק מכל זרעונים ובגדלו יגדל על כל העשבים ונעשה עץ גדול עד שעוף השמים יאצילו באנפא.

³³וידבר להם משל אחר. מלכות שמים דומה לשאור שמביא אותו האלה בשלש סאים קמח ויחמיץ את כולו.

³⁴כל המשלים האלה דבר יש"ו לחבורות ובלי משל לא היה דובר אליהם

³⁵לקיים מה שנאמר ע"פ הנביא אפתחה במשל פי אביעה חדות מני קדם.

## פרק ס"ב

³⁶אז נפרד יש"ו מן החבורות ויבא אל הבית. ויקרבו אליו תלמידיו ובקשו ממנו לפרוש להם משל הזון.

³⁷ויען להם ויאמר להם הזורע זרע טוב הוא האדם

³⁸והשדה הוא העולם הזה ופרי הטוב הם הצדיקים והזון הם הרשעים.

³⁹והשונא שזרע אותו הוא השטן והקמה אחרית העה"ב והקוצרים הם המלאכים.

⁴⁰וכאשר לקטו הקוצרים הזון לשרוף כן יהיה באחרית הימים.

⁴¹ישלח בן אדם את ממלאכיו לעקור ממלכותו כל רשע וכל פועלי און.

⁴²וישליחו אותם במדורת אש ושם יהיה בכי וחרוקת שינים.

⁴³אז יזהירו הצדיקים כשמש במלכות אביהם. למי אזנים לשמוע ישמע.

---

¹³:³¹ ויזרעהו [ויזרעה B

¹³:³² הזרעונים [זרעונים | כל + [השבים G | באנפא [בענפיו ABDEF, עליו G

¹³:³³ האשה [האלה A | שתביא [שמביא ABDEFG | ויאמר להם + [אחר

¹³:³⁴ להם [אליהם ABDEF | דבר [אמר G | האלו [האלה ABCDEFG

¹³:³⁵ אביעה] omit B | קדם . . . אביעה [אביעא F | ישעיה D | פי] + [אביעה

¹³:³⁶ ויבקשו [ובקשו ABDEFG

¹³:³⁷ בן + [הוא A | להם [²להם] omit ABCDEF | ויען להם] omit G

¹³:³⁸ הם] omit ABDG | הטוב [²הם] omit ABCDEF

¹³:³⁹ הוא] omit A | העה"ב [העולם ABDEFG | והקוצרים [וקוצרים A | הם] אלו F

¹³:⁴⁰ לשרוף [להשלך אותו באש G

¹³:⁴¹ האדם [אדם ABDG | ממלאכיו [מלאכיו ABD | און [וכל פועלי און] omit G

¹³:⁴² וישליחו [וישליכו ABDEFG | אותם [אותו G | אש [האש ABDEG | וחריקת [וחריק | שן G | שינים [שנים B

¹³:⁴³ לשמוע] omit A

<sup>31</sup>He set before them another parable.
The kingdom of heaven is like a grain of mustard which a man takes
and sows in the field.
<sup>32</sup>It is smaller than all garden herbs and when it grows up it is greater
than all herbs and is made into a great tree until the birds of heaven
withdraw into (its) branches.
<sup>33</sup>He spoke to them another parable. The kingdom of heaven is like
leaven which (a woman puts) into three measures of flour and it leav-
ens all of it.
<sup>34</sup>All of these parables Jesus spoke to the crowds and without a parable
he did not speak to them,
<sup>35</sup>to fulfill what was said according to the prophet: I will open my mouth
in parables; I will utter riddles from ancient times.
<sup>36</sup>Then Jesus was parted from the crowds and went into the house. His
disciples came to him and asked him to explain for them the parable of
the tares.
<sup>37</sup>He answered them and said to them: The one who sows good seed is
the Man,
<sup>38</sup>the field of this world, the good fruit is the righteous and the tares are
the evil.
<sup>39</sup>The enemy who sowed it is Satan, the standing grain is the latter end,
[namely,] the world to come and the reapers are the angels.
<sup>40</sup>As the reapers gather the tares to burn so will it be at the end of the
days.
<sup>41</sup>The Son of Man will send his angels to uproot from his kingdom all
evil and all who do iniquity.
<sup>42</sup>They will (cast) them into the pyre of fire; there will be weeping and
gnashing of teeth.
<sup>43</sup>Then the righteousness will shine like the sun in the kingdom of their
father. Whoever has ears to hear let him hear.

## פרק ס"ג

⁴⁴עוד אמר יש"ו לתלמידיו מלכות שמים היא דומה לאדם המוציא מטמון אשר יסתירוהו ובשמחת הממון ימכור כל אשר לו ויקנה השדה בעדו.

⁴⁵ועוד מלכות שמים דומה לאדם סוחר המבקש אבנים יקרות.

⁴⁶וכאשר ימצא אחת טובה ימכור כל אשר לו ויקנה אותה.

⁴⁷מלכות שמים דומה לרשת בתוך הים שכל מיני דגים נאספים בה.

⁴⁸וכאשר תמלא יוציאוה לחוץ ויוצאים הדייגים ובוחרים הטובים בכליהם והרעים משליכים חוצה.

⁴⁹כן יהיה באחרית הימים יצאו המלאכים ויבדילו הרשעים מתוך הצדיקים.

⁵⁰וישליכו אותם במדורות אש שם יהיה בכי וחריקת שינים.

⁵¹ויאמר להם הבנתם זה. ויאמרו כן.

⁵²לזאת כל חכם ידמה במלכות שמים לאדם אבי הטף המוציא מאוצרו דברים חדשים גם ישנים.

## פרק ס"ד

⁵³ויהי אחרי זאת כאשר כלה יש"ו הדברים האלה עבר משם.

⁵⁴ובא לארצו והיה מלמד לאנשים בבתי כנסיות. והפרושים נפלאו ויאמרו בלבם מאין בה לזה החכמה וכח לעשות אלו הפעולות.

⁵⁵אין בן זה הנפח ומרים? הלא ידעתם שכל אלו אמו מרים ואחיו ג' יוסף ושמע"ון ויהוד"ה

⁵⁶ואחיותיו. הלא ידעתם שכל אלו עמנו? ומאין בא לזה כל אלה?

⁵⁷והיו נבוכים בו. ויען להם יש"ו אין נביא שאין לו כבוד כ"א בארצו ועירו וביתו.

⁵⁸ולא רצה לעשות שם שום אות למיעוט אמונתם.

---

13:44 היא דומה] 2 1 A, 2 B | המוציא] אשר A | מה שיש A | המוצא ABDEFG | יסתירוהו] יסתירהו ABDEF
13:46 את] אחת G
13:47 דומה] היא + ABEFG, הוא D
13:48 הדייגים] הדגים DEFG | ויוצאים] ויצאו EF
13:49 המלאכים] והם + G
13:50 במדורת] במדורות ADEFG | יהיה] יהי BDG | וחריקת] וחריקות AB
13:51 ויאמרו] + אליו A
13:54 כנסיות] כנסיותהם A בה] בא ABCDEFGH | לזה] + זאת A | ואלו] כאלו EF
13:55 ומרים] אמו מרים שם אין F | מרים DG, שכל אלו אמו] שאמו ABCDEGH, 2 1 ABDEFGH בן זה] 3 2 1 ויוסף ושמעון ויהודה] ABDEGH יאקומו DH | ויוסף] ויוסף ABEFG, גאימי ג' F | שאמרו EF | ויהודה] וידא BCDEGH
13:56 שכל אלו עמנו] שמענו כל אלו D מאין] ומאין ABDEFGH
13:57 נביא] + בעירו BDEFG, + בעירנו H כ"א] אלא A
13:58 שום] omit EF

<sup>44</sup>Again Jesus said to his disciples:
The kingdom of heaven is like a man who finds a treasure which had been hidden and in gladness over the value he sells all which he has and buys the field for himself.

<sup>45</sup>Again the kingdom of heaven is like a certain merchant seeking precious stones.

<sup>46</sup>When he finds a good one he sells all which he has and buys it.

<sup>47</sup>The kingdom of heaven is like a net in the midst of the sea in which are gathered all kinds of fish.

<sup>48</sup>When it is full they draw it out and the fishermen go forth and choose the good for their vessels and the bad they cast away.

<sup>49</sup>Thus it will be at the end of days; the angels will go forth and separate the evil from the midst of the righteous.

<sup>50</sup>Then they shall cast them into the pyre of fire; there shall be weeping and gnashing of teeth.

<sup>51</sup>He said to them: Have you understood this. They said: Yes.

<sup>52</sup>Every wise man in the kingdom of heaven, therefore, is like a certain father of children who brings forth from his treasure things new and old.

<sup>53</sup>It came to pass after this, when Jesus finished these words, he passed on from there.

<sup>54</sup>He came into his own country and was teaching the people in the synagogues. The Pharisees were amazed and said in their heart: Whence (came) to this one the wisdom and power to do these deeds.

<sup>55</sup>(Is this) not the son of the smith and Mary? Do you not know all these: his mother Mary, his three brothers: Joseph, Simon, and Judah,

<sup>56</sup>and his sisters? Do you not know all these who are with us? Whence came to this one all these things?

<sup>57</sup>So they were confused about him. Jesus answered them: A prophet is not without honor except in his own land, city and house.

<sup>58</sup>Then he did not wish to do there any sign because of their little faith.

פרק ס״ה

‏¹בעת ההיא שמע הורוד״וס טִיטְרָא״קָה שמועות יש״ו.

‏²ויאמר לעבדיו הנה אני מאמין שאלו הפלאות עושה יוחנן המטביל.

‏³שהיה לפי שהורוד״וס תפש ליוחנן בימים ההם ויאסרהו במאסר לפי שהיה מוכיחו שלא יקח לאוֹרְדִיסָא לאשה שהיתה אשת אחיו.

‏⁴והיה אומר לו יוחנן אינה ראויה לך.

‏⁵והנה הורוד״וס היה רוצה להורגו לולי יראת העם שלנביא היה ביניהם.

‏⁶ובמשתה יום הולד את הורודוס קרא לגדולי המלכות לאכול עמו ובעוד שהיו אוכלים היתה בתו מרקדת ביניהם וייטב להורודוס.

‏⁷וישבע לה שיתן לה את כל אשר תשאל ממנו.

‏⁸והנערה מיוסרת מיומה שאלה ראש יוחנן המטביל באגן א״.

‏⁹והמלך נעצב מאד בעד השבועה שעשה בפני הקרואים ויצו להעשות כן.

‏¹⁰וישלח לשחוט יוחנן בבית הסוהר.

‏¹¹ויביאו ראש יוחנן באגן ויתנוהו לנערה והנערה נתנה לאמה.

‏¹²ויבאו תלמידי יוחנן וישאו הגוף ויקברוהו והתלמידים הגידו הדבר ליש״ו.

‏¹³וכשמוע יש״ו נסע משם באניה וילך למדבר יהודה. וכשמוע החבורות וילכו אחריו מכל המדינות.

‏¹⁴וכשיצאו ראה אחריו עם רב ויט אליו חסד וירפא כל מחלותם.

‏¹⁵ובעת ערב קרבו אליו תלמידיו ויאמרו לו זה המקום צר עובר. עזוב החבורות שילכו במגדלים ויקחו הצורך אליהם.

‏¹⁶ויען להם יש״ו אינם צריכים לילך תנו להם לאכל.

‏¹⁴:¹ טיטרוקה D, טיטראראקה [טיטראקה B | הורדוס [הורודוס EF

‏¹⁴:² המטביל [omit E | הפעולות A, הנפלאות [הפלאות D | הנהי [הנה אני DG

‏¹⁴:³ לאורדיטא D, לאורדישא AB, לאורדישא [לאורדיסא ABEF | שחיה [שהיה EF, לאורדיסה G

‏¹⁴:⁵ והנה [omit EF | לולי [לולא AG

‏¹⁴:⁶ הולד [הולדת ABDEFG | את [omit ABDEFG | ביניהם [לפנהם AEF

‏¹⁴:⁷ וישבע [ונשבע ABDEFG | את [omit ABDEFG

‏¹⁴:⁸ המטביל [omit F | א״ [omit F | מיומה [מאמה ABDEFG

‏¹⁴:⁹ הקרואים . . . שעשה [omit F | זה G + | בעד [בעד

‏¹⁴:¹⁰ לשחוט [omit EF | יוחנן [ליוחנן ABDEFG

‏¹⁴:¹¹ נתנה [נתנהו A | לאמה [לאמו A

‏¹⁴:¹² תלמידי [תלמידיו G

‏¹⁴:¹³ יהודה [יודא BCDG | ויכלו [הלכו A

‏¹⁴:¹⁵ צר [וצר + | במגדלים [ברגלים G | הצורך [הצריך A | אליו [אליו + ABCDEFG | והעת +

‏¹⁴:¹⁶ להם [אתם + A

# Chapter 14

[1] At that time Herod the Tetrarch heard reports about Jesus.

[2] He said to his servants: Behold I believe that John the Baptizer is doing these miracles.

[3] This happened because Herod had seized John in those days and had bound him in prison because he was reproving him that he should not take Herodias for a wife because she was the wife of his brother.

[4] John was saying to him: She is not suitable for you.

[5] Then behold Herod wished to kill him, except for fear of the people [who believed] he was a prophet among them.

[6] On the feast of Herod's birthday he called the nobles of the kingdom to eat with him and while they were eating his daughter danced among them and it was pleasing to Herod.

[7] He swore to give her whatever she asked from him.

[8] The girl being instructed by (her mother) asked for the head of John the Baptizer in a bowl.

[9] The king was very sad because of the oath which he had made before those invited. But he commanded to do so

[10] and sent to kill John in prison.

[11] They brought the head of John in a bowl and gave it to the girl and the girl gave it to her mother.

[12] Then the disciples of John came and took the body and buried it and the disciples told the matter to Jesus.

[13] When Jesus heard it he departed from there in a boat and went into the wilderness of Judea. When the crowds heard they followed him from all the cities.

[14] When they came out he saw behind him a numerous people; so he extended kindness to [them] and healed all of their diseases.

[15] At evening time his disciples came to him and said to him:
This place is limited (and the time) is advancing. Let the crowds go into the towers that they might take the necessities for themselves.

[16] Jesus answered them: They have no need to go; give them to eat.

¹⁷והם ענו אין לנו בכאן כי אם חמש ככרות שני דגים.

¹⁸ויאמר להם הביאו אותם אלי.

¹⁹ויצו שישובו העם על העשבים. וכשישבו לקח החמש ככרות והשני דגים ובהיותו מביט לשמים ברך אותם ויחלקם ויתנם לתלמידיו והתלמידים חלקו לסייעות.

²⁰ויאכלו כלם וישבעו. וכן מהדגים אכלו כרצונם. ואחר שתכלו לקחו הפתיתים הנשארות וימלאו מהם שנים עשר סאים.

²¹ויהי מספר האוכלים חמשת אלפים אנשים מלבד הנשים והטף.

<u>פרק ס"ו</u>

²²ואחרי זה צוה לתלמידיו לכנס באניה וישליחו קודם ממנו בעיר שהחבורות הולכות.

²³ואחר שעזב החבורות עלה להר והתפלל לדבו ויהי לעת ערב והוא לבדו עומד.

²⁴והאניה באמצע הים וגליהם היו דוחפות אותה לפי שהרוח היה מנגד.

²⁵למשמרה הרביעית מהלילה בא להם יש"ו הולך בים.

²⁶וכאשר ראוהו תלמידיו הלך בים נבהלו בשר בחושבם שהיה שד ומרוב פחדם היו צועקים.

²⁷ואז ענה להם יש"ו ויאמר להם יהיה אמונה בכם שאני הוא ואל תיראו.

²⁸ויען פייט"רוס ויאמר לו אדו' אם אתה הוא צוה אותי לבא אליך במים.

²⁹ויאמר לו יש"ו בא. וירד פייט"רוס מהספינה והלך בים ובא ליש"ו.

---

¹⁴:¹⁷חמש] A חמש' | שני] ושני ABCDEFG

¹⁴:¹⁸להם] omit A

¹⁴:¹⁹שישובו] שישובו ABCDEFG וכשישבו] G ושישבו | החמש] A החמש' | והשני] A ושני | והתלמידים]
לקחו] G וחלקו | אותם] ABDEFG אותם +

¹⁴:²⁰וכן] omit DG

¹⁴:²¹חמשת] AEFG חמש | מלבד] BDEFG לבד | הנשים] מנשים G

¹⁴:²²וישליכו] B, וישליכו אותם A, וילכו] וישליחו ADEF | לכנס] ליכנס EF ואחר כן] ואחרי זה DEFG

¹⁴:²⁴אותה] EFG אותה | וגליהם] G בלב | והגלים] C, וגלהים D, גלי הים AB, באמצע] G
היה] + רצי' מקדם A

¹⁴:²⁵הרביעית] EF ולאשמורה B, ולאשמורת ADG, ולאשמרות] למשמרה AG

¹⁴:²⁶וחשבוהו] ABDEFG הולך] omit ABCG | בשר] בחושבם בחשם ABDEF, G | שהיה] EF כי היה שד שהיה] בשד G | היו] A היה

¹⁴:²⁷ואז] G אז | ויאמר להם] וא"ל B, ואמר להם CD, ואמר] EFG אמונה בכם] EF 1 2 | ואל] אל AEFG

¹⁴:²⁸אותי] לבא] G הוא] omit EF פיטרוס] BDG, פיטרוס A, פיטרוס] פייטרוס CEF

¹⁴:²⁹פייטרוס] EF פיטרוס BDG, פיטרוס A, פיטרו | מהספינה] המספינה G | והלך] וילך G | בים] במים
בא] G בו | BDG במים A,

[17]They answered:

We have nothing here except five loaves (and) two fish.

[18]He said to them: Bring them to me.

[19]Then he commanded that the people should (sit) on the grass. When they sat he took the five loaves and two fish and as he looked into heaven he blessed them, divided them, gave them to his disciples and the disciples made distribution to the groups.

[20]All of them ate and were satisfied. They also ate the fish according to what they desired. After they had eaten they took the fragments which remained and filled with them twelve seahs.

[21]The number of those eating were five thousand men apart from women and children.

[22]After this he commanded his disciples to assemble in a boat that they might (go) before him to the city to which the crowds were going.

[23]After he let the crowds go he went upon a mountain and prayed alone. At the time of evening he was standing alone.

[24]The boat was in the midst of the sea and (the waves of the sea) were driving it because the wind was contrary.

[25]At the fourth watch of the night Jesus came to them walking on the sea.

[26]When the disciples saw him walking on the sea they were alarmed thinking he was a demon and from the greatness of their fear they were crying out.

[27]Then Jesus answered them and said to them:

Let faith be among you because it is I; do not fear.

[28]Peter answered and said to him: Master if it is you command me to come to you on the water.

[29]Jesus said to him: Come. So Peter came down from the boat, walked on the sea and came to Jesus.

‏<sup>30</sup>ובראותו חוזק הרוח פחד מאד ובהתחילו ליטבע צעק‎
‏ואמר אדו׳הושיעני.‎
‏<sup>31</sup>ומיד יש״ו האריך ידו ולקחו ואמר לו אדם מאמונה מעוטה‎
‏למה נסתפקת.‎
‏<sup>32</sup>וכאשר עלו באניה נח הרוח‎
‏<sup>33</sup>ואשר בספינה השתחוו לו ואמרו באמת אתה הוא בן האלקים.‎
‏<sup>35</sup>וכאשר הכירוהו אנשי המקום שלחו אותו בכל המלכות‎
‏והביאו לו כל החולים מכל מדוים‎
‏<sup>36</sup>ויחלו פניו ירצו לעוזבם יגעו בכנך מעילו וכל אשר נגע‎
‏נתרפא.‎

## פרק ס״ז

‏<sup>1</sup>אז בא אל יש״ו החכמים והפרושים ויאמרו אליו‎
‏<sup>2</sup>למה עוברים תלמידך תקנות הראשונות שהם אינם רוחצים‎
‏ידיהם קודם האכילה.‎
‏<sup>3</sup>ויאמר להם יש״ו ולמה אתם עוברים מאמרי האל בעד‎
‏תקנותיכם‎
‏<sup>4</sup>שהאל אמר כבד את אביך ואת אמך ומכה אביו ואמו מות יומת.‎
‏<sup>5</sup>ואתם אומרים שאיזה דבר יאמר האדם לאביו ולאמו שבאיזה‎
‏נדבה שיתן בעד אותו חטא שיכופר לו אותו עון.‎
‏<sup>6</sup>ולא יכבד אביו ואמו ואתם מבזים אמרי אל בתקנותיכם.‎
‏<sup>7</sup>היו חנפים הנה ישעיה ניבא מכם ואמר‎
‏<sup>8</sup>כה אמר ה׳׳ יען כי נגש העם הזה בפיו ובשפתיו כבדוני ולבו‎
‏רחק ממני‎
‏<sup>9</sup>ותהי יראתם אותי מצות אנשים מלומדה.‎
‏<sup>10</sup>ויש״ו קרא לסיעות ויאמר להם שמעו והביטו.‎

---

‏<sup>14:31</sup> זה [אדם G‎
‏<sup>14:33</sup> אלקים A, האלים [האלקים F‎
<sup>14:34</sup> All mss lack vs 34.
‏<sup>14:35</sup> omit EF [מכל מדוים | מיני + ABCDG | מכל [מכל CDEFG | אותו [אותם‎
‏<sup>14:36</sup> נתרפאו [נתרפא ABDEFG | נגעו [נגע AE | לעוזבם [לעוזבם ABG | ירצה [ירצו ABDEFG‎
‏<sup>15:1</sup> בא [באו ABCDEFGH | לישו [אל ישו EF | לו [אליו H‎
‏<sup>15:2</sup> הראשונית [הראשונות ABDEFH | תלמידיך [תלמידך AH‎
‏<sup>15:4</sup> יאמר [אמר EF‎
‏<sup>15:5</sup> החטא [חטה H | שבאיזו [שבאיזה H | אדם [האדם H | שיאמר [יאמר H | באיזה [שאיזה EFH‎
‏<sup>15:6</sup> האל [אל AEF | מאמרי [אמרי EF | אומרים ומבזים [מבזים ACEF |‎
‏בעד תקנותיכם [בתקנותיכם ABDEFGH‎
‏<sup>15:7</sup> נבא ישעיה ניבא [ישעיה ניבא F | החנפים [חנפים ABCDEFG | אוי [הוי ABCDG‎
‏<sup>15:8</sup> כה אמר ה׳׳ [ה׳׳ omit B | ולבו [ולבו omit F | כי [כי omit F | ולבם [ולבם EF‎
‏<sup>15:9</sup> יראתם [. . . מלומדה omit G‎
‏<sup>15:10</sup> הביטו [והביטו EF | דעו [שמעו H | אליהם [להם F‎

³⁰But when he saw the strength of the wind
he feared exceedingly and as he began to sink he cried out and said:
Master save me.
³¹Immediately Jesus stretched out his hand, took him and said to him:
Man of little faith, why did you doubt.
³²When they went up into the boat the wind settled down
³³and those in the boat worshipped him and said: Truly you are the Son
of God.
³⁵When the people of the place recognized him they sent into all that
kingdom and brought to him all who were sick with various kinds of
diseases.
³⁶They implored him that (he) might be pleased to allow them to touch
the skirt of his garment; and each one who touched him was healed.

## Chapter 15

¹Then the sages and the Pharisees came to Jesus and said to him:
²Why do (your disciples) transgress the ordinances of antiquity in that
they do not wash their hands before eating.
³Jesus said to them: Why do you transgress the words of God for your
ordinances,
⁴because God said: honor your father and your mother and he who
smites his father and mother will surely be put to death.
⁵But you say that whatever word a man should say to his father and
mother in regard to any donation he might give for him as a sinner, this
iniquity itself will be made void to him.
⁶So he does not honor his father and his mother and you despise the
words of God by your ordinances.
⁷Woe, hypocrites; behold Isaiah prophesied concerning you and said:
⁸thus the Lord said: because this people has come near with their mouth
and has honored me with their lips, but their heart is far from me
⁹and their reverence toward me is the commandments of men which
have been taught.
¹⁰Jesus called to the crowds and said to them: Hear and consider.

[MT 15:11-27

<sup>11</sup>הנכנס בעד הפה אינו מלכלך האדם אבל היוצא מהפה מלכלך האדם.

<sup>12</sup>אז קרבו אליו תלמידיו ויאמרו לו דע שהפרושים נבוכים בעד דבר זה.

<sup>13</sup>ויען להם יש״ו כל נטיעה שלא נטעה אבי שבשמים תשחת.

<sup>14</sup>הניחו אותם שהעורים מדריכים לעורים ואם עור ידריך עור אחר יפלו שניהם בבור.

<sup>15</sup>ויען לו פייט״רוס אדוני פרוש לנו זאת החדה.

<sup>16</sup>ויען להם יש״ו עדיין אתם מבלי דעת.

<sup>17</sup>לא תבינו אתם שכל הנכנס בעד הפה הולך לבטן והכל הולך בעד המקום הטבעיי?

<sup>18</sup>והיוצא בעד הפה מתנועע מהלב וזהו המלכלך האדם.

<sup>19</sup>לפי שמחלל הלב יוצא התרמית והרציחה והנאופים והגנבות ועדות שקרים והקללות.

<sup>20</sup>וכל אלה הדברים הם המבלבלים האדם. אמנם האכילה בלי רחיצת ידים אינה מלכלכת האדם.

<u>פרק ס״ח</u>

<sup>21</sup>ואחר שאמר יש״ו זה הלך בגלילי צור וסדום.

<sup>22</sup>ותבוא לפניו אשה כנענית באה מארצות מזרח צועקת אליו אדוני בן דוד חנני שבתי אחוזת השדים.

<sup>23</sup>ויש״ו לא ענה דבר. ותלמידיו קרבו אליו ויאמרו לו אדונינו למה אתה מניח לזאת האשה צועקת אחרינו.

<sup>24</sup>ויען להם יש״ו לא שלחוני כי אם לצאן אובדות מבית ישראל.

<sup>25</sup>והאשה משתחוה לו ואומרת אדוני עוזרני.

<sup>26</sup>ויאמר לה יש״ו לא טוב שיקח האדם הפת מבניו ויתננו לכלבים.

<sup>27</sup>ותען האשה פעמים רבים אוכלים הכלבים הפתיתים הנופלים משלחן אדוניהם.

---

<sup>15:11</sup> A מה שיוצא [היוצא | H בפה האדם [בעד הפה

<sup>15:12</sup> A ואמרו [ויאמרו

<sup>15:14</sup> omit A [אחר | E העורים F, את העורים [לעורים | omit EF [אותם

<sup>15:15</sup> G ויאמר DEFG, + פטרוש B, פיטרוש A, פיטרו [פייטרוס

<sup>15:17</sup> EF הטבעים [הטבעי | A עובר [<sup>2</sup>הולך | E בבטן [לבטן | omit G (hap) [הפה . . . הטבעי

<sup>15:19</sup> A ועדיות [ועדות

<sup>15:20</sup> omit G [ידים | ABDEFGH בלא [בלי | BCDEFG המלכלים A, המלכלים [המבלבלים

<sup>15:21</sup> FG וצידון E, וצידון [וסדום

<sup>15:22</sup> A אחוזה [אחוזת | B המזרח [מזרח | omit A [אדוני | G אליו [לפניו

<sup>15:23</sup> EF ללכת [צועקת | ABCDEFG לה + [ענה

<sup>15:24</sup> G שלחני [שלחוני | A הנדחות [אובדות | G ויאמר [ויען

<sup>15:25</sup> BDEFG עוזרני [עוזרני

<sup>15:26</sup> A ותננו [ויתננו | A אליה [לה

<sup>15:27</sup> ADG משולחן [משלחן | EF רבות [רבים

¹¹That which enters through the mouth does not soil the man
but that which goes out of the mouth soils the man.

¹²Then his disciples came to him and said to him:
Know that the Pharisees were perplexed by this word.

¹³Jesus answered them: Every plant which my Father who is in heaven
did not plant will be destroyed.

¹⁴Leave them alone because the blind are leading the blind; but if a blind
man leads another who is blind, both will fall into a pit.

¹⁵Peter answered him: Lord explain to us this riddle.

¹⁶Jesus answered them: Are you still without knowledge.

¹⁷Do you not understand that every thing that enters through the mouth
goes into the belly and all of it goes on to the natural place?

¹⁸But that which goes out through the mouth is moved by the heart; this
is what soils the man.

¹⁹Because the defiled heart brings forth deceitfulness. murder, adulter-
ies, robberies, the witness of liars and curses.

²⁰All these things are what (soil) the man. Indeed eating without washing
the hands does not soil the man.

²¹After Jesus had said this he went into the regions of Tyre and Sodom.

²²Then there came to him a certain Canaanite woman, who came from
the lands of the East, crying out to him: Master, son of David, have
mercy on me because my daughter is possessed by demons.

²³Jesus did not answer (her) a word. So his disciples approached him and
said to him: Our master, why do you leave this woman alone who is
crying out after us.

²⁴Jesus answered them: They did not send me except to the lost sheep
from the house of Israel.

²⁵Then the woman worshipped him and said, Lord help me.

²⁶Jesus said to her: It is not good that a man should take the bread from
his children and give it to the dogs.

²⁷The woman answered: Often the dogs eat the pieces of bread that fall
from the table of their master.

[MT 15:28-16:1

²⁸ויען לה יש״ו אשה גדולה אמונתיך יעשה לך כאשר שאלת. ומהעת ההוא והלאה נרפאת בתה.

## פרק ס״ט

²⁹וכאשר הלך יש״ו משם הלך עבר הגליל להר. בעומדו שם ³⁰ראה עם רב מביטים הרבה צולעים ומנוגעים ופסחים ורבים אחרים ויפלו לרגליו וירפאם. ³¹והעם היו תמהים איך האלמים היו מדברים והפסחים הולכים והעורים רואים וכלם משבחים לאל. ³²אז אמר יש״ו לתלמידיו יש לי רחמנות מהם שהם מיחלים אותי זה שני ימים שעברו ואין להם מה שיאכלו. ואיני רוצה להוליכם בתענית יען לא יחלשו בדרך. ³³ויענו לו תלמידיו ומאין אנו יכולים למצוא לחם במדבר הזה לשביע לעם. ³⁴ויען יש״ו ויאמר להם כמה ככרים לחם לכם. ויענו שבעה ומעט דגים. ³⁵ויצו יש״ו לעם לישב ע״ג העשבים. ³⁶ולקח השבעה ככרות וישברם ונתנם לתלמידיו והם נתנו לעם. ³⁷ויאכלו כולם וישבעו והותר שבעה סאים. ³⁸והאוכלים היו במספר ארבעת אלפים אנשים לבד הנשים והטף.

## פרק שבעים

³⁹אחר זה נכנס יש״ו בספינה ובא לארץ מָאצִידוֹנְיָיא. ¹ויבואו אליו החכמים והפרושים מנסים אותו וילמדם איזה אות מהשמים.

---

15:28 EFG נתרפאת [נרפאת F והלאה + [והלאה A כל + [לך | לך ABDEFG אמונתך [אמונתיך
15:29 EF וכעמדו [בעומדו A מול + [²הלך | A עבר [¹הלך
15:30 A לפניו [לרגליו 2 1 EF, 2 D] הרבה צולעים [מכנים BDEF מביניהם A, מוכנים [מביטים
15:31 2 3 1 G] האלמים היו מדברים
15:32 ABEF יאכלו [שיאכלו A עברו [שעברו | omit EF] אותי
15:33 לשביע לעם B גדול + ADEFG, העם [לעם A לשבוע [לשביע A להם [לחם EF ומאן [ומאין G כדי לשבעם
15:34 והם ענו [ויענו | omit A] לחם ABDEFG] לחם ABDEFG ככרות [ככרים ABDEFG וישו אמר [ויען ישו ויאמר ABDEFG
15:35 F וישבו [לישב
15:36 EF לאכול [לעם G לחם והודה לאל ABDEF, + והודה לאל + [ככרות
15:37 ABDEF, ומהנשאר מלאו [והותר | ACDEFG ושבעו [וישבעו | DEFG ואכלו [ויאכלו G והושאר מלאו
15:38 A מלבד [לבד
15:39 EF, מאסידוני D, מאסידוניאה A, מסאדוניא C, מאצידוניא [מאצידונייא EF לספינה [בספינה G מצדוניאה
16:1 [מהשמים G לעשות D, לאדם ABEF, ילמדם [וילמדם A הפרושים והחכמים [החכמים והפרושים A מן השמים

²⁸Then Jesus answered her:
Woman, great is your faith, let it be done to you as you asked. So from that time on her daughter was healed.

²⁹When Jesus went from there he went to the region across Galilee to a mountain. As he stood there

³⁰he saw many people among whom were many lame, leprous, those who limped and many others; they fell at his feet and he healed them.

³¹The people were amazed at how the dumb were speaking and the lame were walking and the blind were seeing; all of them were praising God.

³²Then Jesus said to his disciples: I have compassion on them because they have remained with me these two days since they came across and they do not have anything to eat. I do not want to lead them fasting [lest] they grow faint in the way.

³³His disciples answered him: Whence will we be able to find bread in this wilderness to satisfy the people.

³⁴Jesus answered and said to them: How many loaves of bread do you have. They answered: Seven and a few fish.

³⁵So Jesus commanded the people to sit upon the grass.

³⁶He took the seven loaves and broke them and gave them to his disciples and they gave to the people.

³⁷All of them ate and were satisfied and (from that which was remaining they filled) seven seahs.

³⁸Those who were eating were by number four thousand men besides women and children.

³⁹After this Jesus entered into a boat and came to the land of Macedonia.

## **Chapter 16**

¹There came to him sages and Pharisees tempting him to teach them some sign from heaven.

**[MT 16:2-16**

²וַיַעַן להם יש״ו חנפים אתם אומרים ערב מחר יום צח יהיה לפי
שהשמים אדומים

³ובבקר אתם אומרים היום ימטיר שהשמים חשוכים. א׳׳כ אתם
יודעים משפט מראים השמים ואין אתם יודעים משפט הזמנים.

⁴זרע מרעים שאל אות ואות לא ינתן להם כי אם אות של יונה
הנביא. ואז נפרד והלך לו.

⁵וכאשר יש״ו היה בשפת הים אמר לתלמידיו שיכינו לחם והוא
נכנס לספינה עם תלמידיו ותלמידיו שכחו ולא הכניסו
שום לחם.

⁸ויש״ו אמר להם אתם מעטי השכל חושבים שאין לכם לחם.

⁹⁻¹²ואין אתם זוכרים מהחמשה ככרות וארבע אלף איש וכמה סאים
נשארו? ולכן תבינו שאיני מדבר מהחלמיש וגם מהלחמים
הטבעיים אבל אני אומר לכם שתשארו מהנהגת הפרושים
והצדוקים.

## פרק ע״א

¹³ויצא יש״ו אל ארץ סוּרִיאָ״ה וארץ פיל״וף נקרא פִּילִיב״וֹס
וישאל לתלמידיו לאמר מה אומרים בני אדם בשבילי.

¹⁴ויאמרו אליו מהם אומרים שהוא יוחנן המטביל ומהם אומרים
שהוא אליהו ומהם ירמיהו או א״ מהנביאים.

¹⁵ויאמר להם יש״ו ואתם מה אומרים בשבילי.

¹⁶ויען שמעון נקרא פייט״רוס ויאמר אתה משיח לעז קְרִיסְטֹ״ו
בן אלקים חיים שבאתה בזה העולם.

---

16:2 שראים השמים G | שהשמים] 3 1 2 A | יום צח יהיה]

16:3 מראית] מראים ABDEFG | אותות] + A | [2]משפט] A ממטיר] ימטיר EF שהיו [היום

16:4 נפרד והלך לו] A | מהם] + A | נפרד AEFG | להם] omit EF

16:5 הכניסו] G והם] [3]ותלמידיו G | לספינה] בספינה EF (between parentheses) | נפרד והלך לו] + EF הכינו

16:6-8a All MSS omit (hap).

16:8b שאין] אין A

16:9-12 וכמה] אלפים AEF | אלף] A | וארבע] וארבעת A | ככרות] דברות D | מהחמש] מהחמשה AG | הטבעיים] הטבעיות omit C | מהלחמים] מהחלמיש וגם G לכן | ולכן] omit ABDEFG ABDEFG | לכם] omit A 2 1 BG | הצדוקים] הפרושים שתשארו] שתשארו ABDEFG B

16:13 סוריאה] בלעז שישיריאה B, + בלעז שישיריאה A, + סוריא לעז שישיריאה DEF, פילוף] פילוף נקרא B ארץ] וארץ H שוריאה, G בלעז שישיראה + | omit H | פיליבוס] פילייפוש ABDEF, מה] + G פיליפוס | הם] + D בני אדם] בני האדם EF

16:14 אומרים] [2]omit G | אליהו] אליה BH | ירמיהו ירמיה BH Whole vs omitted EF

16:15 ואתם מה] מה אתם D | מה] + מה G | בשבילי . . . מה] תאמרו A Whole vs omitted EF

16:16 פייטרוס] פיטרוש A, ויאמר] omit H | משיח] המשיח H לעז] בלעז פיטרו EF קריסטו] קרישטו ADG, קריסטרוס EF | אלקים] אלים A שבאתה] שבאת B | קריסט״ו] קרישטו ACDEFGH

[2]Jesus answered them: Hypocrites, you say in the evening:
tomorrow will be a clear day because the sky is red,

[3]then in the morning you say: today it will rain because the sky is dark.
If so, you know the situation in regard to the appearance of the sky, but
you do not know the situation in regard to the times.

[4]A seed of evil-doers asks for a sign, but no sign will be given them except the sign of Jonah the Prophet. Then he was separated (from them)
and went away.

[5]When Jesus came to the sea shore he told his disciples to prepare
bread. Then he entered a boat with his disciples, but the disciples for-
got and did not bring any bread.

[8b]Jesus said to them: You have little understanding who think that you
have no bread.

[9-12]Do you not remember the five loaves and four thousand men how
many seahs were left over? Therefore you should understand that I
am not speaking of natural loaves but I am saying to you that you
should (beware) of the behavior of the Pharisees and Sadducees.

[13]Then Jesus went out unto the Land of Syria (that is, Caesarea) and the
land of Philoph, called (Philipos), and asked his disciples saying: What
do men say about me.

[14]They said unto him: Some say he is John the Baptizer, some say he is
Elijah and some Jeremiah or one of the prophets.

[15]Jesus said to them: What do you say about me.

[16]Simon, called Petros, answered and said: You are the Messiah, that is,
Kristo, the Son of the living God, who has come into this world.

[MT 16:17-28

‏<sup>17</sup>ויאמרו אליו יש״ו אשריך שמעון בר יונה שבשר ודם לא גלה לך
כי אם אבי שבשמים.

‏<sup>18</sup>ואני אומר לך שאתה אבן ואני אבנה עליך בית תפלתי. ושערי
גהינם לא יוכלו נגדך

‏<sup>19</sup>לפי שאני אתן לך מפתחות מלכות השמים. וכל אשר תקשור בארץ
יהיה קשור בשמים וכל אשר תתיר בארץ יהיה מותר בשמים.

‏<sup>20</sup>אז צוה לתלמידיו לבל יאמרו שהוא משיח.

פרק ע״ב

‏<sup>21</sup>מכאן ואילך התחיל יש״ו לגלות לתלמידיו שהוא צריך ללכת
לירושלם ולשאת עול רבים מהכהנים וזקני העם עד שיהרגוהו
וביום השלישי יקום.

‏<sup>22</sup>ויקחוהו פייט״רוס בינו לבינו והתחיל להוכיח לאמר חלילה
לך להיות לך כן אדו׳.

‏<sup>23</sup>וישב יש״ו ויבט אליו ויאמר לו לך השטן לא תמרה פי שאינך
מכיר דבר האל כי אם דברי האדם.

‏<sup>24</sup>אז דבר יש״ו לתלמידיו מי שירצה לבא אחרי יבזה עצמו
ויקח את השתי וערב ר״ל שקרב עצמו למיתה וילך אחרי.

‏<sup>25</sup>כל הרוצה להושיע נפשו יאבד אותה בעדי והמאבד את חייו
בעה״ז בשבילי יושיע נפשו לחיי העה״ב.

‏<sup>26</sup>מה בצע לאדם אם ירויח את כל העולם אם נפשו יאבד לעד ואיזה
תמורה טובה יעשה האדם אם בעד הדברים ההוים והנפסדים
יתן נפשו לדין גהינם.

‏<sup>27</sup>כי בן האל יבא בכבד אביו שבשמים עם מלאכיו להשיב לכל
איש כמפעלו.

‏<sup>28</sup>אמן אני אומר לכם שיש מהעומדים פה שלא יטעמו מות עד
שיראו בן אלוה בא במלכותו.

‏<sup>16:17</sup>[לך AH שב״ו [שבשר ודם G שבשה [שבשר H בן]בר | BCDEG ויאמר AFH, ויאמ׳ [ויאמרו omit G

‏<sup>16:18</sup>לך A, נגדה [נגדך BD גיהנם [גהינם H ועליך אבנה A, ועל זאת האבן אבנה [ואני אבנה עליך G

‏<sup>16:21</sup>A וביום [ויום EF על [עול omit G [לגלות G

‏<sup>16:22</sup>G לבינו [בינו DEFG פיטרוס [פיטרוס A, פיטרוס B, פיטרוס ADEFG ויקחהו [ויקחהו G ויאמר לו [והתחיל . . . לאמר G אדון להיות לך [להיות . . . אדו׳ A להוכיחו [להוכיח G ויאמר לו [והתחיל . . . לאמר omit C [כן אדו 2 1 A [לך

‏<sup>16:23</sup>omit D [לו ABDEFG שאתה אינך [שאינך ABDEF בי [פי

‏<sup>16:24</sup>ויקרב [ויקח ADG את + [יבזה G אז לקח ישו את תלמידיו ואמר להם שירצה [אז . . . שירצה ABD שיקרב [שקרב omit AG [את EF

‏<sup>16:25</sup>BEFG העולם A, עולם [עולם העה״ב [העה״ב omit D [בשבילי G את נפשו [ונפשו 2 & 1

‏<sup>16:26</sup>[והנפסדים EF בדברים [בעד הדברים A ואיזו [ואיזה omit ABDEFG [את D ירוים [ירוח EF לנפשו [נפשו 2 AB הנפסדים

‏<sup>16:27</sup>G כפעולו ABDEF, כפעלו [כמפעלו omit A [עם מלאכיו ABDEFG אשר בשמים [שבשמים

‏<sup>16:28</sup>omit BEF [בא G האלוה A, האלוה האלים [אלוה ABDEF את + [שיראו EF טעם [יטעמו +

<sup>17</sup>Jesus said to him:

Blessed are you Simon bar Jonah because flesh and blood has not revealed [this] to you but my Father who is heaven.

<sup>18</sup>I say to you: you are a stone and I will build upon you my house of prayer. The gates of Gehenna will not prevail against you

<sup>19</sup>because I will give to you the keys of the Kingdom of heaven. Whatever you bind on earth will be bound in heaven; whatever you loose on earth will be loosed in heaven.

<sup>20</sup>Then he commanded his disciples not to say he is the Messiah.

<sup>21</sup>Henceforth Jesus began to reveal to his disciples that he had to go to Jerusalem and to suffer injustice from many of the priests and the elders of the people until they should kill him; then on the third day he would arise.

<sup>22</sup>Peter took him aside privately and began to rebuke (him) saying: Far be it that it should be like this to you, Lord.

<sup>23</sup>Jesus turned, looked at him and said to him: Go away Satan; do not disobey (me), because you do not regard the word of God but the words of man.

<sup>24</sup>Then Jesus said to his disciples: Whoever wishes to come after me let him despise himself; take the cross, that is, offer himself unto death, and come after me.

<sup>25</sup>Everyone who wishes to save his soul will lose it because of me, and he who loses his life in this world for my sake will save his soul for the life of the world to come.

<sup>26</sup>What profit is there for a man if he should gain the whole world [but] lose his soul forever; what good exchange does the man make if for present things that are spoiled he should give his soul to the judgment of Gehenna?

<sup>27</sup>Because the Son of God will come in the glory of his Father who is in heaven with his angels to reward each man according to his work.

<sup>28</sup>Truly I say to you there are some of those standing here who will not taste death until they see the Son of God coming in his kingdom.

## פרק ע״ג

‎¹אתר ששה ימים לקח יש״ו לפייט״רוס וגם יעקב לעז גאימ״י ויוחנן אחיו ויוליכם אל הר גבוה משם להתפלל הוא.

‎²ובעוד שהיה מתפלל השתנה לפניהם וקרן עור פניו כשמש ומלבושיו לבנים כשלג.

‎³אליהם משה ואליהו מדברים עמו והגידו ליש״ו כל מה שיקראהו בירושלם. ופייט״רוס וחביריו היו נרדמים. נים ולא נים תיר ולא תיר. ראו גופו ושני אנשים עמו.

‎⁴וכאשר הלכו אז אמר פייט״רוס ליש״ו טוב להיות בכאן. ונעשה פה שלש משכנות לך אחד ולמשה אחד ולאלוה אחד שלא היה יודע מה היה דובר.

‎⁵עודנו מדבר והנה ענן שכסה אותם ויבהלו עד מאד ובעוד שהם תחת הענן שמעו מתוך הענן קול מדבר ואומר הנה זה בני יקירי וחפצי בו אליו תשמעון.

‎⁶וישמעו התלמידים ויפלו על פניהם ארצה וייראו מאד.

‎⁷וכאשר נפסק הקול ויאמר להם יש״ו קומו אל תיראו.

‎⁸וישאו עיניהם ולא ראו כי אם יש״ו בלבד.

## פרק ע״ד

‎⁹וירד יש״ו מן ההר ויצו להם לאמר אל תדברו לאיש המראה אשר ראיתם עד שיקום בן האדם מן המות.

‎¹⁰וישאלוהו לו תלמידיו לאמר מה חכמים אומרים שאליה יבא ראשונה.

‎¹¹ויען להם ויאמר אמנם אליה יבא ויושיע כל העולם.

‎¹²אומר אני לכם שכבר בא ולא הכירוהו ועשו בו כרצונם. פן יעשו כבן אדם.

‎¹³אז הבינו התלמידים שבשבל יוחנן המטביל היה מדבר זה.

17:1 ששת] ששת ABDEF לפיטרוס ]לפייטרוס AH, לפיטרו] BDEG ‎וגם יעקב] וייעקב ADH | לעז]
בלעז B | גאימי] גיאימי B | ויוחנן] וגואן D, וגיואני H | אל הר] להר G משם] ממש G, omit H | מאד] G, omit H |
הוא] omit AH

17:2 ‎השתנה] השונה F | כשלג . . . ומלבושיו] omit H

17:3 ‎ופיטרו] ופיטרוס AB, Beginning] + ונגלו | ABDEFG שיקראהו]שיקריהו D שיקרהו B, שיקריהו] +
אותו] גופו A | נים] ‎נים ABDEF מאד] + נרדמים] F ופיטרוס DEG, | פיטרוס G

17:4 ‎אז] omit A | ‎פיטרוס A, פיטרוס BDEG | פיטרו] + לישו] F ‎לישו] + אדוני] אדוני ABDEF, G
‎ולאליהו BDEF, ‎ולאלוה] ולאליה ABDEFG משכנות] משכנים AEF כאן] פה omit A | בכאן] A

17:5 ‎omit AF ‎הנה] omit G אז] + ‎ADG, צח] + EF אחד] ‎כסה] שכסה ADEF ‎ואומר] omit C

17:7 ‎ויאמר] ואומר C | ‎להם] אליהם ABDEFG ‎קומו] omit C

17:8 ‎בלבד] לבד EFG

17:10 ‎וישאלוהו] וישאלו ABDEFG ‎לו] לו תלמידיו A התלמידים | שאליה] שאליהו A

17:11 ‎אליה] אליהו A

17:12 ‎לו] לו G פן] כן AEFG, וכן D כבן] בבן ADG אדם] האדם AEF

17:13 ‎שבשבל] omit F מדבר] אומר G

# Chapter 17

¹After six days Jesus took Peter, James, that is, Jimi, and John his brother and brought them to a high mountain where he might pray.

²While he was praying he was changed before them and the skin of his face shone like the sun and his garments [became] white like snow.

³(Then) Moses and Elijah who were speaking with him (were revealed) to them and they told Jesus all which would happen to him in Jerusalem. Peter and his companions were asleep. Asleep but not asleep; awake but not awake. [Then] they saw his body and the two men with him.

⁴When they went away, then Peter said to Jesus: It is good to be here. Let us make here three tabernacles, one for you, one for Moses and one for Elijah, because he did not know what he was saying.

⁵While he was still speaking behold there was a cloud which covered them and they were greatly alarmed; while they were under the cloud they heard from the midst of the cloud a voice speaking and saying: Behold this is my son, my beloved, my delight is in him, you shall obey him.

⁶The disciples heard [this], fell on their faces to the ground and feared exceedingly.

⁷When the voice ceased, Jesus said to them: Arise, do not fear.

⁸They lifted up their eyes and saw no one except Jesus alone.

⁹Jesus came down from the mountain and commanded them saying: Tell no man the vision you have seen until the Son of Man has risen from death.

¹⁰His disciples asked him saying: Why do the sages say that Elijah will come first.

¹¹He answered them and said: Indeed Elijah will come and will save all the world.

¹²I say to you he has already come, they did not know him and they did to him according to their desire. (So) they will do to the Son of Man.

¹³Then the disciples understood that in regard to John the Baptizer he was saying this.

[MT 17:14-17 **+** MK 9:20-27]

## פרק ע"ה

‏<sup>14</sup>ויהי בבואו אל החבורות ויבא לפניו איש כורע על ברכיו.

‏<sup>15</sup>ויאמר אדוני חנני וחוסה על בני כי נבעת מרוח רעה וחולה מאד וחורק את שיניו ומקטף בפיו ונופל מקומתו ארצה ונופל פעמים באש ופעמים במים.

‏<sup>16</sup>והביאותיו לתלמידיך ולא יוכלו לרפאתו.

‏<sup>17</sup>ויען יש"ו ויאמר דור רע אוי לכם אתם הכופרים עד מתי אהיה עמכם ועד מתי אשא טרחכם. הביאוהו אלי.

## [ MARK ]

‏<sup>9:20</sup>והביאוהו אליו ומיד שיש"ו ראהו השטן מכניעו ומפילו לארץ והתחיל מתעפר ומתקצף.

‏<sup>9:21</sup>ויש"ו שאל לאבי הנער כמה זמן שהשטן לקחו. והאב השיבו מזמן פלוני והלאה.

‏<sup>9:22</sup>והרבה פעמים הפילו באש ובמים בעניין יוכל השמידו. ואם אתה אדו' בשום עניין תוכל לעוזרו עזרהו. וישא האיש חן בעיניו ונתמלא רחמים עליו.

‏<sup>9:23</sup>ואמר לו אם תוכל להאמין כל דבר תוכל להשלים לפי שלמאמין כל הדברים קלים.

‏<sup>9:24</sup>ומיד בכה בצעקה אבי הנער ואמר אדו' אני מאמין אמנם עוזרני לפי אמונתי.

‏<sup>9:25</sup>וכאשר ראה יש"ו שהעם מתקבצים לזה ואמר לו חזק ואלם הנני מצוך שתצא מכאן ומכאן והלאה לא תשוב כאן עוד.

‏<sup>9:26</sup>והשטן יצא צועק ומכאיב והנער נשאר כמת בעניין שרבים היו אומרים שהוא מת.

‏<sup>9:27</sup>ויש"ו לקחו והעמידו וקם.

---

ומקטף B | על B| את] G | עד מאד [מאד EF | וחוס [וחוסה G| חוננ' B, חונני G | חנינו [חנני| לו] G | ויאמר]<sup>17:15</sup> BDEFG | נופל + [ופעמים ABDEFG | ופעמים נופל [ונופל פעמים ABDEFG | ומקצף
לרפאותו [לרפאתו ADEF | יכלו [יוכלו ADEF | לתלמידיך [לתלמידך ADEF | והבאתיו [והביאותיו]<sup>17:16</sup> BD
ABDEFG וכופר [הכופרים omit ABDEFG | לכם אתם] 3 1 2 ABDEFG | דור רע אוי לכם]<sup>17:17</sup>
ומפילו] G | ומה שהביאוהו אליו וישו ראה השטן [והביאוהו . . . השטן] A | ויבאוהו [והביאוהו]<sup>MK 9:20</sup> והפילו G
ומיד + [ומיד ABDEFG | והלאה [והלאה AG | ואביו [והאב ABDEFG | יש + [זמן]<sup>MK 9:21</sup>
| אדון [אדוני A | להשמידו [השמידו G שיוכל A, יוכל [יוכל A | בעניין [בעניין ABDEFG אדון]<sup>MK 9:22</sup>
| עזרהו . . . בשום] עניין עזרו ענין לעזור תוכל EF | ענין [עניין A | לעזרו [לעזור ABCDEFG
F בעיניו [בעיניו A | וישא [וישא ABDEF | עזרנו [עזרני]<sup>MK 9:24</sup> עזרהו
ואם] + אתה [אתה ABDEFG | הדברים] + אצלו ABDEFG | קלה [קלים BDEFG]<sup>MK 9:23</sup>
אדון [אדוני A, omit B | בצעקה] omit G אדון]<sup>MK 9:24</sup>
מבטן ומבטן [מכאן ומכאן DG | שטן + [שטן A | לו + [לו omit G | לזה [לזה ABDEFG צוה לשד [לשד omit G | ראה]<sup>MK 9:25</sup>
G מה הוא ABDEF, שמת הוא [שהוא מת C היה [יצא]<sup>MK 9:26</sup>
B והעמידוהו [והעמידו ABDG, מיד EF | מיד + [מהיד ABDG, מיד EF | לקחו] + מיד]<sup>MK 9:27</sup>

[14]It came to pass when he came to the crowds
there came to him a man bowing upon his knees.

[15]He said: Have mercy on me, Lord, and pity my son because he is terrified of an evil spirit and is very sick. He grinds his teeth, (foams) at his
mouth, falls from his place to the ground and falls sometimes in the
fire and sometimes in water.

[16](I) brought him to your disciple(s), but they were not able to heal him.

[17]Jesus answered and said: Evil generation, woe to you who deny; how
long will I be with you, how long will I bear your trouble. Bring him
to me.

MK 9:20They brought him to him and immediately when Jesus saw him the
satan subdued him and cast him to the ground and he began rolling
in the dust and foaming.

MK 9:21Jesus asked the father of the boy: How long has the satan taken
him. The father answered him: From a certain time and beyond.

MK 9:22Often he casts him into fire or water that he might be able to destroy him. If, Lord, you are able to help him in any way, help him.
Then the man found favor in his eyes and he was filled with compassion for him.

MK 9:23He said to him: If you are able to believe you will be able to ac-
complish anything because to the one who believes all things are
easy.

MK 9:24Immediately the father of the boy cried out with a shout and said:
Lord, I believe, indeed help me according to my faith.

MK 9:25When Jesus saw that the people were gathering together (he commanded the demon) and said to him: Hard and dumb (satan), behold I command you to come out from there and henceforth do not
return here again.

MK 9:26Then the satan came out screaming and inflicting pain and the boy
was left as dead so that many were saying that he was dead.

MK 9:27Jesus took him (by the hand), stood him up and he arose.

<sup>9:28</sup>וכאשר נכנס יש״ו לבית

## [ MATTHEW ]

<sup>19</sup>אז קרבו התלמידים ליש״ו בסתר ויאמרו אליו מדוע לא נוכל אנחנו להוציאו.

<sup>20</sup>ויאמר להם למיעוט אמונתכם. אמן אני אומר לכם אם יהיה בכם מן האמונה כגרגיר חרדל אם תאמינו להר הזה תאמרו סורו ויסור וכל דבר לא יבצר מכם.

<sup>21</sup>וזה המין מן השדים לא יצא כי אם בתפלה וצום.

### פרק ע״ו

<sup>22</sup>המה בגליל ויאמר יש״ו בן האדם ימסר ליד בני האדם.

<sup>23</sup>ויהרגוהו וביום השלישי יקום.

<sup>24</sup>ויבואו כפר נחום מרתה ויקרבוהו מקבלי המכס לפייט״רוס ויאמרו אליהם רביכם אינו נוהג ונותן מכס.

<sup>25</sup>ויאמרו כן. ויבואו בבית והקדים יש״ו לאמר אליו לפייט״רוס מה נראה לך פייט״רוס מלכי ארץ ממי לוקחים מכס מן בניהם או מן הנכרים.

<sup>26</sup>ויען אליו מן הנכרים. ויאמר להם יש״ו אם כן הבנים תפשים. ויאמר לא תהיו בעבר זה נבהלים.

<sup>27</sup>ויאמר לפייט״רוס לך לים והשלך חכה ואותו דג שתקח ראשונה תמצא בפיו מטבע כסף ואותו תתן בעדינו.

### פרק ע״ז

<sup>1</sup>בעת ההיא קרבו התלמידים אל יש״ו ויאמרו אליו מי אתה חושב שהוא גדול במלכות שמים.

<sup>2</sup>ויקרא נער אחד (קטן וישימהו בתוכם.

---

<sup>MK 9:28</sup> וכאשר] + עמד G

<sup>MT 17:19</sup> למה] מדוע G | אליו] לו A | ואליו] + לו F | בסתר] + לו F | לישן] omit AF | וקרבו] + לו A

<sup>17:20</sup> ויאמר] אמר EF | להם] אליהם AB | תאמינו] omit A | להר הזה תאמרו] 3 1 2 AEF | תאמרו] omit | סורו] סור ABEFG | G

<sup>17:21</sup> מן השדים] מהשדים A

<sup>17:22</sup> האדם¹] אדם ABDEFG

<sup>17:24</sup> מרתה] רמתה A | ויקרבוהו] ויקרבו | לפייטרוס] ABCDEFG | לפיטרו A, לפיטרוש BDEFG | אליהם] אליו A | נוהג ונותן] נותן ABDEFG | אליהם] אליו C

<sup>17:25</sup> לפייטרוס] לפיטרו A, | ויבואו] ויבא A | בבית] ביתו G | לאמר אליו] 2 1 ABCDEFG | לפייטרוס] פיטרוס AD, פיטרו BEFG, פיטרוש C | נראה] יראה ABDEFG | לפייטרוס] לפיטרוש BDEFG | מלכי . . . הנכרים] omit C

<sup>17:26</sup> תפשים] חפשים ABDEFG | אליהם] אליו A

<sup>17:27</sup> ומצא] תמצא EF | שתקח] שתצר G, שתמצא A, לפיטרוס C לפיטרוס BDEFG, לפיטרוש A, לפייטרוס | בצד] בצע ABDEFG | בעדינו] בעדנו DEF | מטבע] בצע EF

<sup>18:1</sup> ויאמר אליהם אתם חושבים] ויאמרו . . . | חושב] G | לישן] אל ישן G

<sup>18:2</sup> By haplography (נער אחד . . . נער אחד) all our mss, except A, omit 18:2b-5a. The text printed above in parentheses is according to ms A, which contains all but vs 4.

MK 9:28When Jesus entered the house

19the disciples drew near to Jesus secretly and said to him: Why were we not able to cast it out.

20He said to them: Because of the limitation of your faith. Truly I say to you if there be in you any faith, as a grain of mustard, if you believe, you will say to this mountain depart and it will depart; and nothing will be withheld from you.

21But this kind of demon does not come out except by prayer and fasting.

22They were in Galilee and Jesus said: The Son of Man will be delivered into the hand of men.

23They will kill him and on the third day he will arise.

24They came to Capernaum-Martha and the tax collectors drew near to Peter and said to (him): your teacher does not follow the custom to pay tax.

25Thus they spoke. (He) went into the house and Jesus anticipated him saying to Peter: What is your judgment, Peter, the kings of the earth from whom do they take tribute, from their sons or from foreigners.

26He answered him: From foreigners. Jesus said to them: If so the sons are (free). Then he said: Do not be dismayed because of this.

27He said to Peter: Go to the sea and cast a fishing hook and fish with it because in the mouth of the one you will catch first you will find a silver coin. That you will give for us.

## Chapter 18

1At that time the disciples drew near to Jesus and said to him: Whom do you think is great in the kingdom of heaven.

2He called a (small) lad (and placed him in their midst.

[MT 18:3-15

<sup>3</sup>ויאמר אני אומר אם לא תשובו להיות כנער הזה לא תבואו במ״ש.

<sup>5</sup>והמקבל נער א׳) כזה על שמי מקבל.

<sup>6</sup>ואשר יכשיל אחד מהנערים הקטנים המאמינים בי טוב לו שיקשור פלח רכב על צוארו ויוטל במצולות ים.

<sup>7</sup>(אוי ליושבי תבל מפני המבוכות שצריכות המבוכות לבא.) ויאמר אוי לאדם שיבא בשבלו.

<sup>8</sup>ואם ידך ורגלך יכשילך תכריתהו ותכשילהו ממך. טוב לך לבא בחיים עוד או פסח מהיות לך ידים ורגלים לתתך באש עולמית.

<sup>9</sup>ואם עיניך תכשילך ותקרה ותשליכה ממך. טוב לך לבא בחיים בעין אחד מהיות לך עינים ולתתך בגהינם.

<sup>10</sup>והזהרו פן תדינו אחת מהנערים הקטנים. אומר אני לכם למלאכיהם הם רואים תמיד בני אבי שבשמים.

<sup>11</sup>ובן אדם בטל להושיע האויבים.

## פרק ע״ח

<sup>12</sup>מה יראה לכם אם יהיה לאיש מאה צאן ופרח אחת מהן הלא יעזוב תשעים ותשעה בהרים וילך לבקש הנדחה.

<sup>13</sup>ואם ימצאנה אמן אני אומר לכם שישמח עליה יותר מהתשעים ותשעה אשר לא נדחו.

<sup>14</sup>כן לא ירצה אב שבשמים שיאבד א״ מהנערים.

## פקר ע״ט

<sup>15</sup>בעת ההיא אמר יש״ו לשמעון נקרא פייט׳רוס אם יחטא לך אחיך הוכיחנו בינו לבינך. אם ישמע אליך קנית את אחיך.

---

<sup>18:5</sup> A אותי + | מקבל] EFG | בזה] כזה
<sup>18:6</sup> על צוארו] CG פלס | פלח] omit EF | הקטנים] DG מן הנערים | מהנערים] BDG יכשל | יכשיל] BDG במצולת | במצולות A | בצוארו
<sup>18:7</sup> אוי . . . לבא] omit British Library MS and C. Text printed in parentheses is according to A | ABD, בשבילו] בשבלו A שיבאו | שיבא] DEF לו + | <sup>2</sup>אוי] D תפל | תבל] D לו + | <sup>1</sup>אוי] G המבוכות שצריכות לבא +
<sup>18:8</sup> עוד] עוד ABDEFG ותשליכהו | ותכשילהו B יכשילוך | יכשילך] A ורגליך | ורגלך] A ידיך | ידך A ולתתך | לתתך] A או רגלים | ורגלים] ABCDEFG
<sup>18:9</sup> לבא] A ותשליכהו | ותשליכה] C ונקרה | נקרה A, BDEFG נקרה | נקרהו | ותקרה] BCDEF עינך | עיניך A בגיהנם | בגהינם] BDE לבאו | אחד] B לבאו
<sup>18:10</sup> BEF | שמלאכיהם A, BDG, א A | שמלאכי׳ | למלאכיהם] D מן הנערים | מהנערים] BDG, א A | אחד] אחד פני | בני AB(?)CDEFG
<sup>18:11</sup> G את האויבים | האויבים] omit A, בא BDEFG | בטל
<sup>18:12</sup> DG אחד | אחת] ABCDEFG וברח | ופרח
<sup>18:13</sup> A שלא | אשר לא | A ותשע | ותשעה
<sup>18:14</sup> EF שידחו | שיאבד] DG האב, ABCEF אבי | אב
<sup>18:15</sup> D הוכחנו | הוכיחנו] BDEFG פיטרוס A, פיטרו | פייטרוס

<sup>3</sup>He said: I say if you do not turn to become like this lad
you will not enter the kingdom of heaven.

<sup>5</sup>He who receives a lad) like this in my name receives (me).

<sup>6</sup>He who causes one of the small lads who believe on me to stumble, it
would be good for him to tie a millstone upon his neck and be cast into
the depth of the sea.

<sup>7</sup>(Woe to the inhabitants of the world because of confusion, because
confusion must come.) He also said: Woe to the man who comes because of it.

<sup>8</sup>If your hand or your foot causes you to stumble cut it off and (cast it)
from you; it is better for you to enter into life (blind) or lame than having two hands and two feet for you to be given to everlasting fire.

<sup>9</sup>If your (eye) should cause you to stumble, pick it out and cast it from
you. It is better for you to enter into life with one eye than to have two
eyes and to be given to Gehenna.

<sup>10</sup>Take heed lest you judge one of the small lads. I say to you, their an-
gels always see the sons of my father who is in heaven,

<sup>11</sup>and the Son of Man has stopped saving the enemy.

<sup>12</sup>What is your opinion? If a man has a hundred sheep and one of them
(runs off), will he not leave the ninety-nine in the mountains and go
seek the one which has strayed?

<sup>13</sup>If he should find it truly I say to you he will rejoice over it more than
the ninety-nine which did not go astray.

<sup>14</sup>Thus (my) Father who is in heaven does not wish that any of these lads
should be lost.

<sup>15</sup>At that time Jesus said to Simon, called Petros: If your brother sins
against you reprove him privately. If he listens to you, you have gained
your brother.

[MT 18:16-28

<sup>16</sup>ואם לא ישמע אליך הוכיחנו בפני אחר ואם בכל אלה לא ישמע לך תוסיף עוד אחד או שנים לפנים שנים או שלשה עדים שעל פי שנים או שלשה עדים יקום דבר.

<sup>17</sup>ואם בכל אלה לא ישמע אמור אותו בקהל ואם לא ישמע בקהל חשוב אותו כמנודה ואויב ואכזר.

<sup>18</sup>אמן אני אומר לכם שכל אלה אשר תאסרו בארץ אסור הוא בשמים וכל אשר תתירו בארץ מותר יהיה בשמים.

<sup>19</sup>וגם אני אומר לכם אם ירצו שנים מכם לשים שלים בארץ כל אשר יבקשו יהיה לכם מאת שבשמים.

<sup>20</sup>ובכל מקום שיתחברו שנים או שלשה על שמי שם אנכי בתוככם.

<sup>21</sup>אז קרב פיט״רוס אליו לאמר אדוני אם יחטא לי אחי עד שבע פעמים אמחול לו.

<sup>22</sup>ויאמר לו יש״ו איני אומר לך עד שבע כי אם עד שבעים ושבעה.

<u>פרק פ״</u>

<sup>23</sup>בעת ההיא אמר יש״ו לתלמידיו מלכות שמים דומה היא לאדם מלך יושב לעשות חשבון עם עבדיו ומשרתיו.

<sup>24</sup>וכאשר התחיל לחשוב בא א׳ שהוא חייב כעשרת אלפים זהובים.

<sup>25</sup>ואין לו מה ליתן ויצו אדוניו למכור אותו ואת בניו ואת כל אשר לו לשלם הממון.

<sup>26</sup>ויפול העבד לפני אדוניו ויתחנן לו לרחם עליו ולהמתין לו כי הכל ישלם.

<sup>27</sup>ויחמול עליו אדוניו ומחל לו הכל.

<sup>28</sup>ויצא העבד ההוא וימצא אחד מחביריו שהוא חייב לו מאה מעות ויחזק בו ויפגע לו לאמר

---

18:16 לך] אליך A | תוסיף] הסוף A | לפנים] להיות דבריך לפני A, לפני BCDEF | לפנים שנים] omit G
עדים<sup>2</sup> . . . דבר] דבר] הדבר B | עדים<sup>1</sup>] 1 2 (hap) CD

18:17 בקהל] 1 2 (hap) B

18:18 יהיה] A יהיה | הוא] G 2 1 | אסור הוא] אשר<sup>1</sup>] omit C | אשר<sup>1</sup>] omit ABDEFG | אלה] omit EF | אומר] omit G

18:19 אבי] + מאת EF | תבקשו] יבקשו ABDEFG

18:20 שם] omit C | בתוככם] בתוכם ABDEFG

18:21 פיטרוס] A, פיטרו BDEFG

18:22 פעמים] + EF פעמים | שבעה] שבע A | שבעה] שבע D | ושבעה] + B אליו] לו EF

18:23 היא] הוא A, omit EF | ומשרתיו] משרתיו F

18:24 זהובים] דינרים ABDEF

18:25 ואת<sup>1</sup>] . . . ואת<sup>2</sup>] 1 2 (hap)EFG | שיתן לו, ABDEFG | שיתן G | ליתן] ישלם

18:26 ישלם] אשלם ABDEFG | לאמר חוסה עליו (עלי -D) והמתן (המתן -B) לי והכל] לרחם . . . הכל] ABDEFG (אשלם . . . אשלם)

18:27 אדוני] F | vss 27-29 omitted in DG (hap.

18:28 לאמר] All mss including DG contain a haplography from בו] omit EF | מחביריו] מחבריו AEF | לאמר
לאמר (18:28) to לאמר (18:29). For DG see notes on 18:27 and 18:31.

¹⁶If he does not listen to you, reprove him before another;
   if by every oath he does not listen to you add still one or two (in order
   that your words might be before) two or three witnesses, because by
   two or three witnesses a word will be established.
¹⁷If by every oath he does not listen, tell it in the assembly; and if he
   does not listen to the assembly consider him as ostracised, an enemy,
   and cruel.
¹⁸Truly I say to you that every oath which you shall bind on earth is
   bound in heaven and every [oath] which you shall loose on earth will
   be loosed in heaven.
¹⁹Also I say to you, if two of you wish to make peace on earth everything which (you) ask will be yours from (my Father) who is in
   heaven.
²⁰In every place where two or three are joined together in my name there
   am I in (their) midst.
²¹Then Peter drew near to him saying: Lord, if my brother sins against
   me, shall I forgive him unto seven times.
²²Jesus said to him: I do not say to you unto seven, but unto seventy-
   seven.
²³At that time Jesus said to his disciples: The kingdom of heaven is like a
   certain king who sat to make a reckoning with his servants and minis-
   ters.
²⁴As he began to reckon one came who owed about ten thousand pieces
   of gold.
²⁵But he had nothing to give and his master commanded to sell him and
   his children and all which was his to repay the value.
²⁶The servant fell before his master and implored him to have pity on
   him and to be patient with him because he would repay everything.
²⁷Then his master had pity on him and forgave him everything.
²⁸But that servant went out and found one of his comrads who owed him
   a hundred pieces of money and he grasped him and struck him saying:

²⁹חוסה עלי והמתן לי והכל אשלם.

³⁰ולא אבה לשמוע לו ויוליכוהו לבית הסוהר עד שלם לו הכל.

³¹וראו עבדי המלך את אשר עשה ויחר להם מאד ויבאו ויגידו לאדוניהם.

³²אז קרא אותו אדוניו ויאמר לו עבד ארור הלא מחלתי לך כל חוביך כאשר פייסתני.

³³ומדוע לא מחלת לעבדך בהתחננו אליך כאשר מחלתיך?

³⁴ויחר אף אדוניו בו ויצו לענותו עד ישלם לו כל החוב.

³⁵כן יעשה לכם אבי שבשמים אם לא תמחלו איש את אחיו בלב שלם.

## פרק פ"א

¹ויהי כאשר כלה יש"ו הדברים האלה עבר מן הגליל ויבא לקצות ארץ יהודה אשר בעבר הירדן.

²וילכו אחריו חבורות רבות וירפא את כולם.

³ויגשו אליו את הפרושים לנסותו. וישאלוהו לאמר אם מותר לעזוב את אשתו בשום עניין וליתן לה גט.

⁴ויען להם הלא קראתם לעושיהם מקדם זכר ונקבה בראם.

⁵ויאמר על כן יעזוב איש את אביו ואת אמו ודבק באשתו והיו לבשר אחד.

⁶א"כ אינם שנים כי אם בשר אחד ומה שחבר הבורא אין אדם יכול להפריד.

⁷ויאמר לו אם כן מדוע צוה משה לתת גט כריתות ושלחה מביתו.

⁸ויאמר להם משה לעקשות פה לבבכם אמר לכם לעזוב את נשיכם. ומעולם לא היה כן.

⁹אומר אני לכם שכל העוזב את אשתו ויקח אחרת אם לא בשביל ניאוף הוא נואף והלוקה הגרושה ניאף.

¹⁸:²⁹ Beginning] see note on 18:28. | והכל] + לו B
¹⁸:³⁰ ויוליכהו] ויוליכוהו ABDEFG | שלם] ישלם A | לו²] omit ABDEFG
¹⁸:³¹ את] omit BDEFG | עשה] + vss 27-29 DG (see notes on 18:27 and 18:28 above).
¹⁸:³² חוביך] חובך ABDEFG
¹⁸:³³ לעבדך] לחברך A, לעבדיך B
¹⁸:³⁴ ויצו] ויאמר G | לו] omit A
¹⁸:³⁵ בלב] בלבב A
¹⁹:¹ כלה] כילה B | ישו] + לדבר G | לקצות] לקצה ABDEFG | יהודה] יודא BCDEFG
¹⁹:³ את²] omit A | אדם] + G | לעזוב] omit DG | לנסותו] omit DG | את¹] omit ABDEFG | וישובו ויגשו DG | וליתן] ויתן ADEFG
¹⁹:⁴ לעושיהם] שעושיהם ABDEFG
¹⁹:⁵ איש] האדם G
¹⁹:⁷ ויאמר] ויאמרו A | לתת] + לה ABDEFG | ושלחה] ולשלח G
¹⁹:⁸ להם] אליהם ABDEG | משה] מה F | פה] omit A | ומעולם] ומקדם AB, ומקדם DEFG
¹⁹:⁹ ניאף] ינאף A, נואף EFG | ניאף] omit ABD | את] omit ABD

[29] . . . trust me and be patient with me
and I will repay everything.

[30]But he was not willing to listen to him; so (he) brought him to the
prison until he repaid him everything.

[31]The servants of the king saw that which he did and they were very angry and went and told their master.

[32]Then his master called him and said to him: Cursed servant, did I not
forgive you all your (debt) when you placated me.

[33]So why did you not forgive your servant when he supplicated you as I
forgave you?

[34]His master was angry with him and commanded to afflict him until he
should repay him all the debt.

[35]Thus will my Father who is in heaven do to you if you do not forgive
each man his brother with a perfect heart.

## Chapter 19

[1]It came to pass when Jesus finished these words he passed on
from Galilee and came to the outskirts of the land of Judah across
the Jordan.

[2]There followed him large crowds and he healed all of them.

[3]Then the Pharisees came to him to tempt him. They asked him saying:
Is it permissible for one to leave his wife for any matter and to give her
a bill of divorce.

[4]He answered them: Have you not read that he who made them of old,
male and female he created them.

[5]He said: Therefore a man shall leave his father and his mother and
cleave to his wife and they will become one flesh.

[6]If so, they are not two but one flesh and whatever the creator has joined
together man is unable to separate.

[7](They) said to him: If so why did Moses command to give her a bill of
divorce and to send her away from his house.

[8]He said to them: Moses because of the obstinacy of your heart said for
you to leave your wives. But from eternity it was not so.

[9]I say to you that everyone who leaves his wife and takes another, if not
for adultery, commits adultery; and he who takes her who has been di-
vorced (commits adultery).

[MT 19:10-24

‏<sup></sup>‏¹⁰ויאמרו אליו תלמידיו א״כ דבר אדם עם אשתו לא טוב לקחת אותה.
¹¹ויאמר אליהם אין דבר זה לכל אלא למי שנתן להם.
¹²שיש סריסים מתולדותם אלו הם אשר לא חטאו. ויש סריסים
מעצמם שכובשים את יצרם בשביל מלכות שמים אלו הם חכמים
במעלה גדולה. מי שיוכל להבין יבין.

פרק פ״ב

¹³אז הובאו אליו ילדים לשים ידו עליהם ולהתפלל עליהם
ותלמידיו מגרשים אותם.
¹⁴ויאמר אליהם יש״ו הניחו הנערים לבא אלי ולא תמנעום שמהם
מלכות שמים. באמת אני אומר לכם שלא יכנס במלכות
שמים אם לא כאלה.
¹⁵וישם ידו עליהם וילך משם.
¹⁶ויגש אליו בחור א״ משתחוה לו ויאמר לו ר׳ איזה טוב אעשה
לקנות חיי העה״ב.
¹⁷ויען אליו מה תשאל מטוב אין האדם טוב כי האל לבדו הוא טוב.
ואם תרצה לבא בחיים שמור המצוות.
¹⁸ויאמר לו מה הן. ויאמר לו יש״ו לא תרצח לא תגנוב לא תענה
ברעך עד שקר.
¹⁹כבד את אביך ואת אמך ואהבת לרעך כמוך.
²⁰ויאמר לו הבחור כל אלה שמרתי ומה יחסר לי עוד.
²¹ויאמר אליו יש״ו אם תרצה להיות תם לך ומכור כל אשר לך
ותנהו לעניים ויהיה לך אוצר בשמים ובא אחרי.
²²ויהי כשמוע הבחור הלך לפי שלא היה לו קרקעות רבות.
²³ויאמר יש״ו לתלמידיו אמן אני אומר לכם שכבד לעשיר לבא
במלכות שמים.
²⁴ועוד אני אומר לכם שיותר קל לבא הגמל בעין המחט מן העשיר
במלכות שמים.

‏19:10‏ אליו] לו G
‏19:12‏ שכובשים] ABDEFG | ויש סריסים עשויים בידי אדם + [חטאו | EF שלא [אשר לא | B אילו[1] ואלו]
‏יבין] EF | ומי [מי | ABDEFG הבאים [חכמים | EF בשבילו [בשביל | ABDEFG שהם כובשים omit
EF
‏19:13‏ מקבלים EF, DG | לפניו [אליו | EF הובא [הובאו] מגרשים [מגרשים G | מקבלים
‏19:14‏ יהיה + [אם לא | ולא] DEFG | omit D [לכם | omit D | מניחו] EF, omit G [להם | אליהם]
ABCDEFG
‏19:16‏ משתחוה] וישתחוה ABDEFGH
‏19:17‏ והאל [כי האל H | אדם [האדם H מהטיב [מטוב | H ויאמר + [ויאמר] EFG | אליו + [ואליו] ABDEFGH
‏את + A [שמור | BDEFH הטוב [טוב[2] | omit G [הוא]
‏19:18‏ לא תנאף [לא תרצח | ABDEFGH אמר [ויאמר] D
‏19:20‏ הבחור [החכם] ABDEFG
‏19:21‏ אליו] לו EFG ויהיה [ויהי A | ובא [ולך G
‏19:22‏ הבחור] החכם ABDEFG | הלך [הלך + זעף ABD(?)EF, G(?) [שלא היה [שהיו A | היה [היו DEFG

<sup>10</sup>Then his disciples said to him: If the matter
of a man with his wife is so, it is not good to take her.
<sup>11</sup>He said to them: This matter is not for everyone but for those to whom
it has been given.
<sup>12</sup>Because there are eunuchs from their birth; these are those who have
not sinned. (There are eunuchs made by man) and there are self-made
eunuchs who subdue their desire for the sake of the kingdom of
heaven; these are (those who enter) into great prominence. Whoever is
able to understand let him understand.
<sup>13</sup>Then they brought children to him that he might lay his hand on them
and pray for them, but his disciples were driving them away.
<sup>14</sup>Jesus said to them: Permit the lads to come to me and do not restrain
them, for of them is the kingdom of heaven. Truly I say to you that one
will not enter the kingdom of heaven except (he shall be) like these.
<sup>15</sup>So he laid his hand on them and went on from there.
<sup>16</sup>A young man came to him worshipping him and said to him: Rabbi
what good thing shall I do to acquire the life of the world to come.
<sup>17</sup>He answered them: Why do you ask about good; no man is good; be-
cause God alone is good. But if you wish to enter life keep the commandments.
<sup>18</sup>He said to him: What are they. Jesus said to him: Thou shalt not kill,
thou shalt not steal, thou shalt not bear false witness against your
neighbor.
<sup>19</sup>Honor your father and your mother and love you neighbor as yourself.
<sup>20</sup>The young man said to him: All these I have kept so what yet do I lack.
<sup>21</sup>Jesus said unto him: If you wish to be perfect go and sell all which you
have and give it to the poor and you will have treasure in heaven and
follow me.
<sup>22</sup>It came to pass when the young man heard he went away (angry) be-
cause he did not have much property.
<sup>23</sup>Jesus said to his disciples: Truly I say to you, it is hard for a rich man
to enter the kingdom of heaven.
<sup>24</sup>Again I say to you it is easier for a camel to enter the eye of a needle
than a rich man the kingdom of heaven.

[MT 19:25-20:9

25וישמעו התלמידים ויתמהו מאד ויאמרו ליש״ו א׳׳כ מי יוכל
להושיע.

26ויפן אליהם ויאמר נגד בני אדם הדבר קשה ונגד האלקים הכל
דבר קל להיות.

### פרק פ״ג

27ויען פייט״רוס לו הנה עזבנו הכל לילך אחריך מה
יהיה לנו.

28ויאמר יש״ו אמן אני אומר לכם שאתם ההולכים אחרי שביום
הדין כאשר ישב האדם על כסא כבודו תשבו גם אתם על י״ב
כסאות שנים עשר שבטי ישראל.

29וכל העוזב ביתו גם אחיותיו ואביו ואמו ואשתו ובניו על
שמי יקבל כמותם ומלכות שמים ירש.

30רבים ראשונים יהיו אחרונים ורבים אחרונים יהיו ראשונים.

### פרק פ״ד

1אחר זה אמר יש״ו לתלמידיו מלכות שמים דומה לאדם יחיד
אדון ביתו המשכיר בבקר לשכור פועלים.

2והשכירם בדינר אחד ליום וישלחם לכרמו.

3ויצא בשלישית היום וירא אחרים עומדים בשוק בטלים.

4ויאמר להם לכו גם אתם לכרמי ובראוי אתן לכם.

5וילכו. ויצאו עוד בצהרים וגם בשעה תשיעית ויעש כן.

6ובאחת עשרה שעה יצא ג״כ וימצא אחרים עומדים ויאמר להם
מדוע אתם עומדים בטלים כל היום.

7ויענו לו שלא שכרנו אדם. ויאמר אליהם לכו גם אתם לכרמי.

8ויהי לעת ערב ויאמר בעל הכרם לניצב על הפועלים קרא אותם
ואתן להם שכרם. ויחל באחרונים ויכל בראשונים.

9והאחרונים קבלו דינר אחד.

---

19:25 ויתמהו] ויפלאו ABDEFG | לישו] omit G

19:26 האלקים] האלים A | הדבר [הכל דבר G

19:27 פייטרוס] פיטרוש A, BDEFG פיטרוס C | הנה [הנגנו A | לילך [ללכת A

19:28 ויאמר] + אליהם AG, + להם BDEF | ישראל . . . שנים] omit G | ישראל] omit D

19:29 גם אחיותיו] ואחיותיו ABDEFG | ביתו] + ואחיו A, + אחיו BDEFG | יקבל] + מאה ABDEFG

19:30 ורבים . . . ראשונים] omit A (hap)

20:1 המשכיר] המשכים ABCDEFG | פועלים] + לכרמו ABDEFG

20:3 ויצא] ויבא EF | בשוק בטלים] ABCDEF 2 1

20:4 ובראוי] והראוי ABDEFG

20:5 ויצאו] ויצא ABDEFG | בשעה] בשעת A | תשיעית] התשיעית ABDEF

20:6 ובשנים] ובאחת EF, omit D | שעה] שעת A

20:7 ויענו] ויאמר G | לו] + ויאמרו A, להם G | אליהם] להם AG | לכו] omit G

²⁵The disciples heard and were exceedingly amazed
and said to Jesus: If so who can save [them].

²⁶He turned to them and said: With man the matter is difficult, but with
God everything is easy.

²⁷Peter answered and said to him: Behold we have left all to follow after
you; what will be ours.

²⁸Jesus said: Truly I say to you who follow me, in the day of judgment
when the Man sits upon the throne of his glory also you will sit upon
the twelve thrones of the twelve tribes of Israel.

²⁹Everyone who leaves his house, and (his brothers), also his sisters, his
father, his mother, his wife and his children for my name will receive
(a hundred) like them and will inherit the kingdom of heaven.

³⁰Many who are first will be last
and many who are last will be first.

## Chapter 20

¹After this Jesus said to his disciples: The kingdom of heaven is like a
certain individual who was master in his house (who arose early) in the
morning to hire laborers (for his vineyard).

²He hired them for one dinar a day and sent them into his vineyard.

³He went out at the third [hour] of the day and saw others standing idle
in the market place.

⁴He said to them: Go also you into my vineyard and that which is suitable I will give to you.

⁵So they went. Then (he) came out again at noon and also at the ninth
hour and did the same.

⁶At the eleventh hour he went out also and found others standing and he
said to them: Why do you stand idle all day.

⁷They answered him: No man has hired us. So he said to them: Go also
you into my vineyard.

⁸It came to pass at evening, the master of the vineyard said to the officer
over the laborers: Call them that I might give to them their wages. He
began with the last and finished with the first.

⁹The last received one dinar.

[MT 20:10-24

‏¹⁰והראשונים חשבו לקחת יותר והוא לא נתן לכולם כי אם דינר.
‏¹¹וילונו הראשונים על בעל הכרם
‏¹²לאמר אלו האחרונים עמלו שעה אחת והשוית אותם עמנו שעמלנו כל היום והחורב.
‏¹³ויען לאחד מהם ויאמר לו אהובי איני עושה לך עול. הלא בדינר א״ שכרתיך?
‏¹⁴קחנו ולך. אם אני רוצה לתת לזה האחרון כמותך
‏¹⁵הלא אעשה כרצוני? הידע בעיניך כאשר אני טוב?
‏¹⁶כן יהיה אחרונים ראשונים והראשונים אחרונים. רבים הם הקרואים ומעטים הנבחרים.

פרק פ״ה

‏¹⁷ויקרב יש״ו אל ירושלם ויקח את י״ב תלמידיו בסתר ויאמר אליהם
‏¹⁸הנה אנחנו עולים לירושלם ובן האדם ימסר לגדולי החכמים והכהנים וייחייבוהו למות.
‏¹⁹וגם ימסרו אותו לגוים להכותו ולהשביתו וביום השלישי.
‏²⁰אז בא אשת זבדיאל עם בניה משתחוה ומבקשת בקשה ממנו.
‏²¹ויאמר אליה מה תרצי. ותאמר שתצוה לשבת שני בני אלה האחד לימינך והשני לשמאלך במלכותך.
‏²²ויען להם יש״ו לא תדעון מה תבקשון. התוכל לסבול היסורין והמיתה שאני עתיד לסבול? ויאמרו נוכל.
‏²³ויאמר להם שתו כוסי והושיבו לשמאלי או גם לימיני אין לי לתתה לכם כי אם לאשר הוא נכון לפני אבי.
‏²⁴וישמעו העשרה ויחר בעיניהם בעניין שני אחים.

---

‏²⁰:¹⁰נתן להם דינר אחד [והוא | G נתן G | [חשבו DG | והחושבים [והראשונים G omit | דינר . . . [והוא
‏ABDEF נתן לכל אחד דינר [לא נתן לכולם כי אם דינר
‏²⁰:¹²והשוית] והשויתה A
‏²⁰:¹³G omit [א״ | G omit [לו | A להם | [לאחד מהם G
‏²⁰:¹⁵הרע [והידע ABDG, הירע EF
‏²⁰:¹⁶יהיה] יהיו AB
‏²⁰:¹⁸וייחייבוהו] A | הכהנים והחכמים [החכמים והכהנים A | אדם [האדם A | אל ירושלם [לירושלם A ויחייבוהו ABCDG, ויחריבוהו EF | תמות [למיתה A
‏²⁰:¹⁹השלישי] + יקום | BDEFG | ולהלקותו [ולהלקותו ולתלותו A, וימסרו [וגם ימסרו A | ולהשביתו [ולהשביתו ABDEFG
‏²⁰:²⁰בא] omit AG
‏²⁰:²¹והאחד [והשני D | בניה B, בניה DG | בני אלה [בני אלה B ויאמר [ותאמר G omit
‏²⁰:²²עתיד] C | ביסורים [היסורין G | התוכלו ABDEF, התוכלון [התוכל A | תדעו [תדעון
‏²⁰:²³גם] omit ABDEFG | לשמאלי] EF 1 2 | לימיני . . . לשמאלי EF | ותושיבו [והושיבו EF שתבאו [שתו EF לפני [בעיני EF
‏²⁰:²⁴האחים A | אחים [אחים EF מעניין ABDG, בעינם מעניין | בעיניהם בעניין

<sup>10</sup>So the first thought they would receive more,
but he gave only a dinar to each of them.

<sup>11</sup>Then the first murmured against the master of the vineyard
<sup>12</sup>saying: These last worked one hour and you have made them like us
who have worked all day [in] the heat.

<sup>13</sup>He answered one of them and said to him: My friend, I have done you
no injustice. Did I not hire you for one dinar?

<sup>14</sup>Take it and go. If I wish to give to this last like you
<sup>15</sup>may I not do according to my desire? (Is there evil) in your eyes when
I am good?

<sup>16</sup>So the last shall be first and the first last. Many are called but few are
the chosen.

<sup>17</sup>Jesus drew near to Jerusalem and took his twelve disciples secretly and
said to them:

<sup>18</sup>Behold we are going up to Jerusalem and the Son of Man will be deliv-
ered over to the chief sages and priests and they will condemn him to
death.

<sup>19</sup>Also they will deliver him to the Gentiles to smite and destroy him, but
on the third day (he will arise).

<sup>20</sup>Then came the wife of Zebedeel with her sons bowing down and mak-
ing a request from him.

<sup>21</sup>He said to her: What do you wish. She said: That you command these
my two sons to sit the one on your right and the other on your left in
your kingdom.

<sup>22</sup>Jesus answered them: You do not know what you are asking. Are you
able to endure the suffering and the death that I am going to endure?
They said: We are able.

<sup>23</sup>Then he said to them: Drink my cup, but (that you should sit) on my
left or my right is not for me to grant to you but to the one who is prepared before my Father.

<sup>24</sup>The ten heard [this] and it was a matter of anger in their eyes in regard
to the two brothers.

[MT 20:25-21-5

<sup>25</sup>ויקרבם יש״ו אליו ויאמר להם דעו שנשיאי הגוים רודים בהם וגדוליהם מבקשים לנפשם.

<sup>26</sup>לא כן יהיה ביניכם שהרוצה להיות גדול ביניכם ישקת אתכם.

<sup>27</sup>ואשר ירצה ביניכם להיות ראשון יהיה לכם עבד

<sup>28</sup>כאשר בן אדם לא בא שישרתוהו כי אם הוא לשרת ולתת נפשו כופר לרבים.

<u>פרק פ״ו</u>

<sup>29</sup>המה נכנסים ביריחו ותלך אחריו חבורה אחת.

<sup>30</sup>והנה שני עורים יוצאים אצל הדרך. וישמעו קול ההמון וישאלוהו מה זה. ויאמר להם הנביא יש״ו מנזא״רית בא. אז צעקו לאמר בן דוד חננו.

<sup>31</sup>והחבורה גערו בהם ואעפ״כ הם היו צועקים ואומרים האדון בן דוד חננו.

<sup>32</sup>ויעמוד יש״ו ויקראם ויאמר מה תרצו להעשות לכם.

<sup>33</sup>ויאמרו האדון שתפקחנה עינינו.

<sup>34</sup>ויחמול עליהם יש״ו ויגע בעיניהם ויאמר להם אמונתכם רפאא אתכם. ומיד ראו והודו לאל והלכו אחריו וכל העם הודו לאל על זה.

<u>פרק פ״ז</u>

<sup>1</sup>ויקרבו אל ירושלם ויבואו לבית פאגי להר הזתים וישלח יש״ו שנים מתלמידיו.

<sup>2</sup>ויאמר אליהם לכו אל המבצר אשר הוא נכחכם ומיד תמצאו אתון אחת ועירה אחת. והתירו אותם והביאום אלי.

<sup>3</sup>ואם יאמר לכם איש שום דבר אמרו לו שהאדון צריך להם ומיד יעזוב אתהם.

<sup>4</sup>כל זה לקיים דבר הנביא לאמר

<sup>5</sup>אמרו לבת ציון הנה מלכך יבא לך צדיק ונושע הוא עני ורוסב על אתון ועל עיר בן אתון.

---

<sup>20:25</sup> ABEF ויקריבם [ויקרבם | A לנפשם [לכבשם

<sup>20:26</sup> D ישית ,ABEF ישקת [ישקת | omit EF [<sup>2</sup>ביניכם

<sup>20:28</sup> omit ABCDEFG [הוא | AD האדם [אדם | ABDEFG כאשר [כאשר

<sup>20:30</sup> EF מנזאירית | הנה [הנביא | ABDEF ויאמרו [ויאמר | EF ויאמרו [ויאמר | ABCDG וישאלו וישאלוהו] מנזרת ACDG, מנזרת B מנזרת EF

<sup>20:31</sup> Whole vs 31] omit G | הם . . . הם [ואעפכ | ABDEF לאמר הסו והם [ואומרים | ואמרו EF

<sup>20:34</sup> ומיד [מיד F לאל [<sup>1</sup>לאל | A, א ולא [ולא EF

<sup>21:1</sup> omit H [ישו | AH בהר [להר

<sup>21:2</sup> BEFG עמה ,+ A, עמה [<sup>2</sup>אחת | A אסורה + [<sup>1</sup>אחת | H נכחם [נכחכם | H נכחם [נכחכם G, omit H להם [אליהם והביאו אותם [והביאום EF | A אותה [אותם EF

<sup>21:3</sup> A אמר [ויאמר | לכם [לכם ABDG, omit EF אתכם [אתהם ABDEFG

<sup>21:5</sup> אתונות [<sup>2</sup>אתון | AEFG חמור [<sup>1</sup>אתון | ABCDEFG ורוכב [ורוסב | omit G ונושע הוא [ונושע הוא EF בא [יבא BEF

25Jesus (brought them near) to him and said to them:
Know that the princes of the Gentiles have dominion over them and
their great ones seek (to subdue them).

26It will not be so among you, because he who wishes to be great among
you (will serve) you.

27He who among you wishes to be first will be your servant,

28(just as) the Son of Man did not come that they might serve him but
that he might serve and give himself as a ransom for many.

29They entered into Jericho and a crowd followed him.

30Behold two blind men came out beside the road. They heard the noise
of the multitude and (asked) what this might be. It was said to them:
The prophet Jesus from Nazareth is coming. Then they cried out saying: Son of David, have mercy on us.

31But the crowd rebuked them (saying: Be silent;) they nevertheless were
crying out and saying: Lord, Son of David, have mercy on us.

32So Jesus stopped, called them and said: What do you want [me] to do
for you.

33They said: Lord that our eyes might be opened.

34Jesus had pity on them, touched their eyes and said to them: Your faith
has healed you. Immediately they saw, praised God and followed him
and all the people praised God because of this.

# Chapter 21

1They drew near to Jerusalem and came to Bethpage to the Mount of Olives and Jesus sent two of his disciples.

2He said unto them: Go into the fortress which is opposite you and immediately you will find a she-ass and her colt (with her). Untie them
and bring them to me.

3If anyone should say anything to you say to him the master has need of
them and immediately he will let them go.

4All this was to fulfill the word of the prophet saying:

5Say to the daughter of Zion: behold your king comes to you, just and
victorious is he, humble and (riding) upon a she-ass and upon a colt the
foal of a she-ass.

⁶וילכו ויעשו כאשר ציום יש״ו.

⁷ויביאו האתון והעיר וירכב יש״ו עליה והאחרים שמו עליהם כליהם ומלבושיהם ויעלו למעלה.

⁸ורבים מהחבורה פורשים מלבושיהם בדרך ואחרים הסודרנה ענפי העצים וישליכו לפניו ולאחריו

⁹קוראים לאמר הושענא מושיע העולם ברוך הבא בשם ה״ הושענא מושיענו תתפאר בשמים ובארץ.

פרק פ״ח

¹⁰ויהי אחרי כן בבא יש״ו ירושלם חרדה כל העיר לאמר מי הוא זה.

¹¹ויאמרו העם זה לזה יש״ו הנביא מנאזא׳ריל אשר בגליל.

¹²ויבא יש״ו בית ה״ וימצא שם הקונים והמוכרים. ויהפוך לוחות השולחנים והמושבות מוכרי היונים.

¹³ויאמר אליהם כתיב כי ביתי בית תפלה יקרא לכל העמים ואתם עשיתם אותה מערת פריצים.

¹⁴ויקרבו אליו עורים ופסחים במקדש וירפאם.

¹⁵ויבואו גדולי החכמים והכהנים לראות הפלאות שעשה. והנערים קוראים במקדש ואומרים ישתבח בן האל. והחכמים ילעגו

¹⁶ויאמרו לו הלא שמעת מה אומרים אלו. ויען להם ויאמר שמעתי אלו. הלא קראתם מפי עוללים ויונקים יסדת עוז?

¹⁷ויעזוב וילך חוצה אל בית חנניא וילך שם ושם היה דורש להם ממלכות האל.

¹⁸ויהי בבקר וישב לעיר רעב.

¹⁹וירא תאנה אחת אצל הדרך ויגש אליה ולא מצא בה רק העלים לבד. ויאמר לה אל יצא ממך פרי לעולם. ותיבש התאנה מיד.

²⁰ויראו התלמידים ויתמהו ויאמרו איך יבשה התאנה מיד.

²¹ויען יש״ו ויאמר להם אם תהיה בכם אמונה בלי ספק לא לתאנה בלבד תעשו כי אם תאמרו להר הזה שימוש ויבא בם יעשה.

²¹:⁶ יש״ו] omit G

²¹:⁸ כורתים ]הסודרנא | G ורבים ]ואחרים| ABDEFG

²¹:⁹ מושיע המלך העולם EF, מושיענו עולם ]מושיע העולם| A הושענה ]הושענא| B

²¹:¹⁰ ירושלם ABEF + חרדה]

²¹:¹¹ מנאזריאל G מנזאריאל] A, מנזריאל B, מנזארת DEF, מנאזריאל G

²¹:¹² היונים] omit A, והמושבות] A משם ]שם| A ויוצא ]וימצא| AEF בית ]בית G יונים

²¹:¹⁵ לראות] omit A החכמים והכהנים] 2 1 ABDEF | ויצאו ]ויבואו| EF

²¹:¹⁶ אלו[²] omit A | אלו[¹]] A | אליו A | יאמרו ]אומרים| A | אליהם ]להם| G | ויאמר G | לו[²] omit A

²¹:¹⁷ וילך[²]] ABDEFG | חנניא ]חנניה| BCDEFG | אותם + ]ABDEFG | ויעזוב] + ויעזב

²¹:¹⁹ התאנה מיד] omit G | ויאר G | אחת ]omit G בה[ | בה] + EF תאנים ]לבד| B בלבד]

²¹:²⁰ מיד] A (?), omit G | לאמר ]ויאמרו| G | מאד + ]ויתמהו|

²¹:²¹ כן DG | בים ]בם| AEF | ויאמר להם יש"ו ]ויען| . . . להם]

⁶Then they went and did as Jesus commanded them.

⁷They brought the she-ass and the colt and Jesus rode upon it while the others placed their garments and clothes upon them. Then they made the ascent.

⁸Many of the crowd spread out their garments in the way and others (cut) branches from the trees and cast them before him and behind him

⁹calling out saying: Hosanna, O savior of the world, blessed is he who comes in the name of the Lord; hosanna our savior, may you be glorified in heaven and on earth.

¹⁰It came to pass afterwards, when Jesus entered Jerusalem, all the city quaked saying: Who is this.

¹¹The people said to one another: [it is] Jesus the Prophet from (Nazareth) which is in Galilee.

¹²Jesus entered the house of the Lord and found there those who buy and sell. He overturned the tables of the money-changers and the seats of those who were selling doves.

¹³He said unto them: It is written, my house will be called a house of prayer for all the nations, but you have made it a cave of violent men.

¹⁴Then the blind and lame came to him in the temple and he healed them.

¹⁵The chief sages and priests came to see the wonders which he did. The young boys were calling out in the temple saying: Let the Son of God be praised. The sages mocked

¹⁶and said to him: Have you not heard what these are saying. He answered them and said: I heard them. Have you not read: from the mouth of children and babes you have established strength.

¹⁷He left and went out to Bethany and (spent the night) there and there he was explaining to them the kingdom of God.

¹⁸It came to pass in the morning that he returned to the city hungry.

¹⁹He saw a fig tree near the road and drew near to it but found nothing on it except leaves. He said to it: May fruit never come forth from you. Immediately the fig tree died up.

²⁰The disciples saw and were amazed and said: How is it the fig tree dried up immediately.

²¹Jesus answered and said to them: If you have faith without doubt, not only to the fig tree will you do [thus], but should you say to this mountain that it should depart and go (into the sea), it will be done.

²²וכל אשר תשאלון בתפלה ותהיו מאמינים תקבלון.

## פרק פ"ט

²³ויבא אל המקדש ללמד ויקרבו אליו החכמים והכהנים וקציני
העם לאמר באיזה כח תעשה החיל הזה.

²⁴ויען להם יש"ו ויאמר להם אשאל מכם גם אני שאלה אחת ואם
תאמרו לי אותה גם אני אומר לכם באיזה כח אני עושה.

²⁵טבילת יוחנן מאין היתה מן השמים או מן האנשים? ויתעצבו
ביניהם לאמר מה נאמר. אם נאמר מהשמים יאמר לנו למה לא
תאמינו בו.

²⁶ואם נאמר מן האנשים נירא מן החבורה שכלם מאמינים שיוחנן
נביא היה.

²⁷ויאמרו לא ידענו. ויאמר גם אני לא אומר לכם באיזה כח אני
עושה.

## פרק צ"

²⁸בערב ההיא אמר יש"ו לתלמידיו מה נראה לכם. איש א" היו לו
שני בנים ויגש האחד ויאמר לו לך בני היום לעבוד כרמי.

²⁹ויאמר לו איני רוצה. ואח"כ נחם והלך.

³⁰ויאמר לאחר כמו כן ויען אליו הנני אדו' ולא הלך.

³¹מי משניהם עשה רצון האב? ויאמרו לו הראשון. ויאמר להם יש"ו
אמן אני אומר לכם שהפריצים והקדישות יקדמו אתכם במלכות
שמים.

³²שבא אליכם יוחנן דרך צדקה ולא המנתם. באו הפריצים
והקדישות והאמינו בו ואתם רואים ולא חזרתם בתשובה. גם
אחרי כן לא נחמתם להאמין בו. למי אזנים לשמוע ישמע בחרפה.

---

²¹:²² וכל] ובכל BEFG

²¹:²³ הכהנים והכהנים] החכמים הכהנים B | הכהנים C | תעשה] + (-לך BEF)
ומי נתן לך ADEFGH, גדולי הכהנים הגדולים ABDEFGH

²¹:²⁴ אותה לי] לי ABDEFGH | שאלה אחת] דבר אחד | C omit | שאלה אחת גם אני אומר לכם
CEF אותה לי BDG, אותו לי AH, אליהם] A להם |

²¹:²⁵ אם נאמר מן השמים או מן האנשים] + מאנשים H | לאמר] + ויאמר H מן האנשים] מן האנשים F
H מן השמים] מהשמים | B omit | נאמר אם] ADEFGH omit | נאמר מה |

²¹:²⁶ החבורות] החבורה EF | מהחבורה] מן החבורה A | מהאנשים] מן האנשים AH

²¹:²⁷ ויאמרו] ויאמר H | לא] לא איני A | אני] + לו H | להם

²¹:²⁸ כרמי] לכרמי A, בכרמי BDEFG | הנראה] מה נראה DG | האחד] לאחד D | היום לעבוד] בעת A | A 1 2 | לעבוד] עבוד G |

²¹:²⁹ נחם] נחה A

²¹:³⁰ אדו' הנני] A 1 2

²¹:³¹ ישו] omit EF

²¹:³² יוחנן] ABDEFG | המנתם] האמינתם A, המנתם BDEFG באו הפריצים] בו והפריצים ABDEFG
והאמינו] האמינו ABDEG | חזרתם] G נחמתם | בחרפה] בחכמה A

[22]Everything which you shall ask in prayer while believing, you will receive.

[23]He went into the temple to teach and there came to him the sages, the priests, and the rulers of the people saying: By what power do you do this (and who gave you) this strength.

[24]Jesus answered them and said to them: I also will ask you a question and if you tell me I also will tell you by what power I do [this].

[25]The baptism of John whence was it, from heaven or from men? They grieved among themselves saying: What will we say. If we say from heaven, he will say to us, why did you not believe him.

[26]If we say from men we fear the crowd because all of them believe John was a prophet.

[27]So they said: We do not know. He said: Also I will not tell you by what power I do [this].

[28]In that evening Jesus said to his disciples: what is your opinion. A certain man had two sons; he approached (one) and said to him: go my son today to work in my vineyard.

[29]He said to him: I do not wish to. But afterward he repented and went.

[30]He said to the other likewise and he answered him: here I am, Sir, but he did not go.

[31]Which of two did the will of the Father? They said to him: The first. Jesus said to them: Truly I say to you violent men and harlots will precede you into the kingdom of heaven

[32]because John came to you in the way of righteousness and you did not (believe him). (But) violent men and harlots believed him and you saw it and did not turn in repentance. Also afterward you did not repent to believe him. To the one who has ears to hear let him hear in disgrace.

**[MT 21:33-22:1**

## פרק צ"א

33(בעת ההיא אמר יש"ו לתלמידיו ולסיעת היהודים שמעו נא משל הזורע . אדם אחד נכבד נטע כרם וגדר אותו מסביב ויבן מגדל בתוכו וגם יקב חצב בו ויפקידהו לעובדים וילך לדרכו.

34ויהי לעת אסוף התבואה שלח אל עבדיו אל העובדים לקבל תבואתו.

35ויקחו העובדים את עבדיו ויכו את האחד ויהרגו את השני והשלישי סקלו באבנים.

36וישלח עוד עבדים רבים מהראשונים ויעשו להם כמו כן.

37סוף דבר שלח להם בנו לאמר אולי יראו את בני.

38ויראו העובדים את בנו ויאמרו איש אל רעהו זהו היורש. לכו ונהרגהו ונירש נחלתו.

39ויקחוהו ויוציאוהו מן הכרם ויהרגוהו.

40ועתה כאשר יבא בעל הכרם מה יעשה להם?

41ויענו לו לאמר הרעים יאבדם ברעה וכרמו יתן לעובדים אחרים שיתנו לו חלק תבואתו מיד.

42ויאמר להם יש"ו הלא קראתם הכתוב אבן מאסו הבונים היתה לראש פנה מאת ה"׳ היתה זאת היא נפלאת בעינינו.

43לזאת אני אומר לכם שתתקרע מלכות שמים מעליכם ותנתן לגוי עושה פרי.

44והנופל על האבן הזאת ידחה ואשר יפול עליה יסדק.

45וישמעו גדולי הכהנים והפרושים משליו ויכירו שהוא מדבר בעדם.

46ויבקשו להמיתו ויראו מהחבורות שלנביא היה להם.)

## פרק צ"א (צ"ב)

1ויען יש"ו ויאמר להם עוד בדברי משל.

---

21:33-46Omit Brit. Lib. ms and C. Our basic text for these vss is D.

21:34אל ואת] EG, omit B

21:35G וישלח את השלישי ]והשלישי סקלו באבנים

21:36מהראשונים] omit EF רבים] omit A

21:37G ויאמר ]לאמר ABEF | הדבר ]דבר

21:38A את + ]ונירש A | נלך ]לכו omit A איש אל רעהו]

21:39A ואתה ]ועתה

21:41A הזרים ]אחרים EF ויאמר לו ]ויענו לו לאמר

21:42B נפלאות ]נפלאת omit G מאת] . . . בעינינו]

21:44A יפסק ]יסדק EF והנופל ]EF וראה יפול ]ואשר יפול EF ירחה ]ידחה

21:45G את משליו ]משליו | G החכמים והכהנים ]החכמים והכהנים EF, 2 1 ]הכהנים והפרושים omit EF גדולי]

21:46G ביניהם ]להם A | שכנביא ]שלנביא | A מן החבורות ]מהחבורות BEF ויבקשוהו ]ויבקשו

22:1At this point the Brit. Lib. ms again becomes our basic text; ms C also resumes at this point. Both number this פרק צ"א since the entirety of the last pereq was omitted. All other mss number this פרק צ"ב.

³³(At that time Jesus said to his disciples
and to a company of the Jews: Hear now the parable of the sower. A
certain honorable man planted a vineyard, walled it up on every side,
built a tower in its midst and also dug a vat in it, entrusted it to servants
and went on his way.

³⁴It came to pass at the time of the gathering of the produce, he sent his
servants to those who were working to receive his profit.

³⁵But the workers took his servants, smote the first, killed the second,
and the third they stoned with stones.

³⁶Again he sent many more servants than the first and they did to them
likewise.

³⁷Finally, he sent them his son saying: Perhaps they will honor my son.

³⁸The workers saw his son and said to one another: This is the heir.
Come, let us kill him and we will inherit his estate.

³⁹So they took him, cast him out of the vineyard and killed him.

⁴⁰Now when the lord of the vineyard comes what will he do to them?

⁴¹They answered him saying: As for the wicked he will destroy them in
misery and his vineyard he will give to other workers who will immediately give to him the portion of his profit.

⁴²Jesus said to them: have you not read the scripture, the stone the builders rejected has become the head of the corner; this was from the Lord;
it is a marvel in our eyes.

⁴³Therefore I say to you the kingdom of heaven will be torn from you
and given to a nation producing fruit.

⁴⁴He who falls upon this stone will be cast down; he who falls upon it
will be broken apart.

⁴⁵The chief priests and the Pharisees heard his parables and understood
that he was speaking in regard to them.

⁴⁶They sought to kill him but they feared the crowds to whom he was a
prophet.)

## Chapter 22

¹Jesus answered and spoke to them again
in the words of a parable.

**[MT 22:2-18**

²מלכות שמים דומה למלך אשר עושה חופה.

³וישלח את עבדיו בעד הקרואים לחופה ולא אבו לו.

⁴וישלח עוד עבדים אחרים לאמר אמרו לקרואים הנה הכנתי המשתה וזבחתי שורים ועופות והכל מוכן. בואו אל החופה.

⁵והם בזו וילכו מקצתם בעיר ומקצתם בעסקיהם.

⁶והאחרים (לקחו את עבדיו) והתעללו בם והרגום.

⁷וישמע המלך ויחר אפו וישלח הרוצחים ההם ואת ביתם שרף באש.

⁸אז אמר לעבדיו החופה מוכנת היא רק הקרואים לא היו ראויים.

⁹ועתה צאו אל הדרכים וכל אשר תמצאו קראו לחופה.

¹⁰ויצאו עבדיו אל הדרכים ויקבצו כל הנמצאים טובים ורעים ותמלא החופה מהאוכלים.

¹¹ויבא המלך לראות האוכלים וירא שם אדם אשר לא היה מלובש בגדי החופה.

¹²ויאמר לו אהובי איך באתה לכאן בלא לבושי החופה. והוא החריש.

¹³אז אמר המלך למשרתיו אסרו ידיו ורגליו והשליכוהו בשאול תחתית ושם יהיה בכי וחרוק שינים.

¹⁴הקרואים רבים והנבחרים מעטים.

## פרק צ״ג

¹⁵אז הלכו הפירושים ויועצו לקחתו בדבר.

¹⁶וישליחו אליו מתלמידיהם עם פרושים מהורוד״וס לאמר רבי ידענו שנאמן אתה ותלמוד באמונה דרך האלקים ואינך חושש לשום דבר ולא נושא פנים.

¹⁷אמור מה יראה לך הנכון לתת מס לְצֶיזָא׳רֵי אם אין.

¹⁸ויחרישו את נכלותם ויאמר למה תמיתוני חנפנים.

---

²²:³ לו] לבא ABDEFG, omit C

²²:⁴ הכנתי] הכינותי ABDEFG | שורים ועפות] שור ועוף ABDEFG

²²:⁵ והם בזו] omit C, והם לא באו G | בזו] בא D

²²:⁶ לא] לקחו את עבדיו] בם ABDEFG | בהם G

²²:⁷ וישמע] וישלח A | וישלמ] + וישמיד חיל ABDEFG הרוצחים] ההורגים A

²²:⁹ ועתה] + לכו G

²²:¹⁰ אל הדרכים] הדרכים] + וימצאו G omit EF

²²:¹¹ היה] ראוי לחופה G | מלובש] מלבוש D

²²:¹² אהובי] אדוני A | לכאן] בכאן A | החופה] חופה A

²²:¹³ ורגליו] omit EF בשאול] במחשכי ABDEFG | תחתית] תחתיות ABDEFG | וחרוק] וחריקה C

²²:¹⁴ רבים] מרובים EF | מעטים] מועטים A

At this point the Brit. Lib. ms and ms C number this section פרק צ״ג, leaving out צ״ב, thus bringing their numbering system into line with the other mss. See 21:33 and 22:1. | בדבר] בדברו D

²²:¹⁶ + Beginning] עם פרושים מהורודוס] omit D | וישליחו] וישלחו EF | ויועצו עם תלמידיהם] CF האלקים] האלים A | פרושים] פריצים A

²²:¹⁷ לציסר F לציסר CDEG, לציור B, לציזור A, לשיזר לצייזר] omit G לך] לנו G + | אומר]

²²:¹⁸ חנפנים] חנפים ABDEFG תמיתוני] תסיתוני ABDEFG | ויחרישו] ויכר ישו ABDEFG

²The Kingdom of heaven is like a king
who made a wedding ceremony.

³He sent his servants to those who had been invited to the wedding ceremony, but they did not wish (to come).

⁴He again sent other servants saying: tell those who are invited, behold I
have prepared a feast, I have killed oxen and fowl and all is ready.
Come to the wedding ceremony.

⁵But they scorned and went away, some into the city and some to their
businesses.

⁶Others (took his servants), abused them and killed them.

⁷The King heard this, was angry, sent those murderers away and burned
their house with fire.

⁸Then he said to his servants: The marriage ceremony is ready, but those
who were invited were unworthy.

⁹Now go out unto the roads and all whom you find invite to the marriage
ceremony.

¹⁰His servants went out unto the ways and assembled all those who were
found, good and bad; so the marriage ceremony was filled with those
who were eating.

¹¹The king entered to see those who were eating and saw there a man
who was not clothed in wedding garments.

¹²He said to him: My friend how did you come in here without wedding
garments. He was silent.

¹³Then the king said to his servants: Bind his hands and feet and cast him
to the nether most and lowest hell; there will be weeping and gnashing
of teeth.

¹⁴Many were called but few were chosen.

¹⁵Then the Pharisees came and took counsel to take him in speech.

¹⁶They sent to him some of their disciples, with (violent men) from
Herod saying: Rabbi, we know that you are faithful, you faithfully
study the way of God, you fear nothing and are impartial.

¹⁷Tell us your opinion: Is it right to give tribute to Caesar or not?

¹⁸(But Jesus recognized) their deceit and said: Why do (you entice me,
hypocrites).

‏<sup>19</sup>הראו לי מטבע המס. ויביאו לו.

‏<sup>20</sup>ויאמר אליהם למי הצורה הזאת והרשום.

‏<sup>21</sup>ויאמר לְצֵיזָא״רֵי. אז אמר אליהם יש״ו השיבו לְצֵיזָא״רֵי את אשר לְצֵיזָא״רֵי לְצֵיזָא״רֵי ואשר לאלקים לאלקים.

‏<sup>22</sup>וישמעו ויתמהו ויעזבוהו וילכו.

## פרק צ״ד

‏<sup>23</sup>בום ההוא קראו אליו הצדוקים והכופרים בתחיית המתים. וישאלוהו

‏<sup>24</sup>לאמר ר׳ אמור לנו אמר משה כי ישבו אחים יחדיו ומת אחד מהם ובן אין לו שיקח אחיו את אשתו לקיים זרע אחיו.

‏<sup>25</sup>והנה שבעה אתים היו בינינו ונשא הראשון אשה ומת בלא זרע ויבם אחיו את אשתו.

‏<sup>26</sup>וכן השני ושלישי עד השביעי.

‏<sup>27</sup>ואחריהם מתה האשה.

‏<sup>28</sup>שכבר היה לכולם אל מי מהשבעה תהיה האשה.

‏<sup>29</sup>ויען יש״ו ויאמר אליהם תשגו ולא תבינו הספרים ועוז האלקים.

‏<sup>30</sup>ביום התקומה לא יקחו האנשים נשים ולא הנשים אנשים רק יהיו כמלאכי אלקים בשמים.

‏<sup>31</sup>הלא קראתם מתחיית המתים שאמר ה״ לכם שאמר

‏<sup>32</sup>אני ה״ אלקי אברהם אלקי יצחק ואלקי יעקב. וא״כ אינו אלקי המתים כ״א אלקי החיים.

‏<sup>33</sup>וישמעו החבורות ויתמהו מחכמתו.

‏<sup>22:19</sup>לו] + פשדי EF, + פשוט D, + פשוט אחד AG, + פשדי

‏<sup>22:21</sup>ויאמר] ויאמרו BG, אז אמרו EF | לשיזר<sup>1,2,3</sup>לצֵיזוארי A, לצֵיזור B, לצֵיזור CDE<sup>2,3</sup>G,

‏ואת אשר DEFG | אליהם] להם AEF | את] omit A | לצֵיזורי]<sup>4</sup> omit ABEFG | ואשר] omit A | F<sup>1</sup> לציסר

‏omit B | לאלקים]<sup>2</sup> ולאלים אשר לאלים ואשר לאלקים לאלקים A | לאלקים]<sup>2</sup> omit B

‏<sup>22:22</sup>וישמעו] omit EF

‏<sup>22:23</sup>ביום ההוא] בעת ההיא H | קראו] קרבו A

‏<sup>22:24</sup>אמור לנו] omit A | לקיים זרע אחיו] omit G

‏<sup>22:25</sup>בינינו . . . והנה] omit G | הראשון] + את G

‏<sup>22:26</sup>There is confusion in the text of G.

‏<sup>22:27</sup>ואחריהם] ואחרות B

‏<sup>22:28</sup>שכבר] omit A | היה] שהיתה A, היתה BDEFG | אל מי] למי G

‏ביום התחיה למי משבעהם תהיה לאשה שכבר היתה לכלם אל . . . האשה A

‏<sup>22:29</sup>ויען ישו ויאמר] ויען ישו ויאמר אליהם H | תשגו] תנשו G | ועוז] ועוד EF |

‏האלים A

‏<sup>22:30</sup>אלקים] אלים A | רק] omit G | אלא A | ולא הנשים אנשים] omit G

‏<sup>22:31</sup>שאמר]<sup>2</sup> omit ABEFH, + לכם G | ה״] omit H | שאמר ה״ לכם] omit DG

‏<sup>22:32</sup>אני] omit G | אלקי<sup>1,2,3,4,5</sup>] אלקי]<sup>2</sup> אלהי A | ואלקי H | כי כ״א H

¹⁹Show me a tax coin. They brought (a plain one) to him.

²⁰He said to them: Whose form is this and [whose] impression.

²¹They said: Ceasar's. Then Jesus said to them: Return to Ceasar that which is Ceasar's and to God that which is God's.

²²They heard and were amazed. They left him and went away.

²³On that day there met him the Sadducees and those who deny the resurrection of the dead. They asked him

²⁴saying: Rabbi, Moses surely said to us: when brothers dwell together and one of them dies and has no son, his brother should take his wife to raise up the seed of his brother.

²⁵Behold there were seven brothers among us. The first one took a wife, died without seed and his brother married his wife.

²⁶Likewise the second and third unto the seventh.

²⁷After them the woman died.

²⁸Since (she) had already belonged to all of them, to which of the seven will she be a wife?

²⁹Jesus answered and said to them: You err and do not understand the writings or the power of God.

³⁰In the day of resurrection men will not take women nor women men, but they will be like the angels of God in heaven.

³¹Have you not read concerning the resurrection of the dead that the Lord spoke to you saying:

³²I the Lord am the God of Abraham, the God of Isaac and the God of Jacob. If so, he is not the God of the dead but the God of the living.

³³The crowds heard and were amazed at his wisdom.

## פרק צ"ה

<sup>34</sup>וכאשר ראו הפירושים כי אין מענה לצדוקים התחברו עבדיו.
<sup>35</sup>וישאלוהו חכם א" לנסותו
<sup>36</sup>ר' אמור איזה היא מצוה גדולה שבתורה.
<sup>37</sup>אמר לו ואהבת את ה" ⟨אלקיך⟩ בכל לבבך וכו.
<sup>38</sup>זו היא הראשונה.
<sup>39</sup>שנית דומה אליה ואהבת לרעך כמוך.
<sup>40</sup>ועל שתי המצוות האלה התורה כולה תלויה והנביאים.
<sup>41</sup>ויאספו הפרושים וישאלם יש"ו
<sup>42</sup>לאמר מה יראה לכם מן המשיח ובן מי יהיה. ויאמרו לו בן דוד.
<sup>43</sup>ויאמר להם איך קראו אותו דוד ברוח הקדש לאמר אדון
<sup>44</sup>דכתיב נאם ה" לאדוני שב לימיני עד אשית אויביך הדום לרגליך.
<sup>45</sup>אם דוד קראו אדון איך יהיה בנו?
<sup>46</sup>ולא יכלו להשיבו דבר מכאן ואילך פחדו לשאול ממנו דבר.

## פרק צ"ו

<sup>1</sup>אז דבר יש"ו אל העם ואל תלמידיו
<sup>2</sup>לאמר על כסא משה ישבו הפירושים והחכמים.
<sup>3</sup>ועתה כל אשר יאמר לכם שמרו ועשו ובתקנותיהם ומעשיהם אל תעשו שהם אומרים והם אינם עושים.
<sup>4</sup>ודורשים ונותנים משאות גדולות לא יוכלו לקובלם והם אפי' באצבעם אינם רוצים לנוע.

---

<sup>22:34</sup> אחריו C יחדו EF, יחדו ABDG, עבדיו] יחדיו
<sup>22:35</sup> מהם + [א" | G ואמר + ,EF וישאלהו] וישאלוהו A
<sup>22:36</sup> בתורה] שבתורה F | מצוה גדולה A 21 | גדולה CEFG איזו] איזה | רבי [ר' A
<sup>22:37</sup> ABDEF ובכל נפשך ובכל מאדך :and add וכו omit G וכו] וכו בבל לבבך] A אלהיך] אלקיך
<sup>22:38</sup> הגדולה והראשונה DEF, והגדולה שבמצוות + A, המצוה גדולה C, והגדולה G הראשונה] +
<sup>22:39</sup> ABDEFG והשנית] שנית
<sup>22:40</sup> תורה B התורה] האלו A האלה] האלה
<sup>22:41</sup> omit G ישו]
<sup>22:42</sup> omit A ובן מי יהיה omit G לאמר]
<sup>22:43</sup> 4 1 ברוח הקדש לאמר אדון ABDEFG קרא קראו] A ואיך] איך BEF, omit DG אליהם] להם EFG omit לאמר] G 2
<sup>22:44</sup> omit FG עד . . . לרגליך A לאויביך] אויביך
<sup>22:45</sup> EFG היה] יהיה ABDEF קורא אותו קראו]
<sup>22:46</sup> ABCDEG ומכאן] מכאן
<sup>23:3</sup> וכתקנותיהם ובתקנותיהם G תעשו ותשמרו שמרו] שמרו ועשו ABDEFG יאמרו] יאמר EF מעתה] ועתה omit ABDEFG והם] F וכמעשיכם E, וכמעשיכם ומעשיהם] ומעשיהם F וכתקנותיכם ABDEG,
<sup>23:4</sup> אפילו] אפי' EF שכמי האדם BDG, + שכמי אדם A, + שכמי בני האדם + לסובלם] לקובלם vs 4] omit C BG

[34]When the Pharisees saw that the Sadducees
   had no answer they joined his servants.
[35]Then a sage asked him tempting him:
[36]Rabbi, tell [us] which is the greatest commandment in the Torah.
[37]He said to him: Thou shalt love the Lord your God with all your heart
   (and with all your soul and all your strength).
[38]This is the first.
[39]The second is like it: thou shalt love your neighbor as yourself.
[40]Upon these two commandments the whole law hangs and the prophets.
[41]The Pharisees assembled and Jesus asked them
[42]saying: What is your opinion concerning the Messiah, whose son will
   he be. They said to him: The son of David.
[43]He said to them: How is it that David by the Holy Spirit called him
   saying: Lord,
[44]as it is written: the Lord said to my Lord sit at my right hand until I
   make your enemies the footstool of your feet.
[45]If David called him Lord, how is he his son?
[46]They were not able to answer him a word (and) from then on they
   feared to ask him anything.

## Chapter 23

[1]Then Jesus spoke to the people and to his disciples
[2]saying: Upon the seat of Moses the Pharisees and the sages sit.
[3]Now all which (they) say to you keep and do; but (according to) their
   ordinances and deeds do not do because they say do or not.
[4]They demand and set forth great burdens [which] (the shoulders of
   men) are not able to bear; but they themselves even with their finger
   are unwilling to move.

[MT 23:5-20

⁵וכל מעשיהם עושים למראה עינים ולובשים מלבושים יקרים
וציציות נקראים פִיבְּ״לִיאוֹס גדולים
⁶אהבים להיות מסובים ראשונה בבתי משתאות ולהיות מושבם
בבתי כנסיות בראשונה
⁷ולהשתחוות להם בחוצות ולקוראם רבנים.
⁸ואתם אל תרצו להיות נקראים רבנים. אחד הוא רבכם וכולכם
אחים.
⁹ואב אל תקראו לאדם על הארץ. אחד הוא אביכם שבשמים.
¹⁰ואל תקראו רבנים שרבכם אחד הוא המשיח.
¹¹הגדול ביניכם יהיה משרת אתכם.
¹²ואשר יתרומם ישח ואשר ישח ירום.

## פרק צ״ז

¹³אוי לכם הפרושים והחכמים חנפים מלכות שמים בפני בני אדם
והרוצים לבא אינכם עוזבים אותם לבא.
¹⁴אוי לכם הפרושים והחכמים חנפים שאתם אוכלים וחולקים
נכסי הנשים האלמנות בדרש ארוך ובעבור זה תסבלו עונש ארך.
¹⁵סובבים הים והיבשה לקשור לב איש אחד באמונתכם וכאשר
יהיה נקשר יהיה רע כפלים מקודם.
¹⁶אוי לכם מושבי העורים אשר תאמרו שהנשבע בהיכל אינו חייב
ואשר ידור באיזה דבר שהוא נקדש לבניין ההיכל חייב לשלם
¹⁷משוגעים ועורים איזה יותר גדול ההיכל או דבר הנקדש להיכל
¹⁸ואשר ישבע במזבח אינו חייב והנשבע שיקריב קרבן חייב לתת.
¹⁹איזה יותר הקרבן או המזבח המקדש או הקרבן?
²⁰אשר ישבע במזבח נשבע ובכל מה שבתוכו.

---

²³⁵ פיביליואש A, פיבלאש BF, | פיביליאוס [פיבְּ״לִיאוֹס | G מעשיהם [מלבושים | omit C [וכל . . . עושים | D, בגדהם
EG פיביליאוש D, | להיות [להיותם A | מושבם [מושבים read | מושבים בבתי כנסיות בראשונה [בבתי כנסיות בראשונה | ABDEFG 2 1 3 [בראשונה] ²³⁶
BDEFG ראשונה A, ראשון
G ולקראת להם EF, ולקראם [ולקוראם] ²³⁷
²³⁸ [רבכם . . . אחים omit D (hap)
²³⁹ [ואב . . . הוא omit D (hap—see on 22:8)
²³¹⁰ [אחד omit EF | שרביכם [שרבכם C
²³¹² [יתרומם A | ירום [ישח] omit EF
²³¹³ ABDEFG, אתם אינכם באים + [אדם] | שאתם סוגרים + A, שאתם סוגרים שערו [חנפים] + BDEFG | והרוצה [והרוצים A | והרוצים DEF | האדם
²³¹⁴ [הנשים omit G | זה] omit EF | ארך [ארוך] ABC, omit EF
EF רעב [רע] EF כאשר [וכאשר | G לב] omit G ²³¹⁵
H להיכל ולבנינו [לבניין ההיכל A | נקשר [נקדש | H שתאמרו [אשר תאמרו] ²³¹⁶
G לו [להיכל | ABGH הדבר [דבר | ADEFGH איזהו [איזה] ²³¹⁷
²³¹⁸ נשבע [ישבע] D
²³¹⁹ Beginning of vs] + אוי העורים | ABDEFG איזה [איזה] ACDEFG
A אשר בתוכו [מה שבתוכו | G במה [ובכל מה | A בו + [נשבע] ²³²⁰
²³²¹ Vs 21 omitted by all mss.

[5]All their actions they do for the sake of appearances: they
wear expensive garments and large tassels, called phiblios;

[6]they love to recline first in the banquet halls, to be (seated) first at the
synagogues,

[7]to prostrate themselves in the streets and to be called Rabbi.

[8]But as for you, do not desire to be called Rabbi. One is your Rabbi and
all of you are brothers.

[9]Call no man upon the earth, father. One is your father who is in
heaven.

[10]Do not be called Rabbi, because one is your Rabbi, the Messiah.

[11]The greatest among you will serve you.

[12]He who exalts himself will be humbled; he who is humbled will be exalted.

[13]Woe to you Pharisees and sages, hypocrites (because you close up) the
kingdom of heaven before men; (you yourselves do not enter) and
those who wish to enter you do not permit to enter.

[14]Woe to you Pharisees and sages, hypocrites, because you devour and
divide the wealth of certain widows with lengthy exposition; for this
you will suffer a long punishment.

[15]You encompass sea and land to bind the heart of one man to your faith
and when he is bound he is doubly worse than before.

[16]Woe to you, council of the blind, who say that he who swears by the
temple is not obligated, but he who vows by anything which is consecrated to the structure of the temple is obligated to pay,

[17]—mad and blind men, which is greater, the temple or that which is
consecrated to the temple—

[18]and whoever swears by the altar is not obligated but he who swears that
he will make an offering is obligated to give it.

[19](Woe blind men), which is more, the gift or the altar, the temple or the
gift?

[20]He who swears by the altar swears (by it) and by everything which is in
it.

²²ואשר ישבע בכסא אלקים נשבע בו וביושב עליו.

## פרק צ״ח

²³אוי להם לחכמים ולפרושים המעשרים הנמנע והשבת והרמון והגוזלים ענבים אשר הוא יותר נכבד זהו משפטי התורה והם החסד והאמת והאמונה . אלו המאמרים ראויים לעשות ולא לשכוח אותם.

²⁴זרע מנהיגים העורים מדקדקים בדבר היתוש ובולעים את הגמל. ²⁵אוי לכם הפרושים והחכמים שתקנחו הכוסות והקערות מבחוץ ותוכם מלא נבלה וטומאה.

²⁶רחוף נקה תחלה מה שבתוכו להיות טהור אשר מבחוץ. ²⁷אוי לכם החכמים והפרושים החנפים הדומים לקברים המלובנים שידמו מבחוץ יבין לבני אדם ובתוכן מלאות עצמות מתים ומטונפים.

²⁸כן תראו אתם מבחוץ צדיקים לבני אדם ובקרבכם מלאות חנפות ורשעות.

²⁹אוי להם החנפים והפרושים והחכמים שתבנו קברי הנביאים ותכבדו צאני הצדיקים.

³⁰ותאמרו אם היינו בימי אבותינו לא היינו מניחים בימי הנביאים.

³¹בזאת אתם מעידים על עצמכם שבנים אתם לאשר הרגו הנביאים ³²ואתם נוהגים כמעשה אבותיכם.

³³נחשים זרע צפעונים איך תנוסו מדין גיהנם אם לא תשובו בתשובה.

## פרק צ״ט

³⁴בעת ההיא אמר יש״ו לחבורות היהודים לזאת הנני שולח לכם נביאים וחכמים וסופרים. ומהם תהרגו ומהם תכאיבו בבתי כנסיותכם ותרדפוני מעיר אל עיר.

²³:²² B ביושב |בו וביושב G | וביוצא עליו + |בו A | אלים A | אלקים |אלקים A | נשבע |ישבע

²³:²³ The Brit. Lib. ms and ms C break off at this point. Ms D becomes our basic text from here to the end. | ראויים + הם | omit G והאמת | הנמנע |הנגנע ABEF | ענבים |ועוזבים ABEF, וענבים G | והאמת | להעשות A | אותם| אות B EF |לעשות

²³:²⁵ A 2 1 |והקערות מבחוץ G תקנחו |שתקנחו A, שתנקחו

²³:²⁶ B שבחוץ |מבחוץ EF | החנף נקה |רחוף נקה A, החנף B, החנף מנקה

²³:²⁷ ABEF יפים |יבין EG | האדם |אדם ABEF ובתוכם |ובתוכן

²³:²⁸ A מלאים |מלאות B | בקרבכם |ובקרבכם F | האדם |אדם

²³:²⁹ |צאני A וציוני הצדיקים תכבדו |ותכבדו צאני הצדיקים omit G | והחכמים |לכם ABEFG | ציוני ABEF

²³:³⁰ A להמית |בימי²]

²³:³⁴ |תהרגו B מהם |ומהם G חנפים + BF, |וחכמים F חכמים |וסופרים F סופרים EF אני |הנני A ותרדפום |ותרדפוני A ותתלו +

²²He who swears by the throne of God
swears by it and by the one who sits upon it.

²³Woe to them, the sages and Pharisees, who tithe (mint,) dill, and po-
megranate but who commit robbery (and leave undone) that which is
weightier, that is, the judgments of the Torah which are: kindness,
truth and faithfulness. These are commands worthy of doing; one
should not forget them.

²⁴Offsprings of blind leaders, who are strict in the matter of the gnat and
who swallow the camel.

²⁵Woe to you Pharisees and sages because you cleanse cups and platters
on the outside but inside them is full of wickedness and uncleanness.

²⁶(Hypocrite), cleanse first that which is inside in order that that which is
outside might be pure.

²⁷Woe to you sages and Pharisees, hypocrites, who are like whitened se-
pulchres which appear on the outside to be (beautiful) to men, but on
the inside are full of the bones of the dead and the filthy.

²⁸Thus you appear on the outside to be righteous to men but within you
are full of hypocrisy and wickedness.

²⁹Woe (to you), hypocrites, Pharisees, and sages because you build the
tombs of the prophets and glorify the (monuments) of the righteous.

³⁰You say: If we had been in the days of our fathers we would not have
permitted [them] (to put) the prophets (to death).

³¹In this you bear witness against yourselves that you are sons of those
who killed the prophets.

³²You behave according to the deeds of your fathers.

³³Serpents, seed of vipers, how will you escape the judgment of Gehenna if you do not turn in repentence?

³⁴In that time Jesus said to the crowds of Jews: Therefore, behold I am
sending to you prophets, sages, and scribes. Some of them you will
kill, some of them you will afflict in your synagogues and you will
pursue (them) from city to city.

[MT 23:35-24:9

<sup>35</sup>עליכם דם כל צדיק הנשפך על הארץ מדם הבל הצדיק עד דם
צכריה בן ברכיה אשר הרגתם בין ההיכל ולמזבח.
<sup>36</sup>באמת אני אומר לכם שיבואו כל אלה על הדור הזה
<sup>37</sup>ועל ירושלים ההורגת הנביאים ומסלקת השלוחים כמה פעמים
רציתי לאסוף בניך כאשר תאסוף התרנגולת אפרוחיה תחת
כנפיה ולא רצית.
<sup>38</sup>לכן אתם תעזבו בתיכם חרבות.
<sup>39</sup>באמת אני אומר לכם לא תראוני מכאן ואילך עד שתאמרו ברוך
מושיענו.

## פרק ק׳

<sup>1</sup>ויהי כאשר יצא יש״ו מן המקדש וכשהיה הולך נגשו תלמידיו
להראותו בניני המקדש.
<sup>2</sup>ויאמר תראו כל אלה אמן אני אומר לכם שהכל יהרס ולא ישאר
שם אבן על אבן.
<sup>3</sup>ובשבתו על הר הזתים נגד בית המקדש שאלו לו פיט״רוש ויחנן
ואנדריאה בסתר מתי יהיה כל אלה ומה האות שיהיה כשיהיו
כל אלה הענינים או כשיתחילו ומתי יהיה תכלית העולם
וביאתך.
<sup>4</sup>ויען להם יש״ו השמרו פן יתעה אתכם איש
<sup>5</sup>שרבים יבאו בשמי לאמר אני הוא המשיח ויתעו אתכם.
<sup>6</sup>ואתם כאשר תשמעו המלחמות וחברת הצבאות השמרו פן תהבלו
שכל זה עתיד לבא אבל עדין אין התכלית.
<sup>7</sup>ויקום גוי על גוי וממלכה על ממלכה ויהיו מהומות רבות
ורעב כבד ורעש במקומות.
<sup>8</sup>כל אלה תחלת המכאובות.
<sup>9</sup>אז יאסרו אתכם לצרות ויהרגו אתכם ותהיו לחרפה לכל העמים
על שמי.

---

<sup>23:35</sup>המזבח וההכל [ההיכל ולמזבח | omit B | בן ברכיה [בן ברכיה | מדם EF | עד דם [עד דם | לתת ABEF + | Beginning]
A | והמזבח [ולמזבח B
<sup>23:37</sup>את G + | התרנגולת [התרנגולת A | ומסקלת [ומסלקת G | השלוחם והנבאים [הנביאים ומסלקת השלוחים G
תחת כנפיה [omit G | רצית [רציתם BG
<sup>24:1</sup>בנין הבית והמקדש [בניני המקדש G | את G + | להראותו [להראותו G | מהמקדש [מן המקדש G
<sup>24:2</sup>omit A | שם [שם G | להם EF, + | ואומר [ויאמר
<sup>24:3</sup>פיטרו [פיטרוש AG | שאל [שאלו A | omit ABEF [בית | בהר A | על הר [על הר AG |
EF לו + | כשיתחילו [או כשיתחילו G | omit G [אנדריאוס EF, ואנדריאש [ואנדריאה EF
A | וביאתך [וביאתך F | מתי [ומתי |
<sup>24:4</sup>לכם [אתכם EF | לכם EF + | השמרו [השמרו
<sup>24:5</sup>omit A [הוא | את הרבים [אתכם A
<sup>24:6</sup>תבהלו [תהבלו G
<sup>24:8</sup>omit A [המכאובות
<sup>24:9</sup>ימסרו [ואסרו AEF

³⁵[This is] (to place) upon you the blood of every righteous
one which has been poured out upon the earth, from the blood of Abel
the righteous unto the blood of Zechariah the Son of Barachiah whom
you killed between the temple and the altar.

³⁶Truly I say to you that all these things will come upon this generation,

³⁷and upon Jerusalem who kills the prophets and removes those who are
sent. How many times I wished to gather your children as a hen gathers
her chicks under her wings and you would not.

³⁸Therefore you will leave your houses desolate.

³⁹Truly I say to you, you will not see me henceforth until when you will
say: Blessed is our savior.

## Chapter 24

¹It came to pass when Jesus went out from the temple, as he was going,
his disciples drew near to show him the buildings of the temple.

²He said: You see all these; truly I say to you that all will be destroyed
and there will not be left there one stone upon another.

³As he sat on the Mount of Olives opposite the temple, Peter, John and
Andrew asked him secretly: When will all these things be and what will
be the sign when all these matters will take place or when will they begin and when will be the end of the world and your coming.

⁴Jesus answered them: beware lest anyone should lead you astray,

⁵because many will come in my name saying: I am the Messiah and they
will lead you astray.

⁶As for you, when you hear of wars and a company of hosts, beware lest
you become foolish, because all of this will come but the end will not
be yet.

⁷Nation will rise up against nation and kingdom against kingdom; there
will be great tumults, grievous famine and earthquake in [various]
places.

⁸All of these are the beginning of suffering.

⁹Then they will bind you over for tribulation and will kill you and you
will become a reproach to all the nations for my name.

ואז ירגזו רבים ויבגדו הם בהם ויתקצפו ביניהם.[10]

ויקומו נביאי השקר ויטעו את הרבים.[11]

וכאשר תרבה הרשעות תפוג אהבת רבים.[12]

ואשר יחכה עד התכלית יושע.[13]

ותדרש בשורה לעז אוו"נגילי זאת בכל הארץ לעדות עלי על כל[14]
הגוים ואז תבא התכלית.

זה אנטיק"ריסטוש וזהו שקוץ שומם האמור על פי דניאל עומד[15]
במקום קדוש והקורא יבין.

אז אשר ביודא ינוסו להרים.[16]

ואשר על הבית לא ירד לקרות שום דבר מביתו.[17]

ואשר בשדה לא ישוב לקחת כתנתו.[18]

הוי להרות ולמניקות בימים ההם.[19]

התפללו לאל שלא תהיה מנוסתכם בסתו ובשבת.[20]

שאז תהיה צרה גדולה אשר לא נהיתה מבראת העולם עד עתה[21]
וכמוה לא תהיה.

ולולי היות הימים ההם מעטים לא יושיע כל בשר רק בעבור[22]
הנבחרים ימעטו הימים ההם.

ובאותו הזמן אם יאמר איש לכם הנה המשיח או לשם לא תאמינו.[23]

שיקומו משיחי שקרים ונבאי השקר ויתנו אותות ומופתים[24]
גדולים בענין שאם יוכל להיות יבאו בטעות את הנבחרים.

ואם יאמרו לכם הנו במדבר אל תצאו והנו בחדרים אל תאמינו.[26]

הנני אומרו לכם קודם היותו.[25]

## פרק ק"א

עוד אמר להם יש"ו לתלמידיו כמו שהברק יוצא במזרח ונראה[27]
במערב כן תהיה ביאתו שלבן האדם.

---

ויתקפצו [ויתקצפו BF | באים [בהם | EF ירגשו [ירגזו 24:10 F

שקר [השקר G 24:11

[הגוים | omit A [על | ABEFG אפסי + | [בכל EF אואנגילי [אוונגילי | A, אונגילי [אוו"נגילי B בלעז [לעז 24:14
העם G [תבא | G בא [בא

בדניאל הנביא AG, הנביא + | [על פי דניאל A אנטיקרישט [אנטיקריסטוש | A והוא EF | זהו [זה A, זהו 24:15
EF

ביהודה [ביודה G | ואז [אז AEF 24:16

לקחת G, omit EF | לקח AB, לקחת [לקרות 24:17

הוא [הוי EF 24:19

ושבת [ובשבת BEFH | ביום השבת [בסתו ובשבת A | בסתיו [בסתו | omit G [לאל 24:20

שלא [אשר לא F 24:21

יושיע [יושיע ABEFG | ההם [[1]ההם | omit EF ולילא [ולולי A 24:22

או לשם [אל שם ABEF לכאן + | המשיח [המשיח omit G 24:23

מות [את A | יביאו [יבאו G רבים [שקרים F 24:24

הנו [והנו EF | תשאלו [תצאו A | ואז אם [ואם A 24:26

Vs 25 comes after vs 26 in Shem-Tob. [היותו | omit A 24:25

של בן [שלבן BG | ממזרח [במזרח AEF | [להם omit A 24:27

[10]Then many will be perturbed, will deal treacherously
with each other and will be enraged among themselves.

[11]False prophets will arise and lead many astray.

[12]When wickedness multiplies the love of many will grow faint.

[13]Whoever waits until the end will be saved.

[14]And this gospel, that is, evungili, will be preached in all the earth for a
witness concerning me to all the nations and then the end will come.

[15]This is the Anti-Christ and this is the abomination which desolates
which was spoken of by Daniel as standing in the holy place. Let the
one who reads understand.

[16]Then those who are in Juda let them flee to the mountains.

[17]He who is upon the house let him not come down (to take) anything
out of his house.

[18]He who is in the field let him not turn back to take his garment.

[19]Woe to those who are pregnant and to those who nurse children in
those days.

[20]Pray to God that your flight will not be (on the Sabbath day).

[21]Because then there will be great distress which has not been from the
creation of the world unto now and as will not be.

[22]Except those days were few in number no flesh would be saved; but for
the sake of the chosen those days will be few.

[23]At that time if one should say to you: Behold the Messiah is (here) or
there do not believe it.

[24]Because false messiahs and false prophets will arise and they will give
signs and great wonders so that if it can be they will come to lead the
chosen astray.

[26](Then) if they should say to you: behold he is in the wilderness, do not
go out, and: behold he is in the chambers, do not believe it.

[25]Behold I tell you before it happens.

[27]Again Jesus said to his disciples: As the lightning comes from the east
and is seen in the west so will be the coming of the Son of Man.

[MT 24:28-41

²⁸באיזה מקום שיהיה הגויה שם יתחברו הנשרים.

²⁹ובאותה שעה אחרי הימים ההם יחשך השמש והירח לא יגיה אורו והככבים יפלו מהשמים וחיל השמים יתנודד.

³⁰ואז יראה האות שלבן האדם בשמים ויבכו כל משפחות האדמה ויראו את בן האדם בעבי השמים בחיל רב ובצורה נוראה.

³¹וישלח מלאכיו בשופר ובקול גדול לאסוף את נבחריו מארבע רוחות השמים מקצה השמים עד קצותם.

³²מעץ התאנה תלמדו המשל כאשר תראו ענפיה ועלים צומחים תדעו כי

³³קרוב הוא לשערים.

³⁴אמן אני אומר לכם שלא יעבור זה הדור עד שכל אלו הדברים יהיו עשוים.

³⁵והשמים והארץ יעברו.

³⁶ומהיום ההוא ומהעת ההיא אין מי שיודע ולא מלאכי השמים אלא האב בלבד.

<u>פרק ק״ב</u>

³⁷עוד אמר יש״ו לתלמידיו כאשר בימי נח כן תהיה בימינו שלבן האדם.

³⁸כאשר היו קודם המבול אוכלים ושותים ופרים ורבים עד יום שבא נח בתיבה.

³⁹ולא ידעו עד שבא המבול עליהם וישחיתם כן תהיה ביאתו של בן האדם.

⁴⁰אז אם יהיו שנים חורשים בשדה אחד האחד צדיק והאחד רשע האחד ילכד והאחד יעזב.

⁴¹שתים נשים טוחנות בטחון אחת האחת תלכד והאחת תעזב. וזה יהיה שהמלאכים בתכלית העולם יסירו המכשולים מהעולם ויפרידו הטובים מהרעים.

---

²⁴:²⁸שיהיה [שתהיה A

²⁴:²⁹מהשמים [מן השמים EF | ABEFG צרת + [אחרי

²⁴:³⁰שלבן [של בן A

²⁴:³¹ועד EF [עד | omit AEF [¹השמים | omit E [ובקול

²⁴:³²All mss jump from קרוב vs 32 to קרוב vs 33 (hap.).

²⁴:³³See note on vs 32.

²⁴:³⁴אלו הדברים [הדברים האלו H | עשוים [נעשים H | omit B [אלו

²⁴:³⁷בימינו [ביאתו ABEF

²⁴:³⁸ופרים [פרים A

²⁴:³⁹המבול [מבול EF

²⁴:⁴⁰האחד²[ והתחד B | והאחת²[ והב B, EF והב²[ והאחת B, EF

²⁴:⁴¹שתים [ושתים EF | אחת [אחד G | מהעולם [מן העולם A

[28]Wherever the body is there will be gathered the vultures.

[29]At that time after (the tribulation of) those days the sun will grow dark, the moon will not give forth its light, the stars will fall from heaven and the host of heaven will be shaken.

[30]Then will appear the sign of the Son of Man in heaven and all the families of the earth will weep and will see the Son of Man on the clouds of heaven with a great host and with dreadful appearance.

[31]He will send his angels with a trumpet and with a great shout to gather his chosen from the four winds of heaven from one end of heaven unto the other.

[32]From the fig tree learn the parable; when you see its branches and leaves sprouting know that he is near

[33]to the gates.

[34]Truly I say to you: this generation will not pass away until all these things shall have been done.

[35]Heaven and earth will pass away.

[36]But of that day or that time there is none who knows, not even the angels of heaven, but the Father only.

[37]Again Jesus said to his disciples: As in the days of Noah so will it be in the days of the Son of Man.

[38]Just as before the flood, they were eating, drinking, being fruitful and multiplying until the day when Noah entered the ark.

[39]They did not know until the flood came upon them and destroyed them; so will be the coming of the Son of Man.

[40]Then if there shall be two ploughing in a field, one righteous and the other evil, the one will be taken and the other left.

[41]Two women will be grinding at a mill; one will be taken and the other left. This is because the angels at the end of the world will remove the stumbling blocks from the world and will separate the good from the evil.

The Gospel of Matthew

## פרק ק"ג

42אז אמר יש"ו לתלמידיו לזאת שמרו עמי שלא תדעו אזו שעה אדוניכם בא.

43זאת תדעו אם היה יודע איזו שעה הגנב בא ישמור ולא יעזוב לחבור ביתו.

44כן אתם תהיו נכונים שלא תדעו איזו שעה בן אדם עתיד לבא.

45מה אתם חושבים מהעבד הנאמן והחכם ששם אותו אדוניו על טפיו לתת אכלם בעתו?

46אשרי העבד ההוא שתצווהו אדוניו בבואו עושה כן.

47אמן אני אומר לכם שעל טפיו ישימהו.

48ואם יהיה העבד ההוא רע ויאמר בלבו אדוני מתמהמה ובא

49ויתחיל להכות עבדו אדוניו ויאכל וישתה עם הזוללים

50ובא אדוניו ביום אשר לא יחכה ובעת אשר לא ידע.

51ויפרידהו וישים חלקו עם החנפים שם יהיה בכי וחרוק שינים.

## פרק ק"ד

1עוד אמר יש"ו לתלמידיו מלכות שמים דומה לעשר בתולות שלקחו נרותיהן ויצאו לקראת חתן וכלה.

2חמש מהן היו עצלות כסילות וחמש מהן זריזות וחכמות.

3החמש כסילות הוציאו נרותיהן ולא הוציאו שמן עמהן.

4והחכמות הוציאו שמן בכליהן עם נרותיהן.

5ויתמהמה החתן והנה כלן נתמהמהו ונשנה.

6ויהי בחצי הלילה והנה קול נשמע הנה החתן בא באו לקראתו.

7אז באו הבתולות כולנה והטיבו נרותיהן.

8ותאמרנה הבתולות הכסילות לחכמות תנו לנו משמנכם שנרותינו נדעכו.

---

24:42 שמרו] שמעו G | 2 1 G [אדוניכם בא

24:43 וידע] + אדון הבית A | בא] יבא A | לחבור] לחתור ABEFG

24:44 תהיו] היו EF | אדם] האדם FG | עתיד לבא] בא BG

24:45 והחכם] omit G | לתת] + להם A

24:46 שתצווהו] שימצאהו ABEF

24:47 טפיו] טובו ABEFG

24:48 העבד] העב A | ובא] לבא AEF, לבוא B

24:50 ובא] יבא A

24:51 ויפרידהו] ויפחדהו A

25:2 וחמש] והחמש A | מהן²] מהן A

25:3 כסילות] הכסילות A, העצלות G | הוציאו²] הוציא A | עמהם] omit EF

25:5 נתמהמהו] נתמהמו A | ונשנה] ונשנן EF, ותשנה B, ונשנן G

25:6 והנה קול] וקול A

25:7 הבתולות] + ההן ABEFG

⁴²Then Jesus said to his disciples: Therefore watch with me
because you do not know at what hour your lord is coming.

⁴³This you know, if one knows at what hour the thief is coming he will
watch and not allow him (to dig) into his house.

⁴⁴So you should be prepared because you do not know at what hour the
Son of Man is going to come.

⁴⁵What do you think of the faithful and wise servant whose lord places
him over his children to give (them) food in its time?

⁴⁶Blessed is that servant whose lord (finds) him doing thus when he
comes.

⁴⁷Truly I say to you that he will place him over his children.

⁴⁸But if that servant should be evil and should say in his heart: My lord is
late (in) coming

⁴⁹and should begin to beat the servants of his lord and should eat and
drink with gluttons,

⁵⁰his lord will come in day for which he does not wait and at a time
which he does not know.

⁵¹He will divide him and place his portion with hypocrites; there will be
weeping and gnashing of teeth.

## Chapter 25

¹Again Jesus said to his disciples: The kingdom of heaven is like ten virgins who took their lamps and went forth to meet a bridegroom and a
bride.

²Five of them were lazy fools and five of them were alert and wise.

³The five foolish brought their lamps but they brought no oil with them.

⁴The wise brought oil in their vessels with their lamps.

⁵The bridegroom was late and behold all of them lingered and (slept).

⁶It came to pass at midnight that behold a voice was heard: Behold the
bridegroom is coming; come to meet him.

⁷Then all (those) virgins came and trimmed their lamps.

⁸The foolish virgins said to the wise: Give us some of your oil because
our lamps have gone out.

[MT 25:9-23]

‏⁹ותעננה החכמות לאמר לכו נא אל המוכרים וקנו לכן כי אין די
בשמן שלנו ולכן. נירא שיחסר לנו.

‏¹⁰ויהי כאשר הלכו לקנות בא החתן והמוכנות באו עמו לחופה
ונסגר השער.

‏¹¹ואח״כ באו הכסילות ותקראנה לשער לאמר אדוננו פתח לנו.

‏¹²ויען להן באמת אני אומר לכם איני יודע מי אתן.

‏¹³ועל כן השמרו לכם שלא תדעו היום והשעה שיבא החתן.

### פרק ק״ה

‏¹⁴עוד אמר יש״ו לתלמידיו דמיון אחר מלכות שמים דומה לאדם
הולך בדרך רחוקה ויקרא את עבדיו ויפזר להם ממונו.

‏¹⁵לאחד נתן חמשה זהובים לשני נתן שנים זהובים ולשלישי אחד
איש כראוי לו נתן להם. וילך לדרכו.

‏¹⁶וילך המקבל החמשה זהובים והרויח חמשה אחרים.

‏¹⁷וכמו כן המקבל שנים הלך קנה ומכר והרויח חמשה אחרים.

‏¹⁸והמקבל האחד הלך וחפר בארץ ויטמון את ממון אדוניו.

‏¹⁹ואחר ימים רבים בא אדון העבדים ההם ויבקש מהם חשבון
הממון.

‏²⁰ויגש המקבל החמשה זהובים אמר לו אדוני חמשה זהובים נתת
לי והא לך חמשה אחרים אשר רוחתי.

‏²¹ויאמר לו אדוניו אמנם עבד טוב ונאמן אתה. ויען היית נאמן
במעט אשימך על הרבה בא בשמחת אדוניך.

‏²²וגם המקבל שנים הזהובים נגש ויאמר אדוני שנים זהובים
נתת לי והנה שנים אחרים אשר הרוחתי.

‏²³ויאמר לו אדוניו אמנם עבד טוב ונאמן אתה. וכי היית נאמן
במעט אשימך על הרבה בא בשמחת אדוניך.

---

²⁵:⁹ A ולכן + ]ולכו | EF ]לנו + ]לנו | BEFG נראה ]נירא | EF לכם ]לכן | A לכו + ]שלנו

²⁵:¹² G לכן ]לכם | EF להם ]להן

²⁵:¹³ A שההחתן עתיד לב ]שיבא החתן

²⁵:¹⁴ ABEFG(?) ויפקוד ]ויפזר | A א׳ ]אחר | A היא + ]דומה

²⁵:¹⁵ EF לא ]לו | omit AEFG ]נתן² | ABEF ולשני ]לשני

²⁵:¹⁶ A וירוח ]והרויח | omit F ]זהובים

שָׁנִים A, חמשה שנים ]חמשה | A שהרויח ]והרויח | BEFG קונה ומוכר A, קונה ומוכר עד ]קנה ומכר ²⁵:¹⁷
E [supralinear correction] יותר ]חמשה אחרים F

²⁵:¹⁹ G אלו העבדים ]העבדים ההם F האדון ]אדון . . . ההם | omit F ]רבים | A ואחרי ]ואחר

²⁵:²⁰ A נתתו ]נתת | A מחמשה ]חמשה | ABEFG ויאמר ]אמר | omit G ]זהובים¹ | G מקבל ]המקבל
A הרוחתי ]רוחתי | A עשרה + ]לך

²⁵:²¹ G במועט ]במעט

²⁵:²² ABEFG. After this word F has 3 garbled G ויען מקבל כב ויאמר ]וגם . . . ויאמר | השנים ]שנים¹ | G
words and omits all else down to vs 24. | זהו׳ B omit A, ]הזהובים

²⁵:²³ Vs 23] omit F [see note on vs 22].

⁹The wise answered saying: Go now to those who sell
and buy for yourselves because there is not enough oil for us and you.
We fear that it will be lacking for us.

¹⁰It came to pass when they went to buy, the bridegroom came; those
who were ready went with him into the marriage ceremony and the
gate was closed.

¹¹Afterwards the foolish ones came and called at the gate saying: Our
lord, open for us.

¹²He answered them: Truly I say to you, I do not know who you are.

¹³Be careful, therefore, because you do not know the day or the hour
when the bridegroom will come.

¹⁴Again Jesus told his disciples another example: The kingdom of heaven
is like a man going on a far journey; he called his servants and dis-
persed to them his money.

¹⁵To one he gave five coins of gold, to the second he gave two coins of
gold and to the third one, to each one according to what was suitable
for him he gave. Then he went on his journey.

¹⁶The one who received five coins of gold went and gained five others.

¹⁷Likewise the one who received two went, bought and sold and gained
five others.

¹⁸But he who received the one went and dug in the earth and hid the
money of his lord.

¹⁹After many days the lord of those servants came and sought from them
an accounting of the money.

²⁰The one who received five coins of gold came near and said to him:
My lord, you gave me five coins of gold and behold for you are five
others which I have gained.

²¹His lord said to him: Truly you are a good and faithful servant. Because you have been faithful in a little I will appoint you over much;
enter into the joy of your lord.

²²Also the one who received two coins of gold drew near and said: My
lord, you gave me two coins of gold; here are two others which I have
gained.

²³His lord said to him: Truly you are a good and faithful servant. Because you have been faithful in a little I will appoint you over much;
enter into the joy of your lord.

[MT 25:24-37

²⁴וִיגַּשׁ המקבל האחד ויאמר אדוני ידעתי שעז וקשה אתה ותקצור
אשר לא זרעת ותאסוף אשר לא פזרת.

²⁵ומיראתך הלכתי וטמנתי הזהוב שלך והא לך שלך.

²⁶ויען אדוניו ויאמר עבד רע ועצל אחרי שידעת שקוצר אני אשר
לא זרעתי ואוסף אשר לא פזרתי

²⁷לזאת היית חייב לתת נכסי לשולחני ובבואי הייתי מקבל את
שלי עם ריוח.

²⁸לזאת קחו ממנו הזהב וחנותו לאשר רווח החמשה זהובים.

²⁹לאשר יש לו תנתן לו ולאשר אין לו הראוי לו ילקח ממנו.

³⁰והעבד העצל השליכהו במחשכי תחתיות ושם יהיה לו בכי
וחרוק שנים.

### פרק ק"ו

³¹עוד אמר יש"ו לתלמידיו ובבוא בן האדם במראהו עם מלאכיו
אז ישב על כסא כבודו.

³²ויאספו לפניו כל הגוים ויפריד ביניהם כאשר יפריד הרועה
בין הכשבים ובין העזים.

³³ויציג את הכשבים לימינו והעזים לשמאלו.

³⁴אז ידבר לאשר לימינו בואו ברוכים ברוכי אבי וירשו לכם
ממלכות השמים המוכן לכם מבריאת העולם עד עתה.

³⁵כי רעבתי ונתתם לי לאכול צמאתי ונתתם לי לשתות אורח
הייתי ותאספוני

³⁶ערום ותלבישוני חולה ותבקרוני בבית הסוהר הייתי
ותבואו אלי.

³⁷אז יענו הצדיקים אדוננו מתו ראינוך רעב והשבענוך צמנו
והשקתוך

---

²⁵:²⁴ויאמר] omit G

²⁵:²⁵בארץ + A | ]ושלך

²⁵:²⁶ללא] [²לו EG | ABEF לו + ]ויאמר

²⁵:²⁷שירוח בהם + G | ]לשולחני

²⁵:²⁸חמשה] ABEFG החמשה | A ותנוהו] AEF הזהוב | הזהב] ותנותו

²⁵:²⁹ינתן] תנתן[ ABEF | לו ילקח] תלקח G

²⁵:³⁰לו] [omit A | EF ששם ] ושם[ ABEFG השליכוהו] השליכהו

²⁵:³¹בבא] ובבוא[ B

²⁵:³²הכבשים] הכשבים[ BEF

²⁵:³³הכבשים] הכשבים[ BEF | ויפריד EF, וישיג [G (?) | ]ויציג

²⁵:³⁴שמים] השמים[ G | מלכות] ממלכות G | שבשמים + ]ממלכות ABEF | אבי] B של | ברוכי] B אשר | לאשר] עולם] G | העולם[ G

²⁵:³⁵צאמתי] צמאתי G | ותאספוני רעב ]ותאספוני B רעבתם] רעבתי G

²⁵:³⁶ותבקרוני] A | ותבואו אלי] G הייתי + ]חילה

²⁵:³⁷והשקתוך] ABEF צמא] צמנו[ G ושבענוך] והשבענוך[ G ויאמרו] הצדיקים + ]הצדיקים G | לו ]ויענו + ABEF והשקינוך ABEFG

²⁴Then he who received the one drew near and said:
My lord, I know that you are firm and hard and that you reap what you did not sow and gather what you did not scatter.

²⁵So in fear of you I went and hid your coin of gold and behold you have what is yours.

²⁶His lord answered and said: Wicked and lazy servant, since you know that I reap what I did not sow and gather what I did not scatter,

²⁷therefore, you should have given my wealth to my money-changers so that at my coming I would have received what is mine with profit.

²⁸Therefore, take from him the coin of gold and (give it) to the one who gained five coins of gold.

²⁹To the one who has it will be given but to the one who does not have that which was intended for him will be taken from him.

³⁰As for the lazy servant, cast him into the darkness of the lowest places, there shall be for him weeping and gnashing of teeth.

³¹Again Jesus said to his disciples: When the Son of Man comes in his revelation with his angels then he will sit upon the throne of his glory.

³²All the nations will be gathered before him and he will separate them as the shephard separates the sheep and the goats.

³³He will place the sheep on his right and the goats on his left.

³⁴Then he will say to those on his right: enter blessed (of) my father and inherit for yourselves the kingdom of heaven prepared for you from the creation of the world until now.

³⁵Because I was hungry and you gave me to eat, I was thirsty and you gave me to drink, I was a wayfarer and you took me in,

³⁶naked and you clothed me, sick and you visited me, I was in prison and you came to me.

³⁷Then the righteous will answer: O our Lord, when did we see you hungry and satisfied you, (thirsty) and gave you to drink,

<sup>38</sup>ערום וכסיתוך

<sup>39</sup>חולה ובקרנוך בבית הסהר ובאנו אליך.

<sup>40</sup>ויען המלך ויאמר להם אמן אני אומר לכם שבכל הפעמים אשר
עשיתם לאחד עני מאחד אלו הקטנים כאלו עשיתם לי.

<sup>41</sup>וגם ידבר לאשר לשמאלו סורו ממני ארורים ובאו באש עולמית
במקום מוכן לכם עם השטן ומלאכיו

<sup>42</sup>שרעבתי ולא נתתם לי לאכול צמאתי ולא השקיתם לי

<sup>43</sup>הייתי אורח ולא אספתם אותי ערום ולא כסיתם אותי חולה
ובבית ולא בקרתם אותי.

<sup>44</sup>אז יענו גם הם ויאמרו אליו מתי ראינוך אדוננו רעב וצמא או
אורח וערום וחולה או בבית הסוהר ולא היינו עמך משרתים
אותך.

<sup>45</sup>ויענה אליהם ויאמר אני אומר לכם שכל הפעמים אשר לא עשיתם
זאת לעני אחד מאלו הקטנים כאלו לא עשיתם אלי.

<sup>46</sup>וילכו אלה לדראון עולם והצדיקים לחיי עולם.

פרק ק'ז

<sup>1</sup>ויהי כאשר כלה יש''ו לדבר כל הדברים האלה אמר לתלמידיו

<sup>2</sup>הלא תדעו שאחר שני ימים יהיה הפסח ובן האדם ימסר ביד
היהודים לצליבה.

<sup>3</sup>אז נאספו סגני הכהנים וגדולי העם בחצר נגיד הכהנים ושמו
קאיפש.

<sup>4</sup>ויועצו יחדיו לתפוש את יש''ו בערמה ולהורגו.

<sup>5</sup>ויאמרו לא יהיה בחג פן שאון יהיה בעם.

<sup>6</sup>ויהי כאשר היה יש''ו בכפר חנניה בבית סימון המצורע

---

<sup>25:38</sup> Vs 38] omit FG | וכסינוך [וכסיתוך AB, וכסונוך E

<sup>25:39</sup> Vs 39] omit FG

<sup>25:40</sup> אחד מכל אלו כאלו [מאחד . . . כאלו | BEF מאחי [מאחד | EF שכל [שבכל G

<sup>25:41</sup> המוכן [מוכן G | (?) מרעם + [ממני | EF ואשר [וגם G

<sup>25:42</sup> אותי וכו' [<sup>2</sup>לי | G שבעתם אותי [נתתם לי לאכול G | שרעב היתי [שרעבתי G

<sup>25:43</sup> Vs 43] omit G [see vs 42] | הסוהר + [ABEF | ובבית [ערום ולא כסיתם אותי omit A

<sup>25:44</sup> ובבית [או בבית ABEF | או חולה [וחולה B | אדונינו [אדוננו A 1 2 3 | מתי ראינוך אדוננו B
עמך [omit EF

<sup>25:45</sup> לעני אחד [1 2 A

<sup>25:46</sup> עהב A, ולנצח נצחים + [עולם F

<sup>26:1</sup> את + [לדבר H

<sup>26:2</sup> ביבי [ביד B | ביבא [יבא G | האדם [האדם AH | יהיה [יהיה G

<sup>26:3</sup> קאיפאש [קאיפש A | גדולי העם והכהנים [סגני . . . העם G

<sup>26:4</sup> ולהרגו [ולהורגו G | לתפום [לתפוש G | לב [ויועצו BEF

<sup>26:5</sup> ביום החג [בחג A

<sup>26:6</sup> שימון [סימון ABEF | חנניא [חנניה A

[38]naked and clothed you,

[39]sick and visited you, in prison and came to you.

[40]The king will answer and say to them: Truly I say to you that every
time you did it to one of the needy of these (my brothers), even the little ones like these, you did it to me.

[41]Also he will say to those on his left: Depart from me you cursed and go
into the eternal fire, to the place prepared for you, with Satan and his
angels,

[42]because I was hungry and you did not give me to eat, I was thirsty and
you did not give me to drink,

[43]I was a wayfarer and you did not take me in, naked and you did not
clothe me, sick and in (prison) and you did not visit me.

[44]Then they also will answer and say to him: When did we see you, O
our Lord, hungry, thirsty, or a wayfarer, naked, sick or in prison and
were not with you serving you.

[45]He will answer them and say: I say to you that whenever you did not
do this to one of these needy, even the little ones like these, you did
not do it to me.

[46]Then these will go into eternal abhorrence but the righteous into eternal
life.

## Chapter 26

[1]It came to pass when Jesus finished speaking all these things, he said to
his disciples:

[2]Do you not know that after two days will be the Passover and the Son
of Man will be delivered into the hands of the Jews for the gallows.

[3]Then the rulers of the priests and the great ones of the people were
gathered together in the court of the chief priest whose name was Caiaphas.

[4]They took counsel together to seize Jesus by craftiness and to kill him.

[5]But they said it should not be at the feast lest there be a tumult among
the people.

[6]It came to pass when Jesus was in Cephar-hananyah in the house of Simon the leper

[MT 26:7-22]

7נגשה אליו אשה אחת בפך משיחה יקרה ותיצק אותו על ראשו והוא מסבה לשלחן.

8וירע להם מאד מדוע האבדון הזה

9יוכל למוכרה במחיר רב ולתת לעניים.

10ויש״ו היודע כל דבר לאיזה ענין נעשה אמר להם אתם מאשימים את האשה הזאת. באמת מעשה טוב ונפלא עשתה עמדי.

11כי העניים יחיו עמכם תמיד ואני לא אהיה עמכם תמיד.

12ושמה זאת בגופי רומז לקבורתי.

13אמן אני אומר לכם בכל מקום אשר תקרא בשורה זו לעז אוונגיל בכל העולם יאמר אשר עשה זאת בזכרי.

<u>פרק ק״ח</u>

14אז הלך אחד מהשנים עשר ששמו יודא אשכריוטו לגדולי הכהנים.

15ויאמר מה תתנו לי ואני אמסור יש״ו לכם. ויפסקו אתו שלשים כסף.

16ומכאן ואילך בקש ענין למסור אותו.

17 וביום הראשון של חג המצות קרבו התלמידים ליש״ו לאמר אנה נכין לך אכילת הפסח.

18ויאמר להם לכו אל העיר לאיזה איש שידבנו לבו לעשות ואמרו לו כה אמר הרב זמני קרוב הוא עמך ויעשה פסח עם תלמידי.

20ויהי לעת ערב והוא יושב לשלחן עם י״ב תלמידיו.

21כאמר היו אוכלים אמר להם אומר אני לכם שאחד מכם ימסרני.

22ויתעצבו מאד ויאמרו לו כל אחד לאמר אדוני האני זה.

26:7 EF על השלחן [לשלחן | G מסכב A, מסובה [מסבה | AG אותה [אותו | F ותצוק [ותיצק
26:8 G על אשה שפרה [מדוע האבדון הזה | G עד מאד [מאד
26:9 G וליתן [ולתת | omit G [במחיר רב | G שהיה יכול B, היה יכול [יוכל
26:10 EF | ואמת [ונפלא | A אמר להם [אמר להם | A ענין כל ועשה [ענין נעשה | EF שאיזה [לאיזה | A 2 3 1 [ונפלא עשתה עמדי
26:11 ABEFG יהיו [יחיו | EF העדים [העניים
26:12 B באפי [בגופי
26:13 ABG, omit F עשתה [עשה | omit E [אשר עשה | EF מקום [העולם | B בלעז [לעז | AG זאת [זו | A בזכרתי [בזכרי
26:14 G אסקראוטה AEF, איסכריוטא [אשכריוטו | FG שמו [ששמו | G מי״ב תלמידיו [מהשנים עשר | A בשלשים [שלשים
26:15 A בשלשים [שלשים
26:17 ABEF אנה [אנא BF | ABEF אל ישו [לישו
26:18 ABEF אעשה [ויעשה | EF אדוני + | הרב [EF אשר ידבנו [איש שידבנו
26:19 Vs 19] omit all mss
26:20 EF ב״ [י״ב
26:22 omit EF [אדוני | A האחד מהם [אחד | A לאמר [מאד +

⁷there drew near to him a woman with a flask of costly ointment;
she poured it upon his head while he was reclining at table.

⁸But this waste was very displeasing to them

⁹[since] it would have been possible to have sold it for a great price and
to have given it to the poor.

¹⁰Jesus who knows everything in regard to any matter done, said to
them: Are you making accusation against this woman. Truly she has
performed a good and wonderful deed toward me.

¹¹Because the poor (will be) with you always, but I will not be with you
always.

¹²Her placing this on my body refers to my burial.

¹³Truly I say to you, everywhere this gospel, that is, evungel, is pro-
claimed in all the world, that which this one has done will be said in
reference to my memory.

¹⁴Then one of the Twelve, whose name was Judas Iscariot, went to the
chief priests.

¹⁵He said: What will you give me that I should deliver Jesus over to you.
They settled with him for thirty pieces of silver.

¹⁶From then on he sought a context for delivering him over.

¹⁷On the first day of the festival of unleavened bread the disciples came
to Jesus saying: Where shall we prepare for you to eat the Passover.

¹⁸He said to them: Go into the city to a certain man who will be a volun-
teer for the task and say to him: thus says the teacher, my time is near;
with you (I will observe) the Passover with my disciples.

²⁰It came to pass at the time of evening he was sitting at table with his
twelve disciples.

²¹As they were eating he said to them: I say to you that one of you will
inform against me.

²²They were very sad and spoke each one to him saying:
Lord, is it I.

[MT 26:23-36

²³ויען להם הטובל ידו עמי בקערה הוא ימכרני. וכולם היו
אוכלים בקערה אחת. לכן לא הכירוהו שאלו הכירוהו השמידוהו.
²⁴ויאמר להם יש״ו אמת שבן האדם הולך ככתוב בו אוי לאדם ההוא
אשר בשבילו בן אדם ימסר. טוב לו שלא נולד לאיש ההוא.
²⁵ויען יודא אשר מכרו ויאמר לו רבי האני זה ויאמר אתה דברת.

## פרק ק״ט

²⁶המה אוכלים ויקח יש״ו לחם ויברך ויחלקהו ויתן לתלמידיו
ויאמר קחו ואכלו זה הוא גופי.
²⁷ויקח את הכוס ויתן שבחים לאביו ויתן להם ויאמר שתו מזה
כולכם.
²⁸זהו דמי מברית חדשה אשר ישפך בעבור הרבים לכפרת עונות.
²⁹אומר אני לכם לא אשתה אני מכאן ואילך מפרי הגפן הזאת עד
היום ההוא שאשתה אותו חדש עמכם במלכות שמים.
³⁰וילכו ויצאו להר הזתים.

## פרק ק״י

³¹אז אמר יש״ו לתלמידיו באו כלכם התעצבו עלי הלילה שכן
כתיב הך את הרועה ותפוצינה הרועים.
³²ואחרי קומי מהמיתה אגלה לכם בגליל.
³³ויען פיט״רוש ויאמר לו אם כלם יעצבו עליך אני לא אתעצב
לעולם.
³⁴ויאמר יש״ו אמן אני אומר לך שבזה הלילה קודם קריאת הגבר
תכפור בי ג׳ פעמים.
³⁵ויאמר לו פיט״רוש אם יתכן לי למות עמך לא אכפור בך. וכזה
אמרו לו כל התלמידים.
³⁶אז בא יש״ו עמהם לכפר גיא שמנים ויאמר שבו נא עד שאלך לשם
ואתפלל.

---

²⁶:²³ A שאילו [שאלו | AF ימסרני [ימכרני
²⁶:²⁴ G בשבילו + [ימסר | EF ימסר בן האדם A, בן האדם ימסר [בן אדם | omit G [בשבילו
²⁶:²⁵ EF האתה [האני | ד׳ G or ר׳ + [מכרו | omit G [אשר מכרו
²⁶:²⁶ H ויחלך [ויחלקהו ויתן | EF, omit G אותו + [ויברך | H את + [ישו | omit EF [המה אוכלים | omit H [זה | ABGH הוא [הוא
²⁶:²⁸ H העונות [עונות | G זה הוא [זהו
²⁶:²⁹ אני'[ omit G | לא אשתה אני [omit B אני²[ omit EF | שמים [אבי A
²⁶:³⁰ ABEF וישבו [וילכו
²⁶:³¹ AEFG הצאן [הרועים | F 3 1 2 [כלכם תתעצבו עלי ABEFGH אמר להם ישו [אמר ישו לתלמידין
²⁶:³² EF בהר הגליל [בגליל
²⁶:³³ omit G [כלם | A פיטרו [פיטרוש
²⁶:³⁴ AEF שבזאת [שבזה | ABEF לו + [ויאמר
²⁶:³⁵ G כולם [כל התלמידים | A פיטרו [פיטרוש

²³He answered them: He who dips his hand
with me in the dish will sell me. All of them were eating from one
dish. Therefore, they did not recognize him; because if they had recognized him they would have destroyed him.

²⁴Jesus said to them: Truly the Son of Man goes as it is written concerning him; woe to that man for whose sake the Son of Man is betrayed.
Good would it be for that man not to have been born.

²⁵Judas who sold him answered and said to him: Rabbi am I this one; he
said: You have spoken.

²⁶They were eating and Jesus took bread, blessed, divided it, gave it to
his disciples and said: Take and eat; this is my body.

²⁷He took the cup and gave it to them and said: Drink from this all of
you.

²⁸This is my blood of the new covenant which will be poured out for
many for the atonement of sins.

²⁹I say to you I will not drink henceforth from the fruit of this vine until
that day when I drink it new with you in the kingdom of heaven.

³⁰(They returned) and went out to the Mount of Olives.

³¹Then Jesus said to his disciples: Come all of you, be grieved because
of me tonight because it is written: Smite the shepherd and the (sheep)
will be scattered.

³²After my resurrection from death I will be revealed to you in Galilee.

³³Peter answered and said to him: If all of them are grieved because of
you I will never be grieved.

³⁴Jesus said: Truly I say to you, this night before the cock-crow you will
deny me three times.

³⁵Peter said to him: If it is possible for me to die with you, I will not
deny you. Likewise all the disciples said to him.

³⁶Then Jesus came with them to the village of Geshemonim and said: Sit
now until I go there and pray.

[MT 26:37-51

<sup>37</sup>ויקח את פיטרוש ואת שני בני זבדאל והתחיל להתעצב ולהיות
זעף.

<sup>38</sup>אז אמר להם נפשי מתעצבת עד מות סמכוני ושמרו עמי.

<sup>39</sup>וילך לאט לאט מעט ויפול על פניו ויתפלל ויאמר אם יוכל
להיות הסר נא ממני הכוס הזה. אמנם לא כמו שאני רוצה יהיה
אלא כרצונך.

<sup>40</sup>ויבא אל התלמידים וימצאם ישנים. ויאמר לפיט״רו כך האינך
יכול לשמור עמדי שעה אחת.

<sup>41</sup>שמרו והתפללו פן תבאו בנסיון שהאמת שהרוח נכון לילך לו
ראו את הבשר חלש וחולה.

<sup>42</sup>וילך שנית להתפלל לאמור אם לא תוכל להסיר הכוס הזה אלא
שאשתהו יהיה עשי כרצונך.

<sup>43</sup>וישב אחרי כן וימצאם ישנים שהיו עיניהם כבדים.

<sup>44</sup>ויעזוב אותם וילך להתפלל פעם שלישית כדברים הראשונים.

פרק קי״א

<sup>45</sup>אז בא יש״ו לגליל לתלמידיו ויאמר להם שנו ונוחו הנה הקרב
העת ובן האדם ימסר ביד החטאים.

<sup>46</sup>קומו ונלך שהנו קרוב מי שימסרנו.

<sup>47</sup>עודנו מדבר והנה יודא אסכריוטא אחד מי״ב תלמידיו בא.
ועמו חבורה אחת רבה בחרבות ובשוטים שלוחים מאת גדולי
הכהנים ושרי העם.

<sup>48</sup>ואשר מסרוהו נתן להם אות אשר אשקנו הוא הוא ותפשוהו.

<sup>49</sup>ומיד נגש אל יש״ו ויאמר לו שלום עליך רבי וישקהו.

<sup>50</sup>ויאמר אליו יש״ו אהובי מה עשית. ויקרבו וישלחו ידם בו
ויתפשוהו.

<sup>51</sup>והנה אחד מאשר היה עם יש״ו נטה ידו וישלוף חרבו ויך עבד
אחד מעבדי הכהנים ויכרות אזנו.

<sup>26:37</sup>פיטרוש] פיטרו A | ואת שני] ואשר A | זבדאל] זבדיה B
<sup>26:38</sup>סמכוני] שמרוני EF
<sup>26:39</sup>וילך] omit G | לאט[²] omit A | על] את F | ויאמר] ואומר אבי AEF, + אבי BG |
שאני] שאינך F | נא] omit AB
<sup>26:40</sup>G 2 1 | שעה אחת] omit G | האינך] אינך G | כך] FG | לפיטרוש] E, לפיטרוס omit AEF | לפיטרו
<sup>26:41</sup>חלש] חלוש A | לו ראו את] לבוראו אך A | תבא] תבאו G | פן] + ב ב | פן
<sup>26:42</sup>עשי] עשוי ABEFG | הכוס] כוס A | את] omit AB | להסיר] + את A
<sup>26:43</sup>כבדים] + שהיו A
<sup>26:45</sup>להם] omit G
<sup>26:47</sup>העם] omit E | העם] omit F | ושרי העם] omit F | בא] + A | רבה] + A | בא] omit EF
<sup>26:48</sup>הזה] הוא[¹] A ABEFG | האיש] + F | טרם מסרהו] E, מסרהו | ואשר מסרוהו
<sup>26:50</sup>וישלחו] וישליכו A | אליו] לו EF
<sup>26:51</sup>היה] היו A | היה עם] את G | ויכרות] + את ABG

<sup>37</sup>He took Peter and the two sons of Zebedeel
and began to be sad and to be troubled.

<sup>38</sup>Then he said to them: my soul is grieved unto death; support me and
watch with me.

<sup>39</sup>He slowly went forward a little, fell on his face, prayed and said: (my
father), if it is possible take this cup from me. Indeed, let it not be as I
will but according to your will.

<sup>40</sup>He came to the disciples and found them sleeping. He said to Peter: So
you are unable to watch with me one hour.

<sup>41</sup>Watch and pray lest you enter into temptation, because truly the spirit
is ready to go (to its creator but) the flesh is weak and sick.

<sup>42</sup>He went again to pray saying: If you are not able to remove this cup
except I should drink it let it be done according to your will.

<sup>43</sup>Afterwards he returned and found them sleeping because their eyes
were heavy.

<sup>44</sup>He left them and went to pray a third time according to the first words.

<sup>45</sup>Then Jesus came to where the disciples were and said to them: Sleep
and be at rest; behold the time has come near when the Son of Man
will be delivered into the hand of sinners.

<sup>46</sup>Arise, let us go, for behold he who will betray him is near.

<sup>47</sup>While he was speaking behold Judas Iscariot, one of his twelve disci-
ples, came. With him was a large crowd with swords and whips sent
from the chief priests and the princes of the people.

<sup>48</sup>He who betrayed him had given them a sign: (the man) whom I kiss is
the one whom you are to arrest.

<sup>49</sup>Immediately he drew near to Jesus and said to him: Greetings Rabbi;
then he kissed him.

<sup>50</sup>Jesus said to him: My friend, what have you done. Then they came,
stretched out their hand against him and arrested him.

<sup>51</sup>Behold one who was with Jesus stretched out his hand,
drew his sword, struck one of the servants of the priests
and cut off his ear.

[MT 26:52-66

⁵²ויאמר אליו יש״ו השב חרבך אל נדנה שהשרופים חרב בחרב יפולו.

⁵³הלא תבין שאוכל לפגוע באויבי ואכן לי עתה יתר מי״ב לגיונות של מלאכים?

⁵⁴ואיך ימלאון הכתובים? שכן ראוי לעשות.

⁵⁵אחר אמר יש״ו לחבורה כמו אם היינו גנבים באתם לקחת אותי בחרבות ובשוטים. והלא בכל יום הייתי עמכם במקדש מלמדכם ולא עכבתוני?

⁵⁶אמנם כל זה נעשה יען ימלאו הכתובים מהנביאים. אז כל תלמידיו הניחוהו וברחו.

⁵⁷והם הוליכו ליש״ו לבית קאיפש גדול הכהנים. ואז כל הסופרים והפרושים נקהלו.

⁵⁸ופיט״רוש היה הולך אחריו מרחוק עד בית גדול הכהנים. ונכנס לבית וישב לו אצל האומנים עד יראה התכלית.

⁵⁹וגדולי הכהנים והפרושים היו רוצים עדי שקר נגד יש״ו יען ימיתוהו.

⁶⁰ולא היו מוצאים ואחד אשר הכינו הרבה עדי שקר נגד יש״ו. לסוף באו שני עדים שקרים.

⁶¹ויאמר זה אמר יש לי יכולת להשחית מקדש האל ואחר ג׳ ימים לתקן אותו.

⁶²וגדול הכהנים קם ויאמר לו אינך עונה דבר נגד העדות שאלו מעידים נגדך.

⁶³ויש״ו לא ענה דבר. וגדול הכהנים אמר לו משביעך אני באל חי שתאמר לנו אם אתה משיח בן האל.

⁶⁴ויען לו יש״ו אתה אומר ועוד אני אומר לכם עדין תראו בן האל יושב לימין גבורת האל בא בעבי שחקים.

⁶⁵אז גדול הכהנים קרע בגדיו ואמר זה ברך אלקים. ומה לנו צורך לעדים אחרים? והנה כולכם שמעתם איך ברך האל.

⁶⁶מה יראה לכם שיתכן לעשות? והם ענו שחייב מיתה.

²⁶:⁵² שהשלפים] שהשרופים ABFG

²⁶:⁵³ יתר] ויתר AG

²⁶:⁵⁵ בחרבות ובשוטים] omit G

²⁶:⁵⁶ ימלאון] ימלאו ABEFG | וברחו] + להם G

²⁶:⁵⁷ נקהל] + לשם G

²⁶:⁵⁸ ונכנס . . . המכלית] omit BF | ופיטרו] ופיטרוש A | עד] אל A | המכלית A

²⁶:⁵⁹ וגדולי] omit BFG | רוצים] + למצוא B

²⁶:⁶⁰ באו] omit G

²⁶:⁶¹ ויאמרו] ויאמרו ABG | לתקן אותו] אשוב יאבננהו G

²⁶:⁶³ משביעך אני] 2 1 ABEG, 1 F | ענה] עונה A | ישו לא ענה] 2 3 1 G

²⁶:⁶⁴ ישו] omit A | ועוד אני אומר לכם] לכן G | לימין] + אבו G

²⁶:⁶⁵ אלקים] אלים AG | האל] אלים A, אלקים BEF, את האל G

⁵²Jesus said to him: Return your sword to its sheath
for (those who draw) the sword will fall by the sword.

⁵³Do you not understand that I can meet my enemies and indeed there
will be for me at once more than twelve legions of angels?

⁵⁴But how will the Scriptures be fulfilled? Because thus it is intended to
be done.

⁵⁵Afterwards Jesus said to the crowd: As if we were thieves have you
come to take me with swords and whips. Was I not with you every day
in the temple teaching you without you hindering me?

⁵⁶Surely all this was done because the writings of the Prophets were
being fulfilled. Then all his disciples left him and fled.

⁵⁷They led Jesus to the house of Caiaphas the high priest. Then all the
scribes and Pharisees were gathered together.

⁵⁸Peter was following him at a distance unto the house of the high priest.
He entered the house and sat near the craftsmen until he should see the
end.

⁵⁹The high priest and the Pharisees wished (to find) false witnesses
against Jesus in order to put him to death.

⁶⁰But they did not find even one, though they provided many false witnesses against Jesus. Finally two false witnesses came forward.

⁶¹(They said): This one said I have the power to destroy the temple of
God and after three days to repair it.

⁶²The high priest arose and said to him: Do you not answer anything
against the testimony that these are bearing against you.

⁶³But Jesus answered not a word. The high priest said to him: I adjure
you by the living God that you tell us if you are the Messiah, the Son
of God.

⁶⁴Jesus answered him: You say it; but again I say to you, you have yet to
see the Son of God sitting at the right of the power of God coming on
the clouds of heaven.

⁶⁵Then the high priest tore his garments and said: This one has cursed
God. What need do we have for other witnesses? Behold all of you
have heard how he cursed God.

⁶⁶What do you think can be done? They answered: He is guilty of death.

[MT 26:67-27:8]

67ואז רקקו בפניו והלקוהו על שכמו ואחרים טפחו לו בפניו

68אומרים אמור לנו המשיח מי הכך.

69ופיט״רוש היה עומד לפתח החצר ונגשה אליו שפחה אחת ואומרת לו והלא אתה עם יש״ו הגלילי היית עומד.

70ופיט״רוש כחש לה בפני הכל ואמר לה אשה איני יודע מה את אומרת.

71וכאשר עבר השער ראה שפחה אחרת ואמרת לעוברים שם זה האיש היה עומד עם יש״ו בנאצ״רת.

72ופעם אחרת כחש יש״ו בשבועה שלא הכירו.

73ואחר כן לזמן מעט נגשו אל פיט״רוש העומדים בחצר ויאמרו לו אתה הוא מחבורת זה הנביא שמדברך נכר שאתה מהם.

74אז התחיל לכפור ולישבע שבשום זמן לא הכירו. ומיד קרא התרנגול.

75ופיט״רוש נזכר מאשר אמר לו יש״ו שקודם קריאת הגבר יכפור בו ג׳ פעמים. ואז יצא לחוץ ובכה במרירות נפשו.

## פרק קי״ב

1ויהי בבקר כל גדולי החכמים והקדמונים לקחו עצה נגד יש״ו שמכל וכל יהרגוהו.

2וקשור הוליכוהו לבית פו״טץ פילא״ט שהיה גזבר.

3ואז כאשר ראה יודא אסכריוטא שהיה נדון התחיל לשוב בתשובה. וחזר השלשים דינרים לגדול הכהנים ולזקני העם.

4אמר אני חטאתי ששפכתי דם נקי. והם אמרו לו מה לנו אתה תראה.

5וזרק המעות במקדש והלך לו ולקח חבל אחת ותלה עצמו.

6וגדולי הכהנים כאשר לקחו המעות אמרו לא יתכן שנשים אלו המעות במקדש שדמי דם הם שנתנו בעד דמי יש״ו.

7וייועצו ויתנו אותם בעד שדה אדם יוצר חרס בעד שיגברו שם הגרים.

8ולכן נקרא אותו שדה אהל דם עד היום הזה.

26:67 והלקוהו] והכוהו EF

26:68 הכך] הכה אותך G

26:69 ופיטרוש] ופיטרו A | לפתח] כפתח A | אחת] omit G

26:71 ראה] ראהו ABEF | לעוברים] לעומדים ABEFG | עומד] omit A | בנאצרת] נזארת A, בנזארת BE

26:72 יש״ו] הישו AG, פיטרו G

26:73 שמדברך] שמדבריך A, ומדבריך EF

26:75 נפשו] omit A | במרירות] במרת B | נזכר] omit B | ופיטרוש] ופיטרו A

27:1 החכמים] הכהנים A

27:2 לבת] omit EF | פוטץ] פונץ AB, פריץ EF, פוטס G

27:3 לגדול] אל גדול EF | העם] עם G

27:7 וייועצו] ויתיעצו EF | אדם] של אדם F | חרס] omit EF | שיגברו] שיקברו ABG, שיגררו EF

⁶⁷Then they spit in his face and struck him on the back
and others slapped him in the face

⁶⁸saying: Tell us, Messiah, who struck you.

⁶⁹Peter was standing at the entrance of the courtyard and there came near
to him a maid who said to him: Were you not standing with Jesus the
Galilean.

⁷⁰Peter denied to her before all and said to her: Woman I do not know
what you are saying.

⁷¹When he passed through the gate another maid saw (him) and said to
those who were (standing) there: this man was standing with Jesus in
Nazareth.

⁷²Again he denied Jesus with an oath [saying] that he did not know him.

⁷³After a little while those who were standing in the courtyard drew near
to Peter and said to him: You are from this prophet's group; it is clear
from your speech you are one of them.

⁷⁴Then he began to deny and to swear that at no time had he known him.
Immediately the cock crowed.

⁷⁵Peter remembered what Jesus had said to him, that before the crowing
of the cock he would deny him three times. Then he went outside and
wept with bitterness of soul.

## Chapter 27

¹It came to pass in the morning all the chief sages and elders took counsel against Jesus that they should surely put him to death.

²They led him bound to the house of Pontius Pilate who was commander.

³When Judas Iscariot saw that he had been judged, he began to turn in
repentance. He returned the thirty dinars to the high priest and to the elders of the people.

⁴He said: I have sinned because I have shed innocent blood. But they
said to him: What is that to us; you see to it.

⁵He threw the coins in the temple, went and took a rope and hanged
himself.

⁶When the chief priests received the coins they said: It is not possible
for us to place these coins in the temple because they are the fruit of
blood since they were given for the blood of Jesus.

⁷So they took counsel and gave them for a field of a certain potter of
clay that they might (bury) strangers there.

⁸Therefore that field is called the tent of blood unto this day.

[MT 27:9-23

⁹אז נשלם מאמר זכריה הנביא ואומר להם אם טוב בעיניכם רבו
שכרי ואם חדלו. וישקלו שכרי שלשים כסף. ויאמר ה״ אלי
השליכו אל היוצר. וזהו מהאדם היוצר חרס
¹⁰כאשר אדוני צוה.
¹¹ויש״ו היה עומד לפני פילא״ט ושאל לו האתה הוא מלך
היהודים. ויש״ו אמר אתה אומר.
¹²וכאשר יש״ו היה רודף בעד גדולי הכהנים וזקני העם לשום
דבר שהיו אומרים עליו לא היה עונה.
¹³ופילא״ט אמר לו אינך רואה כמה עדיות יש נגדך.
¹⁴ויש״ו לא ענה אליו דבר ופילא״ט היה נפלא מזה מאד.
¹⁵וביום החג הנכבד של פסח היה מנהגם שגזבר העיר היה לתת לעם
אסור אחד מהאסורים אותו אשר ירצו.
¹⁶וביד פילא״ט היה חבוש אחד שהיה כמעט שוטה שמו ברבא״ש.
ונלקח על רצחה ושם אותו בבור.
¹⁷וכאשר נאספו אמר להם פילא״ט איזה מאלו תרצו שאניח
ברבא״ש או יש״ו שנקרא משיח.
¹⁸לפי שפילא״ט היה יודע שעל שנאת חנם נלקח.
¹⁹ובעודו יושב בכסא אשתו שלחה לו שליח לאמר אחילה אני ממך
שבשום ענין לא תאמר דבר כנגד אותו צדיק שבזאת הלילה
סבלתי ענינים רבים במראה בעדו.
²⁰וגדולי הכהנים וזקני הדת הקהילו לעם ישאלו את ברבאש
וישיש״ו ימית.
²¹ויען להם פילא״ט איזה מהם תרצו שנניח. והם אמרו ברבאש.
²²ויאמר להם פילאט א״כ מה אעשה מיש״ו הנקרא משיח. וכולם
ענו שיתלה.
²³ופילא״ט אמר להם איזו רעה עשה. והם בחוזק היו זועקים
יתלוהו יתלוהו יתלוהו.

²⁷:⁹ ABEF לא + [ואם | ABEF הבו [רבו | A לכם [להם | omit G [ואומר . . . חדלו | omit G [זכריה
[היוצר | AEF השליכהו [השליכו | omit G [ה״ אלי | EF ל׳ שקל [שלשים | EF את + [וישקלו
BEFG חרש [חרס | ABEG וזהו [וזה | EF אדם היקר אשר יקרתי מהם +
²⁷:¹² העם . . . בעד] מגדולי חעם הכהנים G
²⁷:¹³ אינך [אין אתה A
²⁷:¹⁵ העם + [אשר] | AEFG לו + [היה²] | EF שלהם [של פסח A חג [החג G
²⁷:¹⁶ ברבאש [ברבא״ש EF, שברב B, באשרב A, בראבאש [ברבא״ש G
²⁷:¹⁷ ברש A, בראבאש [ברבא״ש | A שתניחוני [שאניח | A השנים + [מאלו] EF
²⁷:¹⁸ פילאט [לפי שפילאט G
²⁷:¹⁹ BG | הצדיק [צדוק | omit G [צדיק] | EF דבר [דבר omit G | עניו [עניי | AEF, אחל [אחל G מחלה [אחילה
A הלילה] + נקרא׳ יום + A
²⁷:²⁰ [את . . . ימות | ABEF שישאלו [ישאלו | G את העם ואמרו להם [לעם | B העם [הדת
omit EF [וששישו ימות | B בארבש A, בראבאש [ברבאש | A את ישו להמית ולא בראבאש
B בארבש [ברבש | omit A (hap) [אזה . . . ברבאש
²⁷:²¹ Vs 21] omit EF | ברבאש [ברבש B
²⁷:²² omit G [פילאט] | omit A (hap. see on vs 21) [ויאמר להם פילאט
²⁷:²³ omit BEF [יתלוהו³] | A מה איזו רעה [איזו רעה

⁹Then was fulfilled the word of Zechariah the prophet:
and I said to them: if it is good in your eyes, multiply my wages, but if
(not), forbear. So they weighed for my wages thirty pieces of silver.
Then the Lord said to me: Cast it unto the potter. This is from the man
who forms clay,

¹⁰as the Lord commanded.

¹¹Jesus was standing before Pilate who asked him: Are you the king of
the Jews. Jesus said: You say it.

¹²When Jesus was harassed by the chief priests and elders of the people
in regard to some word which they spoke against him, he did not reply.

¹³Pilate said to him: Do you not see how much testimony there is against
you.

¹⁴But Jesus did not answer him a word and Pilate was exceedingly
amazed by this.

¹⁵On the day of the honored feast of Passover it was their custom for the
commander of the city to give to the people one of the prisoners whom
they wished.

¹⁶Pilate had a prisoner who was almost crazy: his name was Barabbas.
Taken in a case of murder he had placed him in the dungeon.

¹⁷When they were gathered together Pilate said to them: Which of these
do you wish that I should release, Barabbas or Jesus who is called
Messiah.

¹⁸This was because Pilate knew that due to hatred without cause he had
been taken.

¹⁹While he was sitting upon the throne his wife sent to him a messenger
saying: I implore you that in no matter should you speak a word against
this righteous man because in this night I have suffered many things in
a vision because of him.

²⁰The chief priests and the elders of the law assembled the people (that)
they might ask for Barabbas and that Jesus might die.

²¹Pilate answered them: Which of them do you wish that we should release. They said Barabbas.

²²Pilate said to them: If so what shall I do with Jesus who is called Messiah. All of them answered that he should be hung.

²³Pilate said to them: What evil has he done. Then they vigorously cried
out: let them hang him, let them hang him, let them hang him.

[MT 27:24-38]

‫²⁴ופילא'ט' וש בראותו שלא היה תקומה ולא יכול להשלים שום‬
‫דבר עמהם קודם שיקום שיקום בעד זה קטטה גדולה בעם לקח מים ורחץ‬
‫ידיו בפני העם ואמר אני נקי מהם. שמרו לכם מה תעשו.‬
‫²⁵ויענו כל העם ואמרו דמו יהיה עלינו ועל זרענו.‬
‫²⁶ואז הניח לה ברבאש ומסר להם יש'ו לקוי ומעונה שיתלוהו.‬

## ‫פרק קי''ג‬

‫²⁷אז פרשי החצר לקחו ליש'ו במשמר ויקהלו בפני קהל רב מעמים‬
‫רבים.‬
‫²⁸וילבישוהו ליש'ו בגדי משי ויעטפוהו מעיל משי ירוק.‬
‫²⁹ועשו עטרה מקוצים וישימהו על ראשו ושמו לו קנה אחת ביד‬
‫הימנית וכורעים היו מלעיגים ממנו שלום עליך מלך‬
‫היהודים.‬
‫³⁰ורוקקים לו בפניו והיו לוקחים הקנה ומכים בראשו.‬
‫³¹וכאשר הלעיגו ממנו הפשיטו ממנו המעיל והלבישוהו‬
‫מלבושו וצוו לתלותו.‬
‫³²ועודם יוצאים מהעיר פגעו באיש ששמו שמעון הכנעני.‬
‫ואנסוהו שיוליך הצליבה ר''ל השתי וערב.‬
‫³³ובאו למקים נקרא גולגוטא הוא' הר קאלוואורי‬
‫³⁴ונתנו לו יין מזוג במרה. וכאשר התחיל לשתות הרגישו ולא‬
‫ירצה לשתות.‬
‫³⁵ואחר כאשר שמוהו בצליבה חלקו בגדו בגורל.‬
‫³⁷ואחר הניחו לו על ראשו מכתב אחד שהיה אומר זה יש'ו נאזרת‬
‫מלך ישראל.‬
‫³⁸אז נתלו עמו שני גנבים האחד לימינו והאחד לשמאלו.‬

---

‫²⁷:²⁴ ולא יכול [ולא יכול A | תקומה ולא [omit A G | ובראותו פלאט [ופילאטוש בראותו AEFG | ופילאט [ופילאטוש‬
‫מדם ישו ABEF, מהדם [מהם EF | ויאמר [ואמר A | מעט + [לקח A | כל [שום EF | ולא היה יכול‬
‫G | למדו [שמרו EF‬
‫²⁷:²⁵ זרעינו [זרענו BEF | כולם [כל העם G | והם ענו [ויענו‬
‫²⁷:²⁶ ברבש A, ברבאש [ברבאש EF | להם [לה AEF‬
‫²⁷:²⁸ לישו [omit G‬
‫²⁷:²⁹ בידו [ביד G | אחד [אחת G | וישימו [ וישימו AEF, וישימוה [וישימהו B | ועשה [ועשו ABEF,‬
‫G אומרים + [ממנו G | על ידו‬
‫²⁷:³⁰ והיו רוקקים [ורוקקים A‬
‫²⁷:³¹ ויצוו [וצוו A | מלבושיו [מלבוש A | לו [²ממנו | ABEFG מאד + [¹ממנו‬
‫²⁷:³² והערב [וערב A | שילך [שיוליך ABEF | פשטו [פגעו B‬
‫²⁷:³³ קלוואריאו A, קאלבארי [קאלוואארי EF‬
‫²⁷:³⁴ רצה [ירצה ABEF‬
‫²⁷:³⁵ בגדיו [בגדו ABEFG‬
‫²⁷:³⁶ Vs 36] omit all mss‬
‫²⁷:³⁷ מנזראת [נאזרא A | זהו [זה A | EF 3 4 2 1 [על ראשו מכתב אחד‬
‫²⁷:³⁸ ואחד [והאחד A | והא' [האחד E‬

²⁴Pilate, when he saw that he had no power of resistance
and was unable to make any peace with them, before a great dispute
among the people might arise because of this, took water and washed
his hands before the people and said: I am innocent (of the blood). Be
careful what you do.
²⁵All the people answered and said: His blood will be upon us and upon
our seed.
²⁶Then he released Barabbas (to them), and delivered to them Jesus for
beating and affliction that they might hang him.
²⁷Then the horsemen of the court took Jesus under guard and came together before a great company of many people.
²⁸They clothed Jesus with silk garments and covered him with a greenish
silk robe.
²⁹They made a crown of thorns and placed it on his head and set a reed in
his right hand and were bowing down mocking him [saying]: Peace be
upon you, king of the Jews.
³⁰They spit in his face and took the reed and struck his head.
³¹When they had mocked him (much) they stripped the robe from him,
dressed him in his own clothes and gave orders to hang him.
³²As they were going out from the city they met a man whose name was
Simon the Canaanite. They compelled him to carry the gallows, that is,
"The Cross."
³³They came to a place called Gulgota, that is, Mount Calvary,
³⁴and gave him wine mixed with gall. But when he began to drink it he
perceived [what it was] and would not drink it.
³⁵Then when they placed him on the gallows they divided his garments
by lot.
³⁷Afterward, they set for him over his head a writing which said: This is
Jesus of Nazareth, the king of Israel.
³⁸Then two thieves were hung with him, one on his right and one of his
left.

‏³⁹והעוברים היו מלעיגים ממנו ומניעים ראש

‏⁴⁰ואומרים ראה אפשר חרבת מקדש האל ובעוד שלשה ימים תושיע עצמך ואם אתה בן האל רד מן הצליבה.

‏⁴¹וגדולי הכהנים וזקני העם היו מלעיגים ממנו ואומרים

‏⁴²האחרים הושיע ועצמו לא יוכל להושיע. אם מלך ישראל הוא ירד מן העץ ונאמין.

‏⁴³כי הוא נשען באל יושיעהו עתה אם ירצה שהוא אמר שהוא בן האלקים.

‏⁴⁴ואותם הדברים עצמם אמרו לו הגנבים שהיו נתלים עמו.

‏⁴⁵ולשעה ששית נעשו חשוכות בכל העולם ועמדו עד שעה תשיעית.

‏⁴⁶יש״ו צעק בקול גדול אומר בלשון הקודש אלי אלי למה עזבתני.

‏⁴⁷ואחד מהעומדים שם אמר זה קורא לאליה.

‏⁴⁸ומיד לקח אספוג ומלאהו חומץ ונתן לו לשתות.

‏⁴⁹והאחרים היו אומרים נראה אם יבא אליה ויושיעהו.

‏⁵⁰ויש״ו צעק פעם אחרת בקול גדול ושלח נשמתו לאביו.

‏⁵¹ומיד נקרע פרכת המקדש לשני קרעים מלמעלה למטה ורעשה הארץ ונשתברו האבנים.

‏⁵²והקברים נפתחו ורבים מישיני אדמת עפר קמו.

‏⁵³ויצאו מקבורתם ואחר שחיו באו בעיר הקדש ונגלו לרבים.

‏⁵⁴ושר המאה והעומדים עמו לשמור יש״ו ראו הרעשת הארץ והדברים שנעשו ויפחדו מאד ואומרים באמת זה היה בן האלוק.

‏⁵⁵והיו שם נשים רבות שהיו עומדות מרחוק מאותן אשר שמשו ליש״ו מהגליל עד כה.

‏⁵⁶ובכללן היתה מאריאה מגדלינה ומרים אם יעקב ויוסף ואם בני זבדאל.

‏⁵⁷ולעת ערב בא אדם עשיר שהיה מכרנאסיאה. שמו יוסף והיה תלמיד מיש״ו.

---

‏²⁷:³⁹ ראש [ראשם A

‏²⁷:⁴⁰ איך [אפשר A, אשר BEF | חרבת [אתה חרבת G | האל [אל F | ימים [+ תבנהו A | הצליבה [מן EFG מהצליבה

‏²⁷:⁴² האתרים הושיע [לאתרים רפא והושיע G | ונאמין [+ בו ABG

‏²⁷:⁴³ האלקים [האלים A | כי [בו ABG [to be read with vs 42; see above]

‏²⁷:⁴⁶ ישן [ישו A ולשעה תשיעי׳

‏²⁷:⁴⁷ לאליה [לאלוק EF

‏²⁷:⁴⁸ אספוג [הספוג EF

‏²⁷:⁵¹ מלמעלה [ממעלה EF

‏²⁷:⁵² עפר [העפר B

‏²⁷:⁵³ ונגלו [גלו EF | זה [שחיו E | מקבורתם [מקברוות EF

‏²⁷:⁵⁴ האלוק [האלוה AB ואמר E, AG | ואומרים [ויאמרו G | והדברים שנעשו [וכל הדברים אשר נעשו G

‏²⁷:⁵⁵ מאותן [מאותם G | כה [פה EF

‏²⁷:⁵⁷ שהיה מכרנאסיאה [מכרנאסיאה omit G | מכרנאסיאה [מכרימיסיאה A, מכרמאסי׳ EF | והיה תלמיד מישו omit A

³⁹Those who were passing by mocked him
and shook (their) heads

⁴⁰saying: See, (how) you would lay waste the temple of God and in yet
three days (build it); save yourself; if you are the Son of God come
down from the gallows.

⁴¹The chief priests and the elders of the people mocked him saying:

⁴²Others he saved; himself he cannot save. If he is the king of Israel let
him come down from the tree and we will believe.

⁴³Since he trusted in God let him save him now if he wishes, because he
said he is the Son of God.

⁴⁴The thieves who were hung with him said to him these very same
words.

⁴⁵At the sixth hour darkness came in all the world and it remained until
the ninth hour.

⁴⁶Jesus cried in a loud voice saying, in the holy language: My God, My
God, why have you forsaken me.

⁴⁷One of those standing there said: This one is calling for Elijah.

⁴⁸Immediately he took spongy-bread, filled it with vinegar and gave it to
him to drink.

⁴⁹Others were saying: We will see if Elijah will come and deliver him.

⁵⁰Jesus cried another time in a loud voice and sent his spirit to his father.

⁵¹Immediately the curtain of the temple was torn into two pieces, from
the top downwards; the earth shook and the rocks were broken.

⁵²The graves were opened and many of those asleep in the dust arose.

⁵³They came out of their graves and after (this) they entered the holy city
and were revealed to many.

⁵⁴The captain of the hundred and those standing with him watching Jesus
saw the earthquake and the things which were done and were very
afraid saying: Truly this was the Son of God.

⁵⁵There were there many women standing at a distance from among
those who served Jesus from Galilee unto that time.

⁵⁶Among them were Mary Magdalene, Mary the mother of James and
Joseph and the mother of the sons of Zebedeel.

⁵⁷At evening time a rich man from Karnasiah came. His name was Joseph and he was a disciple of Jesus.

[MT 27:58-28:8

⁵⁸והלך לפילא״ט ושאל לו הגוף מיש״ו. ופילא״ט צוה שיתנוהו לו.

⁵⁹ויוסף לקחו וכרכו בבגד משי חשיב מאד.

⁶⁰ושם אותו בקברו שהיה נחצב חדש מאבן ושם אבן גדולה על פי הקבר.

⁶²וממחרת הפסח גדולי הכהנים והפרושים באו לפילאט.

⁶³ואמרו לו אדוננו אנו מזכירים שזה השקרן היה אומר בעודו בחיים שלקץ שלשה ימים יעמוד ויחיה.

⁶⁴ולכן צוה לשמור קברו עד יום השלישי שבאולי איזה מתלמידיו יבא ויגנוב אותו. ואחר יאמרו לעם שעמד מהמות. ואם זה יעשו גדל יהיה עון האחרון מן הראשון.

⁶⁵ופילאט אמר להם בקשו שומרים שמרו היותר טוב שתוכלו.

⁶⁶והם שלמו בנין הקבר וחתמוהו והניחו שם שומרים.

## פרק קי״ד

¹וביום הראשון מהשבוע בהשכמה באו מרים מגדלינה ומרים אחרת לראות הקבר.

²ונרעשה הארץ שמלאך ה״ ירד מן השמים לקבר והפך האבן ועמד.

³ומראהו היה כשמש ובגדיו כשלג.

⁴ומפחדו נבהלו השומרים ועמדו המתים.

⁵וענה המלאך ואמר לנשים אל תפחדו שאני יודע שאתן מבקשות ליש״ו אשר נתלה.

⁶איננו כאן שכבר חי כמו שאמר. לכן בואו וראו המקום אשר עמד שם האדון.

⁷ולכו מיד ואמרו לתלמידיו שכבר עמד שם האדון. והוא יהיה לפניכם ושם תראוהו כאשר אמר לכם.

## פרק קט״ו

⁸ויצאו הנשים בפחד מהקבר בעבור ראות המלאך ובשמחה רבה לפי שהאדון עמד חי. וירוצו לאמר לתלמידיו.

---

27:58 [ושאל] לשאל B | [הגוף] את הגוף A | [מישו] omit FG

27:60 [הקבר] omit G | [פי] omit B

27:61 Vs 61] omit all mss

27:62 [הפסח] יום הפסח ABEF, + ? G

27:64 [ולכן] ולכה B | [האחרון] אחרון F

27:65 [שמרו] ושמרו ABEFG

28:2 [ה׳] השם B, האל EF | [מן השמים] מהשמים AEF | [ועמד] + עליך A

28:4 [המתים] כמתים AE

28:5 [לנשים] לאותו הנשים G

28:7 [ושם . . . לכם] כאשר אמר אשר תראוהו G | [אמר] דבר A

28:8 [רבה] גדולה G

<sup>58</sup>He came to Pilate and asked him for the body of Jesus.
Pilate commanded that they should give it to him.

<sup>59</sup>Joseph took it and wrapped it in a very fine silk garment.

<sup>60</sup>He placed him in his own tomb which had been freshly hewn from
stone and placed a large stone over the entrance of the tomb.

<sup>62</sup>On the morrow of the Passover the chief priests and the Pharisees came
to Pilate.

<sup>63</sup>They said to him: Sir, we remember that this liar said while still alive
that at the end of three days he would arise and come to life.

<sup>64</sup>Therefore command his tomb to be guarded until the third day since
perhaps one of his disciples might come and steal him. Afterwards they
might say to the people that he arose from death. If they should do this
the last perversion will be greater than the first.

<sup>65</sup>Pilate said to them: Search out guards (and) guard it as well as you can.

<sup>66</sup>So they completed the structure of the tomb, sealed it and placed a
guard there.

## Chapter 28

<sup>1</sup>On the first day of the week, early in the morning, Mary Magdalene
and the other Mary came to see the tomb.

<sup>2</sup>Then the earth shook because the angel of the Lord descended from
heaven to the tomb, overturned the stone and stood still.

<sup>3</sup>His appearance was like the sun and his garments like snow.

<sup>4</sup>From the fear of him the guards were dismayed and stood like dead
men.

<sup>5</sup>The angel answered and said to the women: Do not fear for I know that
you seek Jesus who was hung.

<sup>6</sup>He is not here for he is already alive as he said. Come, therefore, and
see the place where the Lord arose.

<sup>7</sup>Then go immediately and tell his disciples that the Lord has already
arisen there. He will be before you and there you will see him as he
told you.

<sup>8</sup>The women went out of the tomb with fear because they had seen the
angel, but with great joy because the Lord had come back to life. They
ran to tell his disciples.

[MT 28:9-20

⁹והמה הולכות ויש״ו עבר לפניהם אומר השם יושיעכן. והם קרבו אליו ויקדו לו וישתחוו לו.

¹⁰אז אמר להן יש״ו אל תפחדו אמרו לאחי שילכו לגליל ושמה יראוני.

¹¹ובעוד שהן הולכות איזה מהשומרים באו לעיר והגידו לגדולי הכהנים כל הנעשה.

¹²וייעדו לעצה עם זקני העם. ויתנו ממון רב לפרשים.

¹³ואמרו להם אתם תאמרו שבאו תלמידיו לילה וגנבוהו בעודכם ישנים.

¹⁴ואם זה יבא לאוזן פילאט אנו נדבר עמו בענין יניחכם.

¹⁵והם לקחו המטבע ואמרו כן כמו שלמדום. וזה הדבר בסוד בין היהודים עד היום הזה.

¹⁶ואחר זה כאשר השנים עשר תלמידיו הלכו לגליל נראה להם בהר ¹⁷אשר בו התפללו. וכאשר ראוהו השתחוו לו ויש מהם שנסתפקו בו. ¹⁸ויש״ו קרב אליהם ואמר להם לי נתן כל היכולת בשמים ובארץ. ¹⁹לכו אתם

²⁰ושמרו אותם לקיים כל הדברים אשר ציויתי אתכם עד עולם.

28:9 G ה׳, EF האל ]השם | A לפניהן ]לפניהם
28:10 EFG ושם ]ושמה | AEF להם ]להן
28:11 G אשר נעשה ]הנעשה | B לכהני הגדולים ]לגדולי הכהנים | G בא ]באו | G אחד ]איזה
28:12 G וייעצו מה לעשות ]וייעדו . . . העם | G וייעצו AE, יועדו ]וייעדו
28:13 F הלילה ]לילה | G מתלמידיו ]תלמידיו
28:14 G הו׳ + ]בענין
28:15 omit BG הזה ]זה | A ואז ]וזה | F שלמדים A, שלמדים ]שלמדום
28:18 G, omit H אליהם ]להם | H להם ]אליהם | A קרא ]קרב
28:20 AB ולמדו ]ושמרו

⁹As they were going Jesus passed before them saying:
May the Name deliver you. They came near to him and bowed down to
him and worshipped him.

¹⁰Then Jesus said to them: Do not be afraid; tell my brothers that they
should go to Galilee and there they will see me.

¹¹While they were going some of the guards entered the city and de-
clared to the chief priests all that had happened.

¹²They came together for counsel with the elders of the people. Then
they gave much money to the horsemen

¹³and said to them: Say that his disciples came by night and stole him
while you were sleeping.

¹⁴If this should come to the ears of Pilate we will tell him that he should
leave you alone.

¹⁵They took the money and said thus as they instructed them. This is the
word [held] in secret among the Jews unto this day.

¹⁶After this when his twelve disciples came to Galilee he appeared to
them in the mountain where they had prayed.

¹⁷When they saw him they worshipped him, but there were some of them
who doubted him.

¹⁸Jesus drew near to them and said to them: To me has been given all
power in heaven and earth.

¹⁹Go

²⁰and (teach) them to carry out all the things which I have commanded
you forever.

# Part Two

# Analysis
# and
# Commentary

Part two is devoted to a discussion of the Hebrew Matthew contained in Shem-Tob's *Even Bohan*. In this part we seek first to determine the place of Shem-Tob's Matthew within the Hebrew Matthean tradition spoken of by Papias and other early Gentile Christian writers and alluded to or quoted by early Jewish and anti-Christian authors. The conclusion will be that a primitive form of the Hebrew Matthew contained in the *Even Bohan* was known to Jews and perhaps Jewish Christians in the early medieval period, but not to Gentile Christians. Also in this part a profile is given of the Hebrew Matthew in Shem-Tob in order to demonstrate that an old substratum to the Hebrew represents composition, not translation, and to clarify the relationship between the old substratum and the canonical Greek text.

# The Place of
# Shem-Tob's Matthew
# within the
# Hebrew-Matthean Tradition

## Papias and Other Early Gentile Christian Writers

Papias (ca. 60-130 CE), bishop of Hierapolis in Asia Minor, wrote early in the second century that "Matthew collected the oracles in the Hebrew language, and each interpreted them as best he could" (Ματθαῖος μὲν οὖν Ἑβραΐδι διαλέκτῳ τὰ λόγια συνετάξατο, ἡρμήνευσεν δ' αὐτὰ ὡς ἦν δυνατὸς ἕκαστος).[1] Since the time of Widmanstadt,[2] it has

---

[1]Eusebius *H.E.* 3.39.16. The text and translation are taken from *The Ecclesiastical History*, ed. and trans. Kirsopp Lake and J. E. L. Oulton, 2 vols., Loeb Classical Library (Cambridge MA: Harvard University Press, 1926–1932) 1:296-97. Kürzinger's attempt to prove that Papias was speaking only of Matthew's style of writing, not the language in which he wrote, is not totally convincing. See Josef Kürzinger, "Das Papiaszeugnis und die Erstgestalt des Matthäusevangeliums," *Biblische Zeitschrift* 4 (1960): 19-38; "Irenäus und sein Zeugnis zur Sprache des Matthäusevangeliums," *NTS* 10 (1963): 108-15; "Die Aussage des Papias von Hierapolis zur literarischen Form des Markusevangeliums," *Biblische Zeitschrift* 21 (1977): 245-64; "Papias von Hierapolis: Zu Titel und Art Seines Werkes," *Biblische Zeitschrift* 23 (1979): 172-86; *Papias von Hierapolis und die Evangelien des Neuen Testaments* (Regensburg: Friedrich Pustet, 1983). Kürzinger's argument, based on the assumption that Papias was using ancient rhetorical terminology, may ascribe more erudition to Papias than he actually had. Eusebius said that it is obvious that Papias was a man of "very little intelligence" (Eusebius *H.E.* 3.39.13). It is also possible that Papias is quoting the "Presbyter" in regard to Matthew as he is in regard to Mark. The rhetorical abilities of the Presbyter are totally unknown. Papias, on the other hand, may not have been referring to the Hebrew Matthean tradition reflected by Shem-Tob's treatise, but to some apocryphal Semitic Gospel.

[2]Johann Albert Widmanstadt, *Liber Sacrosancti Evangelii de Jesu Christo Domino & Deo Nostro . . . characteribus & lingua Syra, Jesu Christo vernacula, Divino ipsius ore consecrata & a Joh. Evangelista Hebraica dicta, Scriptorio Prelo diligenter Expressa* (Wien:

become commonplace to suppose that by "Hebrew" Papias meant "Aramaic." This supposition was due primarily to the belief that Hebrew in the days of Jesus was no longer in use in Palestine but had been replaced by Aramaic. The subsequent discovery of the Dead Sea Scrolls, many of which are Hebrew compositions, as well as of other Hebrew documents from Palestine from the general time period of Jesus, now show Hebrew to have been alive and well in the first century.[3] There is, therefore, no reason to assume a priori that Papias meant Aramaic.

Whether Papias's "oracles" is a reference to our canonical Matthew or to some other document has been vigorously debated. Kümmel, who surveys the issue, concludes that Papias meant our canonical Matthew but believes that Papias had never actually seen Matthew in a Semitic language and in fact was wrong about the whole matter. "We must concede," he writes, "that the report that Mt was written by Matthew 'in the Hebrew language' is utterly false, however it may have arisen."[4] Whatever the case, the early church writings after the time of Papias are replete with references to an *original Hebrew* Matthew. The following are typical cases.

### Irenaeus, *Adv. Haer.* 3.1.1

Matthew also issued a written Gospel among the Hebrews in their own dialect while Peter and Paul were preaching at Rome and laying the foundations of the Church.[5]

---

M. Cymbermann, 1555). This reference was taken from Jean Carmignac, "Hebrew Translations of the Lord's Prayer: An Historical Survey," in *Biblical and Near Eastern Studies. Essays in Honor of William Sanford LaSor,* ed. Gary A. Tuttle (Grand Rapids MI: Eerdmans, 1978) 71n5.

[3]For an up-to-date discussion of the languages of Palestine see especially Joseph A. Fitzmyer, *A Wandering Aramean: Collected Aramaic Essays* (Missoula MT: Scholars Press, 1979) 29-56. See also Pinchas Lapide, "Insights from Qumran into the Language of Jesus," *Revue de Qumran* 32 (1975): 483-501; James Barr, "Which Language Did Jesus Speak?—Some Remarks of a Semitist," *BJRL* 53 (1970): 9-29; W. Chomsky, "What Was the Jewish Vernacular During the Second Commonwealth?" *JQR* 42 (1951-1952): 193-212; J. A. Emerton, "Did Jesus Speak Hebrew?" *JTS* 12 (1961): 189-202; "The Problem of Vernacular Hebrew in the First Century A.D. and the Language of Jesus," *JTS* 24 (1973): 1-23; Harris Birkeland, *The Language of Jesus* (Oslo: I. Kommisjon Hos Jacob Dybwad, 1954); Jean Carmignac, "Studies in the Hebrew Background of the Synoptic Gospels," *ASTI* 7 (1970): 64-93.

[4]W. G. Kümmel, *Introduction to the New Testament,* rev. ed., trans. Howard Clark Kee (Nashville: Abingdon, 1975) 49, 120-21.

[5]Translation taken from *The Ante-Nicene Fathers,* ed. A. Roberts and J. Donaldson (reprint: Grand Rapids MI: Eerdmans, 1985) 1:414.

### Origen as quoted by Eusebius, *H.E.* 6.25.4

As having learnt by tradition concerning the four Gospels, which alone are unquestionable in the Church of God under heaven, that first was written that according to Matthew, who was once a tax collector but afterwards an apostle of Jesus Christ, who published it for those who from Judaism came to believe, composed as it was in the Hebrew language.[6]

### Eusebius, *H.E.* 3.24.6

Matthew had first preached to Hebrews, and when he was on the point of going to others he transmitted in writing in his native language the Gospel according to himself, and thus supplied by writing the lack of his own presence to those from whom he was sent.[7]

There are other such references but these are sufficient to demonstrate an early belief in the Hebrew originality of Matthew.

In addition to such statements, there are others that refer either to Matthew or to an apocryphal gospel in Hebrew sometimes identified or confused with Matthew. Epiphanius (ca. 315-403 CE), bishop of Salamis, in his *Panarion* (30.13.1-30.22.4; also cited as *Haereses*) speaks of a gospel used by the Ebionites. Elsewhere he says the Ebionites use the Gospel of Matthew and call it "According to the Hebrews" (κατὰ Ἑβραίους; *Panarion* 30.3.7). Epiphanius explains this as an appropriate name since Matthew issued his gospel in Hebrew and with Hebrew letters (Ἑβραϊστὶ καὶ Ἑβραϊκοῖς γράμμασιν; *Panarion* 30.3.7). In another context he again mentions the Gospel of Matthew in Hebrew and says it is preserved in Hebrew letters (*Panarion* 29.9.4). Epiphanius further says it is "incomplete, corrupt, and mutilated" (*Panarion* 30.13.2).

Epiphanius also gives seven quotations from this gospel in his *Panarion* (30.13.2-3, 30.13.4-5, 30.13.6, 30.13.7-8, 30.14.5, 30.16.5, 30.22.4). A recent study of these quotations shows that they do not come from Matthew but from a harmonized account made primarily from the canonical gospels and based on the Greek text of these gospels.[8] Most important for our purposes is the fact that they do not touch base with Shem-Tob's Hebrew Matthew. Whatever the origin of the document used by the Ebionites, it has no particular relationship to our Hebrew Matthew.

---

[6]Translation from the LCL edition, 2:75.

[7]Translation from the LCL edition, 1:251.

[8]See Daniel A. Bertrand, "L'évangile des ébionites: une harmonie évangélique antérieure au Diatessaron," *NTS* 26 (1980): 548-63.

Jerome makes reference to a Hebrew Matthew and to a Gospel according to the Hebrews in such a way as to be unclear as to whether these are one and the same. In *Epist.* 20.5 he writes: "Finally, Matthew, who wrote the Gospel in the Hebrew language, put it in the following way: Osianna barrama, which means ossana in excelsis." The reference is to Matt 21:9 which in the form quoted by Jerome has no particular relationship to the text of Shem-Tob. In *Epist.* 120.8, Jerome writes: "But in the gospel which is written in Hebrew letters we read that not the curtain of the temple but the upper threshold of the temple, being of marvelous size, fell down." It is unclear whether this is the same gospel as the one mentioned above; but, if so, this form of the text has no parallel in Matthew in either the Greek text or that of Shem-Tob. Again, *in Matth.* 12.13, Jerome writes: "In the Gospel which the Nazoraeans and the Ebionites use which we translated recently from Hebrew to Greek and which is called the authentic text of Matthew by a good many, it is written that the man with the withered hand is a mason, praying for help with words of this kind: 'I was a mason earning my living with my hands, I pray you, Jesus, to restore my health lest I must beg shamefully for my food.' " There is no exact parallel to this in Matthew in either the Greek or Hebrew texts. In *adv. Pelag.* 3.2 Jerome writes: "In the Gospel according to the Hebrews which was written in the Chaldaic and Syriac language but with Hebrew letters, and is used up to the present day by the Nazoraeans, I mean that according to the Apostles, or, as many maintain, according to Matthew. . . . "[9] In the quotations that follow there is no particular relationship to Shem-Tob.

There are many other such references in Jerome and elsewhere but further citation of these would be of little benefit. The fact is that the quotations from the so-called Hebrew Matthew, the Gospel of the Hebrews, the Gospel of the Nazoraeans, the Gospel of the Ebionites, or the Gospel of the Twelve Apostles[10] mentioned in early church writings, yield little evi-

---

[9]The above quotations from Epiphanius and Jerome have been taken from A. F. J. Klijn and G. J. Reinink, *Patristic Evidence for Jewish-Christian Sects* (Leiden: Brill, 1973).

[10]For a discussion of these see Edgar Hennecke, *The New Testament Apocrypha,* ed. W. Schneemelcher, trans. R. McL. Wilson (Philadelphia: Westminster, 1959) 1:118-65. In addition to the bibiliography already cited above, see A. S. Barnes, "The Gospel according to the Hebrews," *JTS* 6 (1905): 356-71; M. E. Boismard, "Évangile des ébionites et problème synoptique (Mc, I, 2-6 ET Par.)," *Revue Biblique* 73 (1966): 321-52; Oscar Cullmann, "Ebionitenevangelium," *RGG,* Zweiter Band, 298; Jean Daniélou, *The Theology of Jewish Christianity,* trans. J. A. Baker (London: Darton, Longman, and Todd,

dence of any relationship to Shem-Tob's Matthew. This is true with two possible exceptions:

### 1. Jerome *in Matth.* 2.5

And they said to him: "In Bethlehem of Juda." Here there is an error on the part of the copyist: for we believe that the evangelist in his first edition wrote, as we read in the original Hebrew: "Juda" and not "Judea" (Iudae, non Iudeae).[11]

This corresponds to the reading of Shem-Tob (according to mss BDEFG) at Matt 2:5, יודא.

### 2. Jerome *in Esaiam* 11.2

And it came to pass, when the Lord had come up from the water, the entire

---

1964) 55-64; Martin Dibelius, *Geschichte der urchristlichen Literatur* (Berlin/Leipzig: Walter de Gruyter, 1926); E. Fabbri, "El bautismo de Jesús en el Evangelio de los Hebreas y en de los Ebionitas," *Revista de Teologia* 6 (1956): 36-55; Joseph A. Fitzmyer, "The Qumran Scrolls, the Ebionites, and Their Literature," *TS* 16 (1955): 335-72 (reprinted in Fitzmyer's *Essays on the Semitic Background of the New Testament* [Missoula MT: Scholars Press, 1974] 435-80); Rudolf Handmann, *Das Hebräer-Evangelium. Ein Beitrag zur geschichte und Kritik des hebräischen Matthäus* (Leipzig: J. C. Hinrichs, 1888); Adolf Harnack, *Geschichte der altchristlichen Literatur bis Eusebius*, 2nd ed. (Leipzig: J. C. Hinrichs, 1958) 205-209; Harris Hirschberg, "Simon Bariona and the Ebionites," *JBL* 61 (1942) 171-91; M. R. James, *The Apocryphal New Testament* (Oxford: Clarendon Press, 1924) 8-10; A. F. J. Klijn, "The Question of the Rich Young Man in a Jewish-Christian Gospel," *Novum Testamentum* 8 (1966): 149-55; M. J. Lagrange, "L'Évangile selon les Hébreux," *Revue Biblique* 31 (1922): 161-81, 321-49; Adolf Hilgenfeld, *Evangeliorum secundum Hebraeos,* etc. (Lipsiae: T. O. Weigel, 1866, 1884); Allan Menzies, "Gospel according to the Hebrews," in *A Dictionary of the Bible,* ed. James Hastings (Edinburgh: T. & T. Clark, 1904) 5:338-43; W. G. Most, "Gospel of the Ebionites," in *Encyclopedic Dictionary of Religion,* ed. P. K. Meagher et al. (Washington DC: Corpus Publications, 1979) A-E:215; J. Munck, "Jewish Christianity in Post Apostolic Times," *NTS* 6 (1959-1960): 103-16; Johannes Quasten, *Patrology* (Utrecht-Antwerp: Spectrum, 1964) 1:113-14; A. Schmidtke, *Neue Fragmente zu den judenchristlichen Evangelien,* TU 37 (Leipzig, 1911); "Zum Hebräerevangelium," *ZNW* 35 (1936): 24-44; H. J. Schoeps, *Theologie und Geschichte des Judenchristentums* (Tübingen: Mohr, 1949); *Jewish Christianity* (Philadelphia: Fortress, 1969); G. Strecker, *Das Judenchristentum in den Pseudoklementinen,* TU 70 (1958) D:117-36; J. L. Teicher, "The Dead Sea Scrolls—Documents of the Jewish-Christian Sect of Ebionites," *JJS* 2 (1951): 67-99; H. Waitz, "Das Evangelium des zwölf Apostel," *ZNW* 14 (1913): 48ff.; "Neue Untersuchungen über die sogenannten judenchristlichen Evangelien," *ZNW* 36 (1937): 60-81; L. St. Alban Wells, "Gospels (Apocrypha)," in *Encyclopedia of Religion and Ethics,* ed. James Hastings (New York: Scribner's, 1928) 5:347-48; B. F. Westcott, *An Introduction to the Study of the Gospels* (London: Macmillan, 1895) 471-73; Theodor von Zahn, *Geschichte des Neutestamentlichen Kanons* (Erlangen: A. Deichert, 1888-1892).

[11]Klijn and Reinink, *Patristic Evidence,* 214-15.

fountain of the Holy Spirit descended and *rested* upon him (et requievit super eum) and said to him.[12]

This reference is to Matt 3:16, where the word "rested," contrary to the Greek ἐϱχόμενον, agrees with Shem-Tob' וישרתה "and dwelt" and Sy[s.c] וקוית "and abode."

The question is, do these minor readings establish a relationship between Shem-Tob's Matthew and the Hebrew Matthew or apocryphal Hebrew gospels referred to in early Gentile Christian literature? It seems they do not. The overlaps are too few and insignificant to establish such a relationship. The evidence strongly suggests that none of the gospels referred to in early Gentile Christian literature relates in any particular way to the Hebrew Matthew in Shem-Tob. This text stands apart from all others.

## Du Tillet, Münster,
## and Allusions to and Quotations from Matthew
## in Early Jewish and Anti-Christian Writings

Although the Hebrew Matthew of Shem-Tob is the earliest complete Hebrew text of the Gospel known, earlier Jewish and anti-Christian writings quote Matthew in Hebrew suggesting the possibility of an earlier date for a Hebrew text than the fourteenth century. Four of the most important of these writings to which we will refer are: (1) the Book of Nestor (perhaps between the sixth and ninth centuries);[13] (2) the Milhamot HaShem by Jacob ben Reuben (1170);[14] (3) Sepher Joseph Hamekane by Rabbi Joseph ben Nathan Official (thirteenth century);[15] and (4) the Nizzahon Ve-

---

[12]Taken from Edward Byron Nicholson, *The Gospel according to the Hebrews* (London: C. Kegan Paul, 1879) 43.

[13]This is according to Pinchas E. Lapide, *Hebrew in the Church*, trans. E. F. Rhodes (Grand Rapids MI: Eerdmans, 1984) 23. The text may be found in J. D. Eisenstein, ישראל (אוצר ויכוחים), 1969) 310-15. The editor there (310) dates it in the ninth century.

[14]ישראל, 1963) viii. מוסד הרב קוק) יהודה רוזנטאל, יעקב בן ראובן. מלחמות השם. See also Judah Rosenthal, תרגום של הבשורה על-פי מתי ליעקב בן ראובן, *Tarbiz* 32 (1962): 48-66.

[15]Judah Rosenthal, ספר יוסף המקנא (Jerusalem, 1970) 17. Ms. Or. #53 of the Biblioteca Nationale Centrale in Rome includes material quite close to the Paris manuscript of Sepher Joseph Hamekane. See E. E. Urback, "Études sur la littérature polémique au moyen-âge," *Revue des études juives* C (1935): 49-77. Judah Rosenthal published the material on the gospels in Ms. Or. Rome #53 in בקורת יהודית של הברית החדשה מן המאה הי"ב in *Studies in Jewish Bibliography, History, and Literature in Honor of I. Edward Kiev*, ed. Charles Berlin (New York: KTAV, 1971) 123-39.

tus (latter part of the thirteenth century).[16] A comparison of the quotations from Matthew in these writings with the text of Shem-Tob reveals an occasional unique textual link between them. Examples of this will be given below. For now it may be stated with some certainty that at least some portions of the Hebrew Matthew contained in Shem-Tob's *Even Bohan* predate the fourteenth century, being reflected sporadically in these earlier anti-Christian writings.

Considerable confusion exists between the Hebrew Matthew contained in Shem-Tob's *Even Bohan* and the Hebrew versions of Matthew published by Sebastian Münster and Jean du Tillet. Münster's versions appeared in 1537 under the title תורת המשיח (The Torah of the Messiah).[17] Published in a folio volume, it was dedicated to King Henry VIII of England. In the letter of dedication Münster reported he had received the Hebrew Matthew from the Jews in defective form with many lacunae and had, from necessity, restored what was lacking in the manuscript. Münster failed, however, to mark the passages he had restored so that now, unfortunately, his work is of limited value.

Du Tillet's version of Matthew in Hebrew appeared in print in 1555. Accompanied by the Latin translation of Jean Mercier, it was published in Paris by the firm of Martin Le Jeune. The letter of dedication to the Cardinal of Lorraine, Charles de Guise, explains that the basis for the text is a manuscript that du Tillet found among the Jews in Italy in 1553. The manuscript now resides in the Bibliothèque Nationale in Paris catalogued under Hebrew Mss. No. 132.[18]

As early as 1690 Richard Simon mistakenly identified the text of Matthew in Shem-Tob with the versions of Münster and du Tillet.[19] This confusion has persisted since the time of Simon. In 1879 Adolf Herbst issued a new printing of du Tillet's text accompanied by an introduction and vari-

---

[16]David Berger, *The Jewish-Christian Debate in the High Middle Ages* (Philadelphia: Jewish Publication Society of America, 1979) 33.

[17]Sebastian Münster, *Evangelium secundum Matthaeum in lingua Hebraica, cum versione latina atque succinctis annotationibus* (Basiliae, 1537).

[18]For more information on this version, including my assessment of it, see George Howard, ''The Textual Nature of an Old Hebrew Version of Matthew,'' *JBL* 105 (1986): 49-63. For an English translation see Hugh J. Schonfield, *An Old Hebrew Text of St. Matthew's Gospel* (Edinburgh: T. & T. Clark, 1927).

[19]Richard Simon, *Histoire Critique des Versions du Nouveau Testament* (Rotterdam: R. Leers, 1690) 231.

ants from Münster's text in a volume entitled *Des Schemtob ben Schaphrut hebraeische Übersetzung des Evangeliums Matthaei nach den Drucken des S. Münster und J. du Tillet-Mercier*.[20] The title gives away the author's belief that the texts of Münster and du Tillet are basically reproductions of Shem-Tob's Hebrew Matthew. Herbst also stated his conviction that the source for the Hebrew text was the Latin Vulgate.[21] His conclusions were not drawn from his own extensive research into the textual nature of the Hebrew but from earlier scholars whom he cited at length. He excused himself from making an extensive study into the variants because of his lack of materials and opportunity for doing so.[22] As late as 1967 Herbst's confusion of these texts was followed by Matthew Black who says in regard to du Tillet's version that "the author of the Hebrew Matthew was probably a certain Shem-Tob ben Shaprut, a famous Jewish polemical writer who flourished in Spain in the fourteenth century."[23]

The present edition of Shem-Tob's Hebrew Matthew should forever dispel any belief in its identity with the texts of Münster and du Tillet. Shem-Tob's independent nature was, of course, already proven in 1929 by Alexander Marx in his comparison of texts in a few passages.[24] A comparison now of all the texts will support his previous conclusion. An extensive comparison, however, will reveal something in addition: despite their vast differences in vocabulary and style, a large number of unique or almost

---

[20]Göttingen: Dieterichsche Verlagsbuchhandlung, 1879.

[21]Ibid., 16.

[22]"Die Quelle der Übersetzung ist, wie schon einige theologische Einleitungen bemerkt haben, die Vulgata. Es ist mire nicht möglich, mich auf eine genauere Durchforschung der Varianten einzulassen, welche die von mir edierte Übersetzung darbietet. Einmal nicht, well mir die nöthingen Hülfsmittel oder doch die Musse und Gelegenheit sie aufzusuchen und zu benutzen fehlt, sodann nicht, weil eine erschöpfende Behandlung des Gegenstandes zu umfänglich werden würde. Ich beschränke mich daher auf einige wenige Bemerkungen, welche irgend welche Ansprüche nicht machen." Ibid., 16.

[23]Matthew Black, *An Aramaic Approach to the Gospels and Acts*, 3rd ed. (Oxford: Clarendon Press, 1967) 295. Cf. Robert L. Lindsey, *A Hebrew Translation of the Gospel of Mark* (Jerusalem: Dugith Publishers, n.d.) 67, who identifies S. Münster's edition as a version of "Ibn Shaprut's translation."

[24]Marx, "The Polemical Manuscripts in the Library of the Jewish Theological Seminary of America," 270-73. Cf. Lapide, *Hebrew in the Church*, 55: "And yet with even the most superficial comparison of the two works the radical differences between their vocabulary, style, and diction would have demonstrated the impossibility of a common origin."

unique readings exists between Shem-Tob and du Tillet (and occasionally Münster). These are sufficiently important to justify the following sampling of passages.[25]

## MATT 2:12

| | |
|---|---|
| Greek | VOID |
| Shem-Tob | מהמלאך by the angel |
| du Tillet | המלאך the angel |
| Protev. Jocobi | ὑπὸ τοῦ ἀγγέλου by the angel |
| Geo[B] | ab angelo |

## MATT 2:22

| | |
|---|---|
| Greek | εἰς τὰ μέρη τῆς Γαλιλαίας into the region of Galilee |
| Shem-Tob | אל ארץ הגלגל unto the land of Gilgal |
| du Tillet | אל ארץ הגליל unto the land of Galilee |
| Münster | אל ארץ גליל unto the land of Galilee |

## MATT 3:11

| | |
|---|---|
| Greek | αὐτὸς ὑμᾶς Βαπτίσει ἐν πνεύματι ἁγίῳ καὶ πυρί<br>he will baptize you with the Holy Spirit and fire |
| Shem-Tob | והוא יטביל אתכם באש רוח הקדוש<br>he will baptize you with the fire of the Holy Spirit |
| du Tillet | והוא יטבל אתכם באש ריח הקדש<br>he will baptize you with the fire of the Holy Spirit |

## MATT 6:16

| | |
|---|---|
| Greek | ἀπέχουσιν τὸν μισθὸν αὐτῶν<br>they have received their reward |
| Shem-Tob | שכבר קבלו שכרם<br>they have already received their reward |
| du Tillet | כבר קבלו שכרם<br>they have already received their reward |

---

[25]For Münster I have relied on the apparatus in Herbst's edition of du Tillet.

**MATT 8:21**

| | |
|---|---|
| Greek | ἕτερος δὲ τῶν μαθητῶν αὐτοῦ another of his disciples |
| Shem-Tob | ואחד מתלמידיו one of his disciples |
| du Tillet/ Münster Joseph/ Ms Or Rome #53 | ואחד מתלמידיו one of his disciples |

**MATT 9:2**

| | |
|---|---|
| Greek | θάρσει τέκνον courage child |
| Shem-Tob | תתחזק בני courage my son |
| du Tillet/ Münster | בטח בני trust my son |

**MATT 10:2-3**

| | |
|---|---|
| Greek | James and John . . . Philip and Bartholomew |
| Shem-Tob | Philip and Bartholomew . . . James and John |
| du Tillet/ Münster | Philip and Bartholomew . . . James and John |

**MATT 10:5**

| | |
|---|---|
| Greek | καὶ εἰς πόλιν Σαμαρειτῶν μὴ εἰσέλθητε<br>and do not enter into the city of the Samaritans |
| Shem-Tob | ובערי השמרונים אל תבואו<br>and do not enter into the cities of the Samaritans |
| du Tillet/ Münster | ואל ערי השמרונים לא תבואו<br>and do not enter into the cities of the Samaritans |

**MATT 14:21**

| | |
|---|---|
| Greek | οἱ δὲ ἐσθίοντες ἦσαν ἄνδρες ὡσεὶ πεντακισχίλιοι<br>those who ate were about 5,000 men |
| Shem-Tob | ויהי מספר האוכלים חמשת אלפים אנשים<br>the number of those who ate was 5,000 men |
| du Tillet/ Münster | ומספר האוכלים היה חמשת אלפי איש<br>the number of those who ate was 5,000 men |

Such agreements can hardly be the result of coincidence. This list of readings, which could easily be expanded to include scores of other examples, establishes a textual link between Shem-Tob, du Tillet, and occasionally Münster. The situation suggests that the texts of du Tillet and Münster rest on an earlier literary Hebrew tradition, reflected to some degree by Shem-Tob. Generally speaking, however, these texts as a whole have undergone extensive modification and revision away from the older base primarily in two ways: (1) stylistic modification and (2) revision designed to bring the Hebrew into closer harmony with the current Greek and Latin texts. Most stylistic modification consists of improvements in grammar and the substitution of synonymous words and phrases. Revisions designed to bring the Hebrew into closer harmony with the Greek and Latin were apparently for the purpose of establishing a common textual base for discussion and debate between Jews and Christians.

These changes are best understood when they are placed in a chronological sequence beginning with Hebrew quotations from Matthew in early Jewish and anti-Christian writings, continuing through Shem-Tob, and ending with readings from du Tillet. When these texts are placed together in this order a gradual evolution in the Hebrew tradition becomes evident including both stylistic changes and changes that bring the Hebrew into closer harmony with the current Greek and Latin. Logic would suggest that each successive stage in the chronological sequence would produce a text closer to the Greek and Latin and further from the dissident primitive Hebrew. Although this is generally true, the stages of development do not always arrange themselves quite so neatly, thus indicating that individual manuscripts of our documents are not themselves related directly to each other but rather reflect a complicated literary Hebrew tradition. The following examples are typical cases. In each instance two things will be evident: (1) a textual relationship running throughout all or part of the Hebrew tradition; and (2) a textual evolution (generally based on chronological sequence of documents) in the direction of the Greek/Latin tradition.[26]

---

[26]Some clarification is needed at this point. Although these examples are typical and represent a sampling of a larger whole, it is not the case that each Hebrew quotation from Matthew in medieval Jewish documents shows a relationship to the Shem-Tob Matthean tradition. In many instances the quotations appear to be ad hoc translations of the Greek or Latin texts freshly prepared for the occasion. It is in fact the tendency to translate directly from the Greek or Latin that eventually contaminated the primitive Hebrew Matthean tradition when it too was subjected to the influence of the canonical text through the process of revision.

### Sequential Evolution in the Literary Hebrew Tradition

MATT 3:5

| Greek ( = Vg) | καὶ πᾶσα ἡ περίχωρος τοῦ ᾿Ιορδάνου<br>and all the region about the Jordan |
| Joseph | וממלכות על הירדן<br>and the kingdom by the Jordan |
| Ms Or Rome #53[27] | וכל הממלכות עד הירדן<br>and all the kingdom unto the Jordan |
| Nizzahon Vetus #160 | וכל המלכות עד הירדן<br>and all the kingdom unto the Jordan |
| Shem-Tob | ומכל המלכות סביבות הירדן<br>and from all the kingdom about the Jordan |
| du Tillet | וכל מחוז הירדן<br>and all the district of the Jordan |

The unusual textual link running throughout the Hebrew tradition (with
the exception of du Tillet) is the reading of הממלכות/ממלכות in Joseph and
Ms Or Rome # 53 and המלכות in Nizzahon Vetus and Shem-Tob. Modification toward the Greek and Latin appears in the reading of וכל or ומכל
in Ms Or Rome #53, Nizzahon Vetus, Shem-Tob, and du Tillet in agreement with πᾶσα. Shem-Tob further reads סביבות in correspondence with
περίχωρος. Finally, du Tillet abandoning the unique מלכות/ממלכות and
reading the Medieval מחוז ( = περίχωρος) converges with the Greek
and Latin.

MATT 4:1

| Greek ( = Vg) | τότε ὁ ᾿Ιησοῦς ἀνήχθη εἰς τὴν ἔρημον ὑπὸ<br>τοῦ πνεύματος περιπασθῆναι ὑπὸ τοῦ διαβόλου<br>then Jesus was led up into the wilderness<br>by the Spirit to be tempted by the devil |
| Nestor | ישו היה בורח מן השטן<br>Jesus was fleeing from Satan |
| ben Reuben | אז נוהג אל המדבר ברוח שטן להתנסות<br>then he was led unto the wilderness<br>by the spirit of Satan to be tempted |

---

[27]See n. 15 above.

| Nizzahon Vetus #162 | שהובא ישו במדבר וניסהו השטן<br>Jesus was led into the wilderness<br>that Satan might tempt him |
|---|---|
| Shem-Tob | אז לוקח ישו ברוח הקדוש למדבר להתנסות מהשטן<br>then Jesus was taken by the Holy Spirit<br>to the wilderness to be tempted by Satan |
| du Tillet | אז הובא ישו במדבר יהודה על ידי רוח למען ינסה מהשטן<br>then Jesus was led into the wilderness of Judea<br>by the Spirit to be tempted by Satan |

An element of continuity in the Hebrew tradition is the reading of "Satan" rather than "devil." This agrees with the parallel in Mark 1:13 and may represent an early harmonistic tendency in the Hebrew or a primitive form in the gospel tradition reflected by these two independent compositions. Another element of continuity in the Hebrew is the peculiar reading of בורח ("fleeing") in Nestor and the visually similar ברוח ("by the Spirit") in ben Reuben and Shem-Tob. The difference represents only a metathesis of letters that brings the latter two into harmony with the Greek ὑπὸ τοῦ πνεύματος. The similarity of Nestor's reading with the theoretical Hebrew substratum to the Greek, reflected by ben Reuben and Shem-Tob, suggests the existence of variant forms based on a visual similarity of letters in the earliest period of the synoptic tradition. Revision toward the Greek and Latin is evidenced by various elements in the Hebrew. אז in ben Reuben, Shem-Tob, and du Tillet corresponds to τότε. All Hebrew texts except Nestor have a correspondent for ἀνήχθη: ניהג, לוקח, and הובא. All Hebrew texts except Nestor have correspondents for πειρασθῆναι and εἰς τὴν ἔρημον by reading some form of נסה ("to tempt") and מדבר ("wilderness"). The revisions, however, are gradual. After Nestor, ben Reuben is farthest from the Greek and Latin by lacking "Jesus," and in reading "by the spirit of Satan." Nizzahon Vetus is next in distance by lacking "by the Spirit," and by reading the active "Satan tempted him." Although Shem-Tob and du Tillet are close to the Greek and Latin, the former reads "Holy" and the latter "Judah" against the canonical text. Du Tillet is slightly the closer of the two by containing the order "wilderness . . . Spirit" in agreement with the Greek and Latin against Shem-Tob's "Spirit . . . wilderness."

MATT 5:17-18a

| | |
|---|---|
| Greek ( = Vg) | μὴ νομίσητε ὅτε ἦλθον καταλῦσαι τὸν νόμον ἢ τοὺς προφήτας· οὐκ ἦλθον καταλῦσαι ἀλλὰ πληρῶσαι. ἀμὴν γὰρ λέγω ὑμῖν<br>Think not that I have come to abolish the law and the prophets; I have come not to abolish them but to fulfil them. For, truly, I say to you |
| b. Shabb. 116 | אנא לא למיפחת מן אורייתא דמשה אתיתי<br>ולא לאוספו על אורייתא דמשה אתיתי<br>I am not come to take away from the Law of Moses and I am not come to add to the Law of Moses. |
| Nestor | אני לא באתי לסתור ולא להחסיר דבר מתורת משה<br>והנביאים כי אם באתי להשלים בדברי אמת<br>I have not come to cancel or to subtract from the Law of Moses and the prophets but I have come to fulfil the words of truth. |
| Ms. Or Rome #53 | אל תחשבו שבאתי לעקור התורה והנביאים לא באתי<br>כ״א לקיים אמת. אני אומר לכם<br>Do not think that I have come to abolish the law and the prophets; I have not come except to fulfil truth. I say to you |
| Nizzahon Vetus # 157 | לא באתי לחסור על תורת משה<br>I have not come to diminish the Law of Moses |
| Nizzahon Vetus #71 | לא באתי לבטל תורת משה ודברי הנביאים אלא להשלימם<br>I have not come to abolish the Law of Moses or the words of the prophets but to fulfil them |
| Nizzahon Vetus #221 | שלא בא לעקור תורת משה ולא דברי הנביאים<br>I have not come to remove the Law of Moses of the words of the prophets |
| Shem-Tob | אל תחשבו שבאתי להפר תורה אלא להשלים באמת אני<br>אומר לכם<br>Do not think that I have come to annul the law but to fulfil. Truly I say to you |
| Shem-Tob (Comment after 6:1) | אין בכל אלו המאמרים להוסיף דבר על<br>דברי תורה ולא להסר<br>in all these words not to add a word to the words of the law nor to subtract any |
| du Tillet | אל תחשבו שבאתי לבטל את התורה או את הנביאים<br>לא באתי לבטל אלא למלא אמן אני אומר לכם<br>Do not think that I have come to abolish the law or the prophets; I have not come to abolish but to fulfil. Truly I say to you |

The Aramaic statement found in b. Shabb. 116[b] is among the few such quotations or allusions to the New Testament in the Babylonian Gemara.[28] It says: "I am not come to take away from the Law of Moses and I am not come to add to the Law of Moses." It appears within an anecdote about a judge, probably a Jewish Christian, who refers to the gospel in his decisions. That his quotation is actually from Matt 5:17 is doubtful since an earlier "gospel" quotation from him, that is, "A son and a daughter shall inherit alike," is not from Matthew or any of the canonical gospels, and since the present quotation is said to come at the end of the book. Herford suggests the saying may have come from a logia source in which various sayings of Jesus were collected.[29] Whatever the case, the saying is close enough to Matt 5:17 to suggest a connection to it. There are three major elements of continuity between the Aramaic and the Hebrew. The first is the name "Moses," which appears in the Gemara reading as well as in Nestor and Nizzahon Vetus. It is lacking in Ms Or Rome #53, Shem-Tob, and du Tillet. The second is the Gemara reading of למיפחת, "to take away," and the reading of להחסיר in Nestor, לחסור in Nizzahon Vetus # 157, and להסר in Shem-Tob's comment, all of which have the same basic meaning. The third is the similarity between the Gemara reading and the allusion to it in Shem-Tob's comment after 6:1. In his comment Shem-Tob says that the intention of Jesus was "in all these words not to add a word to the words of the law nor to subtract any." This, of course, differs from Shem-Tob's reading in 5:17 in the biblical sequence, but in all probability reflects his original text. It was common for scribes to revise a lemma citation of a biblical text in ancient documents without bothering to revise in a corresponding way subsequent comments that repeat the quotation or parts of it or, at least, allude to it.[30] The evidence, therefore, suggests that Shem-Tob knew this passage in its Gemara form (though with some variation, as, for example, the transposition of the order of "add . . . subtract") and

---

[28]For a discussion of these see R. Travers Herford, *Christianity in Talmud and Midrash* (Clifton NJ: Reference Book, 1966).

[29]Ibid., 151.

[30]A good example of this is to be found in mss UF and sometimes L of Philo. See Peter Katz, *Philo's Bible. The Aberrant Text of Bible Quotations in Some Philonic Writings and Its Place in the Textual History of the Greek Bible* (Cambridge: Cambridge University Press, 1950). For some corrective to Katz see George Howard, "The 'Aberrant' Text of Philo's Quotations Reconsidered," *HUCA* 44 (1973): 197-209.

that the reading, as it stands in his text at Matt 5:17, is due to scribal alteration designed to make it correspond more closely to the Greek/Latin.

Modification toward the Greek and Latin is evidenced in the sequence
of Hebrew readings. All the documents except Shem-Tob's comment after
6:1 read the following: (1) some form of "abolish" (that is, לעקור, לסתור,
להפר, לבטל) in agreement with καταλῦσας, (2) "prophets" (mss A and
D only in Shem-Tob's revised text) in agreement with προφήτας, (3)
"fulfil" (that is, למלא, להשלימם, לקיים, להשלים) in agreement with
πληρῶσαι. A further revisionary element appearing in some Hebrew
readings seems to be אמת in Nestor and Ms Or Rome #53, באמת in Shem-
Tob's revised text, and אמן in du Tillet—all in some way or other corresponding to ἀμήν in 5:18. Of all the texts cited, du Tillet is the closest to
the Greek and Latin and apparently represents the end result of a long revisionary process.

The relationship between the various texts involved—the Aramaic,
Hebrew, and Greek/Latin—is an interesting one. The most important difference between the Greek/Latin and Hebrew (including Shem-Tob's revised text), on the one hand, and the Aramaic and the reading in Shem-
Tob's comment, on the other, is that the former read both a negative and
a positive statement in regard to the purpose of Jesus' coming. The Greek/
Latin, for example, says that Jesus came not "to abolish" but "to fulfil."
All the Hebrew documents follow suit (Nizzahon Vetus #157 and #221
lack the second element, but #71 contains it), reading both the negative
and the positive. The Aramaic and the reading in Shem-Tob's comment
contain only a double negative statement, that is, Jesus came not "to subtract or to add." The positive element apparently belongs to the Greek/Latin
tradition only, and the correspondence to it in the Hebrew readings represent textual accommodation to the Greek/Latin. Accommodation, however, came gradually. Nestor, the earliest Hebrew witness, reads, "I have
not come to cancel (= καταλῦσαι) or to subtract (= Aramaic למיפחת).
All other Hebrew witnesses, except Shem-Tob's comment, read "cancel/
abolish/remove/annul" but not "subtract." The element "to subtract" in
most readings thus was eliminated in the revisionary process reflected in
most readings in the Hebrew tradition. It is not possible to explain all the
factors involved in the separation of the Greek and Aramaic forms, but
conceivably an original Aramaic לאוספי ("to add") was misread for לאספי
("to end") and this gave rise to the Greek καταλῦσαι ("to abolish").[31]

MATT 5:39

| Greek (not = Vg) | ἀλλ' ὅστις σε ῥαπίζει εἰς τὴν δεξιὰν σιαγόνα σου, στρέψον αὐτῷ καὶ τὴν ἄλλην<br>But whoever strikes you on the right cheek, turn to him the other also |
|---|---|
| Nestor | אם יכך אדם בצד ימין התר לו את שמאלך להכות בו<br>If a man should strike you on the right side permit him to strike your left |
| ben Reuben | אם יכך אדם על לחיך נטה לו האחרת<br>If a man should strike you on your cheek turn to him the other |
| Nizzahon Vetus #232 | אם יכך יהודי בלחי נטה לו לחי האחרת<br>If a Jew should strike you on the cheek turn to him the other cheek |
| Shem-Tob | אבל המכה בלחיך הימין הכן לו השמאל<br>But whoever strikes your right cheek provide for him the left |
| du Tillet | אלא אם יהיה שיכך על הלחי הימנית תטה אליו האחרת<br>But if there shall be one who strikes you on the right cheek turn to him the other |

Nestor's text differs from the Greek in several respects. Primary for our purpose is his reading of (1) אם ("if") for ἀλλ' ὅστις ("but whoever"), (2) (ב)צד ("side") for σιαγόνα ("cheek"), (3) התר ("permit") for στρέψον ("turn"), and (4) שמאלך ("your left") for ἄλλην ("other"). Nestor's text is in basic agreement (though not exactly) with certain Old Latin manuscripts and even less with Vg which read, *Sed si quis te percusserit in dexteram maxillam tuam, praebe illi et sinistram*. In addition, Nestor agrees with Marcion's reading at Luke 6:29: ἐὰν τίς σε ῥαπίσῃ εἰς. (Cf. Did. 1:4: ἐὰν τίς σοι δῷ ῥάπισμα).

Continuity in the Hebrew tradition is in the readings of אם (Nestor, ben Reuben, Nizzahon Vetus, du Tillet), אדם (Nestor, ben Reuben), and שמאלך (Nestor, Shem-Tob).

Various elements of revision appear in the Hebrew readings. לחי ("cheek") in agreement with σιαγόνα appears in ben Reuben, Nizzahon Vetus, Shem-Tob, and du Tillet. נטה ("turn") in agreement with στρέψον appears in ben Reuben, Nizzahon Vetus, and du Tillet. האחרת ("the

---

[31]A similar confusion of the Hebrew roots סוף ("to end") and יסף ("to add") appears in Amos 3:15: MT וספו is rendered by LXX καὶ προστεθήσονται = ונוספו.

other'') in agreement with την ἄλλην appears in ben Reuben, Nizzahon Vetus, and du Tillet. אבל המכה in agreement with ἀλλ' ὅστις appears in Shem-Tob and אלא = ἀλλ' in du Tillet.

## MATT 8:4

| | |
|---|---|
| Greek (= Vg) | ὃ προσέταξεν Μωϋσῆς εἰς μαρτύριον αὐτοῖς<br>which Moses commanded for a witness to them |
| Nestor | כאשר ציה ה׳ את משה<br>as the LORD commanded Moses |
| Joseph | כאשר ציה משה בתורתו<br>as Moses commanded in his law |
| Ms Or Rome #53 | כאשר צוה משה בתורתו<br>as Moses commanded in his law |
| Nizzahon<br>Vetus #166 | כאשר ציוה משה בתורתו<br>as Moses commanded in his law |
| Shem-Tob | כאשר צוה משה בתורתכם<br>as Moses commanded in your law |
| du Tillet | כאשר ציה משה להם לעדות<br>as Moses commanded them for a witness |

A continuity in the Hebrew tradition is seen in the reading כאשר (''as'') in agreement with καθώς in the Lukan parallel (Luke 5:14) and in disagreement with ὅ (''which'') in Matthew. Continuity is again seen in the Hebrew tradition, with the exception of Nestor (who simply breaks off after משה leaving us in doubt whether his text read further at this point or not) and du Tillet, in the unique reading of ''in his/your law'' in disagreement with the Greek and Latin ''for a witness to them.'' Du Tillet's להם לעדות is clearly a revision toward the Greek and Latin.

The first difference between the Greek and Hebrew may be explained by a confusion in an early Hebrew tradition based on אשר (''which''), reflected in Matthew's ὅ, and כאשר (''as''), reflected in Luke's καθώς and the Hebrew quotations listed above. The second difference may be explained as a confusion in an early Hebrew tradition of the roots תורה (''law'') and תעודה (''witness''). The difference in these words is the additional ayin in ''witness'' and the reading of daleth instead of resh. The latter two letters are often confused in ancient manuscripts.

| | |
|---|---|
| Greek (= Vg) | ³⁰καὶ ὁ μὴ συνάγων μετ' ἐμοῦ σκορπίζει . . .<br>³²καὶ ὃς ἐὰν εἴπῃ λόγον κατὰ τοῦ υἱοῦ τοῦ ἀνθρώπου<br>ἀφεθήσεται αὐτῷ<br>³⁰and he who does not gather with me scatters . . .<br>³²And whoever says a word against the Son of Man<br>will be forgiven |
| Nestor | . . . אשר קלל את האב והבן ורוח הקדש<br>המקלל את הבן והתחרט האב יכפר לו<br>who has cursed the Father and the Son and the Holy Spirit<br>. . . he who curses the Son and repents,<br>the Father will make atonement for him |
| ben Reuben | ³⁰ומי שאינו מאסף עמי הוא מפזר<br>³²ומי שילעיג מהבן יכופר עליו<br>³⁰whoever does not gather with me scatters<br>³²And whoever mocks the Son will be forgiven for it |
| Joseph (ט) | החוטא באב ובבן יש לו מחילה<br>He who sins against the Father and the Son has forgiveness |
| Joseph (מא) | החוטא באב יתכפר לו וכן החוטא בבן<br>He who sins against the Father will be forgiven;<br>so also he who sins against the Son |
| Ms Or Rome #53 | . . . מי שחטא נגד האב יש לו כפרה אם ישוב בתשובה<br>מי שחטא נגד הבן יש לו מחילה<br>Whoever sins against the Father has forgiveness if he re-<br>pents. . . . Whoever sins against the Son has forgiveness |
| Shem-Tob | ³⁰(מי) שלא יתחבר עמי יכפור (בי)<br>³²וכל האומר דבר נגד בן האדם ימחל לו<br>³⁰Whoever does not join with me denies me<br>³²And everyone who says a word against the Son of Man<br>it will be forgiven him |
| Shem-Tob<br>(Comment<br>after 12:37) | הנה האב והבן ימחלו לו אבל הרוח לא ימחול לו<br>Behold the Father and the Son will forgive him<br>but the Spirit will not forgive him |
| du Tillet | ³⁰ומי שלא יאסוף עמי הוא יפזר<br>³²וכל איש שיאמר דבר על בן אדם יסלח לו<br>³⁰And whoever does not gather with me scatters<br>³²And every man who says a word against the Son of Man<br>it shall be forgiven him |

Gospel | Whoever blasphemes against the Father will be forgiven, and
of Thomas 44 | whoever blasphemes against the Son will be forgiven.[32]

Unfortunately, verse 30 is lacking in Nestor, Joseph, and Ms Or Rome #53. Nevertheless their reading of "Father" in verse 32, along with the text reflected in Shem-Tob's comment, shows a continuity running throughout this part of the Hebrew tradition. As stated before,[33] the reading reflected in Shem-Tob's comment is to be preferred to that in his biblical text since the latter apparently represents scribal revision toward the Greek and Latin. The antiquity of the reading "Father" is supported by its appearance in the Coptic Gospel of Thomas.

Another possible continuity in the Hebrew tradition is the unique reading in Shem-Tob of יכפור ("denies") and the root כפר meaning "to forgive" that appears in Nestor, ben Reuben, Joseph (מא) and Ms Or Rome #53. Allowing for scribal alteration in the transmission of the Hebrew tradition, it is conceivable that a word connection based on the root כפר stood in the original text. A possible reconstruction of the Hebrew is:

He who does not join me denies (יכפור) me . . .
He who blasphemes the Father and the Son will be forgiven (יכופר).

A final continuity in the Hebrew tradition is the concept of 'repentance" mentioned in Nestor and Ms Or Rome #53.

Revision toward the Greek and Latin is found (1) in the absence of "repentance" in all documents other than Nestor and Ms Or Rome #53, (2) in the absence of "Father" in ben Reuben, Shem-Tob's revised text, and du Tillet, and (3) in the reading פזר ("scatters") in ben Reuben and du Tillet. Again du Tillet is closest of the Hebrew texts to the Greek and Latin and apparently represents the end result of a long evolutionary process.

---

[32]Translation by Thomas O. Lambdin in *The Nag Hammadi Library,* ed. James M. Robinson (New York: Harper & Row, 1977) 123.

[33]See on Matt 5:17-18a above and n. 30.

MATT 13:57

| | |
|---|---|
| Greek ( = Vg) | οὐκ ἔστιν προφήτης ἄτιμος εἰ μὴ ἐν τῇ πατρίδι καὶ ἐν τῇ οἰκίᾳ αὐτοῦ<br>A prophet is not without honor except in his homeland and in his own house. |
| Mark 6:4 | οὐκ ἔστιν προφήτης ἄτιμος εἰ μὴ ἐν τῇ πατρίδι αὐτοῦ καὶ ἐν τοῖς συγγενεῦσιν αὐτοῦ καὶ ἐν τῇ οἰκίᾳ αὐτοῦ<br>A prophet is not without honor except in his own homeland and among his own kin and in his own house. |
| Luke 4:24 | οὐδεὶς προφήτης δεκτός ἐστιν ἐν τῇ πατρίδι αὐτοῦ<br>No prophet is acceptable in his own homeland. |
| Nestor | הנביא אינו מתקלל כי אם במדינתו<br>No prophet is cursed except in his own city/land. |
| Nizzahon Vetus #167 | אין נביא בלא כבוד אלא בעירו ובביתו<br>No prophet is without honor except in his own city and in his own house. |
| Nizzahon Vetus #207 | לא יהיה נביא מבוזה ולא יתחרף כי אם במדינתו ובקום שמכיריו אותו<br>A prophet is not held in contempt or abused save in his own city/land and in a place where he is recognized. |
| Shem-Tob | אין נביא שאין לו כבוד כ"א בארצו ועירו וביתו<br>No prophet is without honor except in his own land and in his own city and in his own house. |
| du Tillet | אין נביא בלא כבוד אלא במקום מולדתו ובביתו<br>No prophet is without honor except in the place of his homeland and in his own house. |

The synoptic gospels reflect a variegated tradition in regard to the locality of a prophet's dishonor: (1) Luke says "homeland"; (2) Matthew, "homeland and house"; and (3) Mark, "homeland, kin, and house." There is some ambiguity in the word πατρίς which can mean "homeland" or "hometown." Usually, however, the reference is broader than "town" and is best understood as "homeland." A similar ambiguity exists in Nestor's במדינתו which can mean "in his land" or "in his city." This reading is preserved in Nizzahon Vetus #207 which, however, is only a rough paraphrase of our passage. Elsewhere the Nizzahon Vetus (#167) reads בעירו which clearly means "in his city." Shem-Tob reads בארצו ועירו, "in his land and in his city," a doublet apparently based on the ambiguity of ‏במדינתו‏. Du Tillet returns to the concept of "homeland," reading ‏מולדתו‏. Thus we see an interconnection running throughout the Hebrew tradition oscillating between the ideas "homeland," "city," and combinations of them.

One may argue that the earliest form of the tradition was the ambiguous πατρίς ("homeland/hometown") or ‏מדינה‏ ("land/city") which eventually gave rise to the doublet ‏בארצו ועירו‏ in Shem-Tob. This may not be the case, however, in view of the parallel in the Gospel of Thomas 31 which reads, "No prophet is acceptable in his village; no physician works cures on those who know him." The reading of "acceptable" in Thomas corresponds to Luke. The reading of "village" corresponds to Nizzahon Vetus #167 and Shem-Tob. We cannot know the original (whether Greek or Syriac) that stands in the background of Thomas in order to judge the specificity of the word "village" (*time*). Thomas 32, however, reads, "Jesus said: A city (πόλις) that is built on a high mountain (and) fortified cannot fall nor can it remain hidden." A catchword connection appears to exist between the two sayings in Thomas based on the idea "village/city." The order of sayings in Thomas, then, suggests that a very early form of Matt. 13:57, perhaps the original, read "city" rather than "homeland." In view of this the following development in the tradition is suggested:

1. ‏עיר‏ stands as an original Hebrew base (Nizzahon Vetus #167).
2. ‏עיר‏ gave rise to the ambiguous synonym ‏מדינה‏ "city/land" (Nestor).
3. ‏מדינה‏ gave rise to Greek πατρίς "homeland/hometown" and in Hebrew to the doublet ‏בארצו ועירו‏ "in his land and his city" (Shem-Tob).

Finally, it is clear that du Tillet of all the Hebrew texts is the closest to the Greek and Latin of Matthew and again appears to represent a revision.

These examples show that in some way the First Gospel in Shem-Tob fits into a process of textual evolution that began in primitive times and culminated in du Tillet in the sixteenth century, or possible later if our survey should include subsequent Hebrew texts of Matthew. The suggestion made here is that the gospel text incorporated into the *Even Bohan* was not a freshly made translation of the First Gospel by Shem-Tob, but was a reproduction, possibly with some revision by Shem-Tob himself, of an already existing literary Hebrew tradition that had been in the process of evolution for some time.

## The Evidence from Shem-Tob Himself

Two comments made by Shem-Tob himself further suggest that his Hebrew text of Matthew was not a freshly made translation but one that was already in existence. The first comment comes from his brief introduction to section twelve (in the British Library ms) of the *Even Bohan*.[34]

אמר המחבר שם טוב בן יצחק בן שפרוט ראיתי להשלים
חבורי זה אשר (קראתיו) אב"ן בוח"ן להעתיק ספרי
האוונג"יילִיון עם היותם שהספרים היות אסורים לנו
לקרוא בהם פן יבואו התלמידים שלא שמשו כל צרכם וישתו
מהמים ההם, עם כל זה ראיתי להעתיקם לשתי סיבות ה"א
להשיב מתוכם לנוצרים ובפרט למומרים שמדברים בעניין
אמונתם ואינם יודעים דבר אמונה ומפרשים פסוקי תורתינו
הקדושה בעניין זה הפך האמת והפך אמונתם ובזה יגיע שבח
ליהודי לאותו המתווכח עמהם כאשר ילכדם בשוחתם

ח"ב להראות לבעלי אמונתם (הרמה) חסרון הספרים ההם
והשגיאות הנופלות בתוכם ובזה ידעו ויבינו יתרון
ומעלת אמונתינו על שאר האמונות, לפי שלא יודע גודל מעלת
הדבר כי אם בבחינת הפכו, ואני נשען בשית (באל ית') שלא
יצא מזה רק טוב טוב כמו שכוונתי לטובה, ואכתוב בכל פרק ופרק
ההשגות אשר יראו לי בתוכן, והנני משביע לכל מעתיק בחי
העולם לבל (יעתיק) ספרי האוונגיילִיוס אם לא (יכתוב)
בכל מקום ההשגות אשר כתבתי כפי אשר סדרתים וכתבתים הנה

The author, Shem-Tob ben-Isaac ben-Shaprut, says: I have chosen to complete this my treatise which (I have called) *Even Bohan* by transcribing (להעתיק) the books of the gospel in spite of the fact that the books are forbidden for us to read, lest the disciples should come without having sufficient practice and should drink from those waters. Nevertheless, I have chosen to transcribe them (להעתיקם) for two reasons: The first is to answer the Christians from them and especially proselytes who speak in regard to their faith but do not know the word of faith and explain the Scriptures of our holy law in regard to that which is contrary to the truth and contrary to their faith. In this way glory will come to the Jew who debates with them whenever he captures them in their own pit.

The second is to show to the faithful the degree of defect in these books and the errors that occur in them. By this they will know and understand the superiority and virtue of our faith to the other religions. Since the greatness of the virtue of the word is not known except by an examination

---

[34]The words in parentheses come from ms A; otherwise the text is from the British Library ms.

of that which is contrary to it, I depend on God, blessed be he, that there
come from this nothing but good since I have aimed at that which is good.
I have written section by section all the objections that appear to me to be
in them. I adjure by God every copyist (מעתיק) that he not copy (יעתיק)
the books of the gospel unless (he write) in every place the objections that
I have written just as I have arranged them and written them here.

The root translated "transcribe" or "copy" above is עתק which can
mean either "to transcribe/copy" or "to translate."[35] In its first two oc-
currences modern scholars ordinarily have taken it to mean "to translate,"
with the result that Shem-Tob is reputed to be the first rabbi to produce a
complete translation of a gospel into Hebrew.[36]

Since the context is not completely clear, the following need to be considered. (1) Shem-Tob says he has chosen to complete the *Even Bohan* by
transcribing/translating the books of the gospel. If he meant to "transcribe" rather than to "translate," this might presuppose the existence of
more than one gospel in Hebrew by the fourteenth century (although as a
matter of fact Shem-Tob reproduced Matthew only). Epiphanius in the
fourth century speaks of a Hebrew translation of John and Acts as well as
the original Hebrew Matthew.[37] From the gospel quotations from the *Pugio
Fidei* by Raymund Martini, written about 1278 and based on Hebrew
manuscripts confiscated earlier from the Jews in Aragon, Alexander Marx
concludes: "we learn that a Hebrew translation of the Gospels already existed in thirteenth-century Spain."[38] The existence of Hebrew gospels in
the fourteenth century is thus a probability. On the other hand, it is possible that ספרי האוונגיילױן refers to the various sections of Matthew, rather
than to the four canonical gospels. In this case Shem-Tob had only the
Gospel of Matthew in mind.

(2) In the last paragraph of Shem-Tob's introduction the root עתק appears twice more but here it seems to require the meaning of "copy" with
no ambiguity at all. He writes: "I adjure by God every copyist (מעתיק)

---

[35]Kutscher pointed out that Maimonides used the word to mean "transmit," an Arab-
ism. See E. Y. Kutscher, *A History of the Hebrew Language* (Leiden: Brill, 1982) 165.

[36]Lapide, *Hebrew in the Church,* 46. Cf. Black *An Aramaic Approach to the Gospels
and Acts,* 295; Lindsey, *A Hebrew Translation of the Gospel of Mark,* 67.

[37]*Panarion* 30.3.6.

[38]Marx, "The Polemical Manuscripts in the Library of the Jewish Theological Seminary
of America," 271. See also Rosenthal, תרגום של הבשורה על-פי מתי ליעקב בן ראובן, 49.

that he not copy (יעתיק) the books of the gospel unless'' he include the objections as well. That Shem-Tob envisioned his work to be ''translated'' into other languages is hardly likely. He wrote in Hebrew in the first place in order to prepare the Jewish people to defend their faith against Christian antagonists. The root עתק can hardly be understood in this context other than with reference to Jews who may *copy* Shem-Tob's work. But lest he be hopelessly confusing, Shem-Tob must also use עתק in the beginning of his introduction to mean ''copy.''[39]

The preponderant weight of evidence, therefore, suggests that Shem-Tob only copied, not translated, his Matthew and that his Matthew was already in Hebrew when he got it.

The second comment by Shem-Tob that suggests his Hebrew text of Matthew was not a freshly made translation comes in a section after Matt 21:9. He writes:

הנה יוחנן פרק כ״ח כתב שישו עצמו לקח האתון שאמר הכתוב
אל תראי בת ציון הנה מלכך יבא לך יושב על עיר בן אתונות
גיואן (ומטיב) שנו הכתוב ולא הסכימו בשנוי כי הכתוב
אומר עני ורוכב על חמור ועל עיר בן אתונות

Here John perek 28 wrote that Jesus himself took the ass (האתון) because that which is written says: do not fear, daughter of Zion, behold, your king comes to you sitting upon a colt (עיר) the foal of asses (אתונות). John (and) Matthew have changed the Scripture and do not agree in the change because the Scripture says: humble and riding upon an ass (חמור) and upon the colt (עיר) the foal of asses.

Shem-Tob's objection to John and Matthew is not totally clear. It is clear, however, that he accuses them of reading אתון instead of the Masoretic Text of Zech 9:9 which reads חמור.[40] But since he criticizes the gospel reading at this point, the reading must not have been made by Shem-Tob. The conclusion is inescapable: this section of Matthew was not translated into Hebrew by Shem-Tob.

---

[39]It is interesting to note that Lapide is inconsistent in translating the root עתק. For the initial להעתיקם he renders ''Übersetzung'' (''translation''), but for the following מעתיק and יעתיק he renders ''Abschreiber'' (''copyist'') and ''zu kopieren'' (''to copy'') respectively. See Pinchas E. Lapide, ''Der 'Prüfstein' aus Spanien,'' *Sefarad* 34 (1974): 231-32.

[40]Since both אתון and חמור are legitimate Hebrew correspondents for the Greek ὄνον (f. m.), his objection to אתון is not that it mistranslates the Greek; his objection is that it varies from the Hebrew of the Masoretic Text.

From the above we may draw the following conclusions:

1. The text of the Hebrew Matthew in Shem-Tob is not the same as the Hebrew Matthean texts in du Tillet and Münster. There are, however, textual links between them that suggest the latter two evolved from a text base that was similar to Shem-Tob.

2. The text of Shem-Tob is not a freshly made translation by Shem-Tob. When compared to Hebrew and Aramaic quotations of Matthew from earlier Jewish and anti-Christian writings, it appears to have been based on a primitive Hebrew literary tradition. Comments by Shem-Tob himself further suggest that he made use of an already existing Hebrew Matthew.

3. The evidence as a whole presupposes a Hebrew text of Matthew that existed from ancient times and was used among the Jews for polemical purposes against Christians. Through centuries of use this text went through a process of evolution which included stylistic modification and changes designed to bring the text into closer harmony with the canonical text used by Christians. The latter changes were presumably for the purpose of facilitating discussion and debate.

# Shem-Tob's Hebrew Matthew:
# A Literary and Textual Profile

In this section[1] a literary and textual profile of Shem-Tob's Hebrew Matthew will be presented in order to clarify, as much as possible, its relationship to the Greek Matthew. Three basic possibilities for this relationship exist: 1. The Hebrew text is a translation of the Greek (or one of its versions such as the Latin). 2. The Greek is a translation of the Hebrew. 3. Both the Hebrew and the Greek represent original compositions in their own respective languages with one serving as a literary model for the other. The discussion will conclude that number 3 is to be preferred without, however, determining which—the Greek or the Hebrew—served as a model for the other. In addition the discussion will make it clear that the Hebrew

---

[1]The article by Pinchas E. Lapide ("Der 'Prüfstein' aus Spanien," *Sefarad* 34 (1974): 227-72) should be consulted at this point. It is a detailed analysis of Shem-Tob's Hebrew Matthew. Of particular importance is the discussion (on pp. 246-49) of "Romanismen" which reflect late revisions. Unfortunately Lapide believes the Hebrew Matthew is a translation of the Latin Vulgate, perhaps partly because he used the Neofiti ms which shows considerable assimilation to the Vulgate in places where other mss do not. (See for examples 2:1 Magi, Neofiti מאגוס, Brit Lib ms BCDEFGH void [all reading simply חוזים [בכוכבים]; 3:9 filios Abrahae, Neofiti בנים לאברהם, Brit Lib ms ABCDEFG בנו אברהם; 4:21 Zebedaeus, Neofiti זבדיאוש, D זבאדאו, BC זבדאו, EF זבאדו; 6:28 lilia agri, Neofiti ליריו, Brit Lib ms גילון, BC גיליין, DG גילין; 15:2 traditionem seniorum, Neofiti תקנות הראשונים, Brit Lib ms BCDEFG תקנות הראשונות, AH תקנות הראשונית; 16:18 tu es Petrus, et super hanc petram aedificabo, Neofiti אתה אבן ועל זאת האבן אבנה, Brit Lib ms CDEFG שאתה אבן ואני אבנה עליך; 24:47 super omnia bona sua, Neofiti על טובו, D שעל טפיו.) Lapide himself notes many differences in Shem-Tob and the Vulgate without, however, recognizing the true nature of the oldest layer of the Hebrew text. Other problems with the article are: (1) It fails to note Shem-Tob's relationship to the Old Syriac and the Diatessaron against the Latin tradition, and to the Old Latin against the Vulgate (see below). (2) It shows no recognition of Shem-Tob's relationship to the Coptic Gospel of Thomas. (3) It fails to note most of the puns, word connections, and alliterations that are so characteristic of Shem-Tob's Matthew. (4) It lacks a discussion of the abbreviation/ circumlocution for the divine name. (5) Finally, a general misunderstanding of the nature of Shem-Tob's Matthew, even in specific contexts (e.g., 12:28—see below), characterizes the article. Nevertheless, in spite of these difficulties, Lapide's study can be read with profit.

text of our manuscripts has been corrupted by a series of revisions and modifications designed to present the Hebrew in a more grammatically acceptable form and to make it conform more closely to the Greek and Latin texts of Matthew. It will be argued that despite the revisions and modifications by medieval scribes, an old substratum to the Matthean text reflects Hebrew composition, not translation.

The discussion will include: (1) linguistic characteristics of the Hebrew text; (2) late revisions to the Hebrew text; (3) textual relationships of Shem-Tob's Matthew; (4) puns, word connections, and alliteration; (5) the Divine Name; (6) theological tendencies in Shem-Tob's Matthew; (7) different interpretations in Shem-Tob's Matthew; (8) passages suggesting a variant Hebrew substratum for the Greek; (9) Shem-Tob's text and synoptic variation; and (10) other interesting readings in Shem-Tob's Matthew.

## Linguistic Characteristics of the Hebrew Text

It is difficult to assess the language of the text of Matthew in Shem-Tob since it is a Christian writing preserved in a Jewish polemical treatise. The question is, would a Jewish polemist of the fourteenth century translate a Christian document from Greek or Latin and render it into standard biblical Hebrew (BH) with a mixture of Mishnaic Hebrew (MH) and even late medieval vocabulary. If it were a matter of an original Jewish composition in the late Middle Ages one would expect BH or even archaic BH to play a dominant role, as is the case with most texts written during this time.[2]

But the fact is what we have is a Christian text in Hebrew appearing in a Jewish polemical treatise designed specifically to point out its errors and the general fallacious nature of Christianity. Yet the linguistic nature of the gospel text is basically BH with a healthy mixture of MH and later rabbinic vocabulary and idiom.

In many ways the linguistic situation of Shem-Tob's Matthew is analogous to the Masada fragments of Ben Sira[3] when compared to the late fragments of the same document from the Cairo Geniza.[4] Kutscher ex-

---

[2]See Kutscher, *A History of the Hebrew Language,* 88.

[3]See Y. Yadin, *The Ben Sira Scroll from Masada* (Jerusalem: Israel Exploration Society, 1965).

[4]These were published in Israel Lévi, *The Hebrew Text of the Book of Ecclesiasticus* (Leiden: Brill, 1904). See also A. A. di Lella, *The Hebrew Text of Sirach* (The Hague, 1966).

plains the original Ben Sira as written primarily in BH without escaping, however, the influence of MH, an occasional parallel to the Dead Sea Scrolls, and contemporary Aramaic. The medieval fragments from the Cairo Geniza, in addition to this, show numerous changes due to the corrections of medieval scribes designed to bring the text into a more contemporary form in regard to spelling, vocabulary, and other linguistic phenomena.[5]

The Hebrew Matthew of Shem-Tob is similar. We already have demonstrated that the basic text predates the fourteenth century, in some instances going back to very early times. Our evidence for this is its connection with quotations of Matthew in early Jewish polemical treatises and in one case in the Talmud. Assuming that the basic text of Shem-Tob's Hebrew Matthew is a primitive Hebrew text, we have in this case what one might expect, a writing composed primarily in BH with a mixture of MH elements, but which has undergone scribal modification designed to bring it more into harmony with later linguistic forms. In addition, the text reflects considerable revision designed to make it conform more closely to the standard Greek and Latin texts of the Gospel during the Middle Ages.

This means that Shem-Tob's Matthew, as printed above, does not preserve the original Hebrew in a pure form. It has been contaminated by Jewish scribes during the Middle Ages. Nevertheless, enough of the original text is left intact to observe its primitive nature. It is clear to see that its base is biblical and Mishnaic Hebrew and that it is written in unpolished style. It is filled with ungrammatical constructions and Aramaized forms and idioms. Some of these points will be demonstrated in the following discussion.

## The Verb

The most pronounced difference in BH and MH is the virtual disappearance of the consecutive tenses in MH.[6] The earliest possible date assignable to Shem-Tob's Matthean text is the first century CE, a time when BH had ceased to be spoken and MH had become dominant. In accordance

---

[5]Kutscher, *A History of the Hebrew Language*, 87-93. See also the cautious remarks of Isaac Rabinowitz, ''The Qumran Hebrew Original of Ben Sira's Concluding Acrostic on Wisdom,'' *HUCA* 42 (1971): 173-74.

[6]M. H. Segal, *A Grammar of Mishnaic Hebrew* (Oxford: Clarendon Press, 1927, 1958) 72. Cf. E. Y. Kutscher, *The Language and Linguistic Background of the Isaiah Scroll (1 QIsaᵃ)* (Leiden: Brill, 1974) 41-42.

with this, Shem-Tob's text appears to be an imitation of BH in regard to
tense. The consecutive tense system, for example, dominates the language
throughout. The following are typical cases.

ויקץ יוסף . . . ויעש 1:24
ויקבוץ כל גדוליו ויבקש 2:4
ויען ישו ויאמר 3:15
וילך ישו . . . וירא 4:18
ויהי לעת הערב ויבאו 8:16
ויבאו תלמידי יוחנן וישאו 14:12
יעזוב איש . . . ודבק באשתו 19:5
וישמעו העשרה ויחר בעיניהם 20:24

Although BH is clearly being written, lapses in the consecutive tenses
show that the writer and/or later scribes of Shem-Tob's Matthew were not
completely at ease with this usage. Occasional examples exist of noncon-
secutive tenses where the *waw* is merely a connective:

ותלד בן ותקרא שמו ישוע 1:21
שלחו בכל אותו המלכות והביאו לו 14:35
ולקח השבעה ככרות וישברם ונתנם 15:36
נכנס ישו בספינה ובא לארץ 15:39
ויקום גוי על גוי . . . ויהיו מהומות רבות 24:7
הלך קנה ומכר והרויח חמשה אחרים 25:17

Another difference between BH and MH occurs in the use of the infinitive with the prepositions ב and כ. The construction appears in BH while
MH uses כש– with the finite verb as כאשר in BH.[7] All forms appear in
Shem-Tob's Hebrew Matthew: (1) infinitive plus preposition: 1:20 ובחשבו,
14:14 :כש– (2) ;בבואו 17:14, בעומדו 15:29, ובראותו 14:30, בהתפללך 6:6
וכשיצאו 14:19, וכשישבו; (3) כאשר: 2:10 ויהי כאשר ראו 5:48, היו אתם
וכאשר ראוהו תלמידיו 14:26, כאשר תעשו צדקה 6:2, תמיהים כאשר.

The infinitive absolute is not used at all in MH[8] and may appear once
in Shem-Tob, at 22:24 (although the form is possibly an imperative here).

An interesting form of the infinitive construct plus לא, used for pro-
hibition, appears at 23:23, ולא לשכוח אותם. It occurs in late BH and the
Dead Sea Scrolls but rarely if ever in standard BH. Kutscher says it "is all
the more interesting since it crops up in the languages spoken in Jerusalem

---

[7]Segal, *A Grammar of Mishnaic Hebrew*, 165.

[8]Kutscher, *The Language and Linguistic Background of the Isaiah Scroll*, 41.

at the time, as we see from Aramaic and Greek inscriptions of Jerusalem (and also in Punic, that is, late Canaanite of North Africa).'"[9]

## Pronouns

In the first person singular אני is dominant in MH while both אני and אנכי are found in BH.[10] The form אני is dominant in Shem-Tob with אנכי occurring in 18:20. In regard to the plural, MH always uses אנו while BH uses אנחנו except for the kᵉtib at Jer 42:6.[11] The short form is used in Shem-Tob, although אנחנו appears occasionally (see 6:12). Of the two forms הם and המה, the latter is found only in biblical quotations in MH.[12] Both occur in Shem-Tob: (1) המה: 2:13, 5:8, 11:7; (2) הם: 13:13, 38, 39, 23:23.

The plural demonstrative pronoun אלה, standard for BH, becomes אלו in MH. Both forms occur in Shem-Tob: (1) אלה: 10:2, 5, 15:20, 24:8; (2) אלו: 7:24, 28, 23:23.

The possessive is regularly expressed in MH by the combination of ש plus the preposition ל. Although in older texts it is attached to the noun it governs, it eventually came to exist as a separate particle, של.[13] Though rare, של occurs in Shem-Tob at 10:20, 12:39, 26:17, and 27:15. (Cf. שלכם at 12:27, שלך at 25:25, שלי at 25:27, and שלקץ at 27:63.)

## Vocabulary

The vocabulary in Shem-Tob's Hebrew Matthew[14] comes from various levels of the history of the language including BH, MH, and later rabbinic Hebrew. (1) Typical words occurring in BH and Shem-Tob but not in MH are: אולי 11:23, 27:64; אז 9:1, 6, 14, 37, 10:1, 11:20, 12:13, 14, 22, 44, 45, 13:36, 43; רק 9:6, 10:28, 11:30; אמנם 25:21, 26:56; אכן 8:17, 10:22; בעד 2:8, 5:11, 6:2, 6, 10:18, 11:10; למען 5:45; פן 6:1, 8:4, 25, 9:16, 30, 13:15, 29; אשר 8:27, 9:36, 10:4, 11:4, 12:18; כי 9:2, 13, 11:18, 26, 12:41; גם 8:29. (2) Typical words occurring in MH and Shem-Tob but not in BH are: מיד 21:41; כתיב 22:44; מוכן 22:8, 25:33; רבן 23:7; זהוב 18:24; מֶתָר 12:10, 19:3; מעוט 14:31, 17:20; כריתה 19:7; זון 13:25; חרדל

---

[9]Kutscher, *A History of the Hebrew Language*, 99.

[10]Segal, *A Grammar of Mishnaic Hebrew*, 39.

[11]Ibid., 39-40.

[12]Ibid., 40.

[13]Ibid., 43-44.

[14]Cf. ibid., 46-57.

13:31; ממון 13:44; נים 17:3; בשביל 17:13. (3) Typical words occurring
only in later rabbinic writings and Shem-Tob are: מאסר 4:12; תמידית 6:11;
טבעי 15:17, 16:9-12; הנהגה (= behavior) 16:9-12; שתי וערב (= cross)
16:24; עולמית 18:8, 25:41; שום דבר 21:3, 24:17, 27:12; סוף דבר 21:37;
חנפן 22:18; רשום (= impression) 22:20.

## Late Revisions to the Hebrew Text

There are clear examples of late revisions in the Hebrew Matthew of
Shem-Tob such as explanatory additions in other languages and alterations
designed to clarify or bring the Hebrew into harmony with the standard
Greek and Latin texts. One example is 1:23 where the following redun-
dancy occurs: ותקרת שמו עמנואל שר״ל עמנו אלקים "and you will call
his name Emmanuel, that is, God with us." It is the Greek and Latin that
need explanation for Emmanuel, not the Hebrew. Another example is 27:33
which reads: ובאו למקום נקרא גולגוטא הוא הר קאלוווארי "then they came
to a place called Golguta, that is, Mount Calvary." "Calvariae" is read
by the OL and Vg. A host of revisions in individual manuscripts may be
gleaned from the critical apparatus. Examples are: 12:39 [יונה + הנביא A
= Greek and Vg; 21:12 ויוצא A [וימצא = Greek and Vg; 24:6 [תהבלו
תבהלו G = Greek and Vg; 24:43 [יודע + אדון הבית A = Greek; 27:40
אשר [אפשר BEF = Greek and Vg.

Other examples of revision are interpolated explanations of names and
places usually following (ב)לעז "in another language," transliterated into
Hebrew from Greek, Latin, and other languages. A list of these follows.

| | | | |
|---|---|---|---|
| מירא | 2:11 | מאטיאו | 9:9 |
| פאריזיאי | 3:7 | טיראו דיטיר או סדומה ,בורוזואים | 11:21 |
| שאטאנאס | 4:10 | פאן סאגרה | 12:4 |
| מאריטמה | 4:13 | ריזינה די אישטריאה | 12:42 |
| זבאדאו וזאבאדה | 4:21 | ברייאגה | 13:25 |
| מאוונגייליו | 4:23 | פיליבוס ,סוריאה | 16:13 |
| ליבי״ל ריפודייו | 5:31 | קריסטו ,פייטרוס | 16:16 |
| איפוקראטיס | 6:2 | גאימי | 17:1 |
| גיליון | 6:28 | פיבליאוס | 23:5 |
| פינן | 6:30 | אוונגילי | 24:14 |
| פיראלשיזה | 8:6 | אוגיל | 26:13 |
| גארגיזאני | 8:28 | קאלוווארי | 27:33 |
| פאראלטיקו | 9:2 | | |

From the distribution of these transliterations throughout the gospel it appears the interpolator's interest in the task waned substantially after six-

teen chapters. Only five occur after that part of the text. The secondary nature of these readings is shown by an occasional disruption they make in the syntax. An example is 24:14 which reads: ‏בשורה לעז אוונגילי זאת‎. The words ‏בשורה‎ . . . ‏זאת‎ which go together are separated by ‏לעז‎ and a transliteration of the Greek or Latin word for "gospel."

## Textual Relationships of Shem-Tob's Hebrew

It is also difficult to assess the relationship of Shem-Tob's Hebrew Matthew to already known textual traditions. In many respects it is different from all known traditions in that it contains many unique readings. In the absence of a thorough comparison of Shem-Tob with other texts, which would involve far more research than this preliminary report, it can be stated that a clear relationship exists between Shem-Tob and the Latin and Syriac traditions, the latter including the Diatessaron of Tatian. Thus Shem-Tob contains many readings in common with the Old Latin (OL) in company with the Vulgate (Vg) and with the Old Syriac (OS or Sy[s.c]) in company with the Peshitta (Sy[p]). Of particular interest is a moderate number of readings in which Shem-Tob agrees only with the OL or OS without joint agreement with Vg or Sy[p]. The following lists contain typical examples of these readings.

$$\text{Shem-Tob} = \text{OL} \neq \text{Vg}^{15}$$

| | | |
|---|---|---|
| | Greek | τὴν ἄλλην (the other) |
| 5:39 | Shem-Tob | ‏השמאל‎ (the left) |
| | abg[1] | sinistram (the left) |
| | Greek | ὁ εὑρών (who finds) |
| 10:39 | Shem-Tob | ‏האוהב‎ (who loves) |
| | ff[1] | qui amat (who loves) |
| | Greek | καὶ γραμματέων (and scribes) |
| 16:21 | Shem-Tob | VOID |
| | a | VOID |

[15]For the Old Latin the following have been consulted: Adolf Jülicher, *Itala. Das Neue Testament in Altlateinischer Überlieferung. I Matthäus-Evangelium*, ed. W. Matzkow and K. Aland, 2nd ed. (Berlin: Walter de Gruyter, 1972); S. C. E. Legg, *Novum Testamentum Graece . . . Evangelium Secundum Matthaeum* (Oxford: Clarendon Press, 1940).

| 27:21 | Greek | ὁ ἡγεμών (the governor) |
|---|---|---|
|  | Shem-Tob | פילאט (Pilate) |
|  | aur f | Pilatus (Pilate) |

## Shem-Tob = OS ≠ Sy^p[16]

| 3:9 | Greek | καὶ μὴ δόξητε λέγειν (and do not think to say) |
|---|---|---|
|  | Shem-Tob | ואל תאמרו (and do not say) |
|  | Sy^s.c | ולא תאמרון (and do not say) |

| 4:18 | Greek | παρὰ τὴν θάλασσαν (by the sea) |
|---|---|---|
|  | Shem-Tob | על שפת הים (by the shore of the sea) |
|  | Sy^s | על גנב ספתה דימא (by the shore of the sea) |

| 5:12 | Greek | τοὺς προφήτας τοὺς πρὸ ὑμῶν (the prophets who were before you) |
|---|---|---|
|  | Shem-Tob | הנביאים (the prophets) |
|  | Sy^s | לנביא (the prophets) |

| 12:45 | Greek | ἑπτὰ ἕτερα πνεύματα (seven other spirits) |
|---|---|---|
|  | Shem-Tob | שבעה רוחות (seven spirits) |
|  | Sy^s | שבע רוחא (seven spirits) |

| 16:17 | Greek | ἀποκριθεὶς δὲ ὁ Ἰησοῦς εἶπεν αὐτῷ (Jesus answered and said to him) |
|---|---|---|
|  | Shem-Tob | ויאמר אליו ישו (Jesus said to him) |
|  | Sy^c | אמר לה ישוע (Jesus said to him) |

| 20:14 | Greek | θέλω (I wish) |
|---|---|---|
|  | Shem-Tob | אם אני רוצה (If I wish) |
|  | Sy^s | אן צביא (If I wish) |
|  | Sy^c | ואן צבא אנא (And if I wish) |

## Shem-Tob = the Diatessaron of Tatian

There are a number of readings in Shem-Tob's Hebrew Matthew that correspond to Tatian's Diatessaron. As is well known, Tatian, a native of Assyria, came to Rome in the middle of the second century and became a disciple of Justin Martyr. About 172 he left Rome for the Euphrates Valley and is said to have founded the sect of Encratites. He died a few years later. Sometime either shortly before leaving Rome or after returning to Mesopotamia, he constructed a harmony of the gospels in which the texts

---

[16]For Sy^s.c the following have been used: Agnes Smith Lewis, *The Old Syriac Gospels or Evangelion Da-Mepharreshe* (London, 1910); F. C. Burkitt, *Evangelion Da-Mepharreshe,* vol. 1: *Text* (Cambridge: Cambridge University Press, 1904).

of Matthew, Mark, Luke, and John were woven together into a continuous narrative. This was called the Diatessaron of Tatian.

It is notoriously difficult to identify true Diatessaric readings due to the fact that no copy of the original has ever been discovered.[17] The surest witness to its text is Ephraem's commentary on the Diatessaron (EC). About three-fifths of the original Syriac of this work was published in 1963 by Dom Louis Leloir.[18] An Armenian version of this same work also exists (vEC) and will be cited where necessary below.[19] Other witnesses to the text of the Diatessaron are problematic since they suffer from defects which impair their value for reconstructing the original text of the Diatessaron.[20] In the matter of sequence, however, as opposed to the actual wording of

---

[17]The original language of the Diatessaron has been the subject of endless debate. If Tatian made his composition after his departure from Rome (ca. 172) he probably made it in Syriac, although Kraeling argues that it was composed in Greek even if it was written in Mesopotamia. See Carl H. Kraeling, *A Greek Fragment of Tatian's Diatessaron from Dura* (London, 1935) 15-18. If Tatian wrote it while he was in Rome he could have made it in Greek, Syriac, or Latin. For the latter see F. C. Burkitt, "The Dura Fragment of Tatian," *JTS* 36 (1935): 257-58. Many hold that it was written in Greek and was soon translated into Syriac. Among others see Adolf von Harnack, "Tatian's Diatessaron und Marcion's Commentar zum Evangelium bei Ephraem Syrus," *ZKG* 4 (1881): 494-95; *Chronologie der altchristlichen Literatur* (Leipzig, 1897) 1.289; H. J. Vogels, *Die Harmonistik von Evangelientext des Codex Cantabrigiensis,* TU 36 (Leipzig, 1910): 45-46; M.-J. Lagrange, "L'ancienne version Syriaque des Évangiles," *RB* 29 (1920): 326; Adolf Jülicher, "Der echte Tatiantext," *JBL* 43 (1924): 166. Others think the evidence points to a Syriac original. Notable among these are A. Baumstark, "Das griechische Diatessaronfragment von Dura Europos," *OrChr* 32 (1935): 250; Arthur Vööbus, *Studies in the History of the Gospel Text in Syriac* (Louvain, 1951) 12; G. A. Weir, "Tatian's Diatessaron and the Old Syriac Gospels. The Evidence of MS Chester Beatty 709" (Ph.D. diss., University of Edinburgh, 1969) xiv-xv.

[18]Louis Leloir, *Saint Ephrem, Commentaire de l'Evangile Concordant, Texte Syriaque (Manuscript Chester Beatty 709)* (Dublin, 1963).

[19]Louis Leloir, *Saint Ephrem, Commentaire de l'Evangile Concordant, Version Arménienne,* CSCO 137, Scriptores Armeniaci 1 (Louvain, 1953); Latin trans. 145, Scriptores Armeniaci 2 (Louvain, 1964). An English translation is by J. Hamlyn Hill, *A Dissertation on the Gospel Commentary of S. Ephraem the Syrian* (Edinburgh: T. & T. Clark, 1896).

[20]See esp. ch. 3 in Vööbus, *Studies in the History of the Gospel Text in Syriac,* 25-45. The great collection of quotations of early Syriac fathers and the attempted reconstruction of the Diatessaron by Urbina must be viewed with caution since it uses early Syriac sources without sufficient discrimination. Ignatius Ortiz de Urbina, *Vetus Evangelium Syrorum, et exinde excerptum Diatessaron Tatiani,* Biblia Polyglotta Matritensia, Series 6 (Madrid, 1967). Cf. the critical review of this work by Robert Murray, "Reconstructing the Diatessaron," *HeyJ* 10 (1969): 43-49.

the text, the Arabic Diatessaron is generally considered reliable[21] as well as when it agrees with the Syriac tradition against the canonical Greek. In several examples below where these criteria are met an English translation of the Arabic will be cited as a witness.[22]

The first two examples will consist of Tatianic readings (that is, readings involving the actual wording of the Diatessaron) in the Hebrew text of Shem-Tob.

| 5:14 | Greek | οὐ δύναται πόλις κρυβῆναι ἐπάνω ὄρους κειμένη |
| | | (A city *set* on a hill cannot be hidden.) |
| | Shem-Tob | עיר בנויה על ההר לא תוכל להסתר |
| | | (A city *built* on a hill cannot be hidden.) |

Evidence for "built" being a Diatessaric reading is: (1) Sy[s.c.p] read "built" (**בניא**). (2) The Coptic Gospel of Thomas (32), which often shares readings with Tatian's Diatessaron,[23] reads "A city being *built* on a high mountain and fortified cannot fall, nor can it be hidden."[24] A Greek counterpart to this is Pap. *Oxyrhynch.* 1.7: πόλις οἰκοδομημένη ἐπ᾽ ἄκρον [ὄ] ὑψηλοῦς καὶ ἐστηριγμένη οὔτε πε[σ]εῖν δύναται οὐδὲ κρυ[β]ῆναι. (3) Arabic Diatessaron 8.41: "It is impossible that a city *built* on a mountain should be hid."

| 5:30 | Greek | ἡ δεξιά σου χείρ | (your right hand) |
| | Shem-Tob | ידך | (your hand) |
| | vEC[25] | | (your hand) |

In addition to these readings there are several lengthy passages involving order and mixture of synoptic parallels rather than wording that correspond to the Diatessaron. The following is a sampling.

---

[21]See Bruce M. Metzger, *The Early Versions of the New Testament* (Oxford: Clarendon Press, 1977) 10-36.

[22]The translation is that of Hope W. Hogg, "The Diatessaron of Tatian" in *The Ante-Nicene Fathers,* vol. 10, 5th ed., ed. Allan Menzies (reprint: Grand Rapids MI: Eerdmans, 1965) 35-138.

[23]T. Baarda, *Early Transmission of the Words of Jesus: Thomas, Tatian, and the Text of the New Testament,* ed. J. Helderman and S. J. Noorda (Amsterdam: VU Boekhandel/ Uitgeverij, 1983) 38. For a discussion of the relationship between the two and further bibliography see Metzger, *The Early Versions of the New Testament,* 29-30.

[24]Translation by Lambdin in *The Nag Hammadi Library,* 122.

[25]See Hill, *Gospel Commentary of S. Ephraem,* 84n5.

| Shem-Tob | Arabic Diatessaron 7.37-38 |
|---|---|
| (Matt 12:1) and his disciples | his disciples |
| being hungry began to pluck | hungered. And they were |
| the ears | rubbing the ears |
| (Luke 6:1) and to crush them | |
| between their hands | with their hands, |
| (Matt 12:1) and to eat them | and eating |
| | vEC |
| | began to pluck the ears, |
| | to rub and to eat |

The Diatessaron at this point appears to have been a combination of Matthean and Lukan readings. The major differences in the two synoptics are: (1) Matthew reads ''hungered'' (ἐπείνασαν) and ''began'' (ἤρξαντο). Neither of these elements appears in the majority text of Luke. (2) Luke reads ''to crush them between their hands.'' These words are lacking in the majority text of Matthew. A comparison of the Arabic Diatessaron[26] and Ephraem's Armenian commentary on the Diatessaron demonstrates that at least parts of these three elements occurred in Tatian's harmony. The reading in Shem-Tob concurs with Tatian since it too includes all three elements.

| Shem-Tob (Ms A) | Sy^c |
|---|---|
| (Matt 5:3) Blessed are the | (Matt 5:3) Happy is it for the |
| humble of spirit for theirs | poor in their spirit, that theirs |
| is the kingdom of heaven. | is the kingdom of heaven. |
| (Matt 5:5) Blessed are the | (Matt 5:5) Happy is it for the |
| meek for they shall inherit | lowly, that they shall inherit |
| the earth. | the earth. |
| (Matt 5:4) Blessed are | (Matt 5:4) Happy is it for the |
| those who wait for they | mourners, that they shall be |
| shall be comforted. | comforted.      (Burkitt translation) |

In this particular instance Sy^c, accompanied by Shem-Tob, appears to follow the order of the Diatessaron of 5:3, 5:5, and 5:4. Hill argues that Ephraem and Aphraates did the same: ''Ephraem quotes this beatitude [5:5—GH] before the preceding one, as if his Diatessaron had it in the or-

---

[26]The Arabic has not been revised toward the Peshitta in this instance. The latter reads according to the majority Greek text of Matthew.

der of the Curetonian Syriac and Aphraates."[27] The Arabic Diatessaron
follows the Greek order and probably represents an accommodation to it.

| Shem-Tob | Arabic Diatessaron 4.18-25 |
|---|---|
| (Matt 3:10) Already the axe has reached the root of the tree; the one which does not produce good fruit will be cut down and burned in the fire (Luke 3:10-15) The crowds asked him: if so what shall we do. John answered them: he who has two shirts let him give one to him who has none. | Behold, the axe hath been laid at the roots of the trees, and so every tree that beareth not good fruit shall be taken and cast into the fire. And the multitudes were asking him and saying, What shall we do? He answered and said unto them, He that hath two tunics shall give to him that hath not; and he that hath food shall do likewise. |
| So they came to be baptized. Many asked him: what shall we do, and he answered them: be anxious for no man. | And the publicans also came to be baptized, and they said unto him, Teacher, what shall we do? He said unto them, Seek no more than what ye are commanded to seek. And the servants of the guard asked him and said, And we also, what shall we do? He said unto them, |
| and do not chastise them and be pleased with your lot. And all the people were thinking and reckoning in their circumcised heart, John is Jesus. (Luke 3:16) John answered all of them: (Matt 3:11) behold I truly baptize you in the days of repentance, but afterwards another comes mightier than I (Luke 3:16) the thong of whose sandal I am not worthy to unfasten | Do not violence to any man, nor wrong him; and let your allowances satisfy you. And when the people were conjecturing about John, and all of them thinking in their hearts whether he were haply the Messiah, John answered and said unto them, I baptize you with water there cometh one after me who is stronger than I the latchets of whose shoes I am not worthy to loose; |

---

[27]Hill, *Gospel Commentary of S. Ephraem* 83n4. For a translation of Aphraates see F.
C. Burkitt, *Evangelion Da-Mepharreshe*, vol. 2: *Introduction and Notes* (Cambridge:
Cambridge University Press, 1904) 181.

| (Matt 3:11 ‖ Luke 3:16) He will baptize you with the fire of the Holy Spirit. | he will baptize you with the Holy Spirit and fire. |

| Shem-Tob | Arabic Diatessaron 11.44-50 |
|---|---|
| (Matt 8:29) They cried out to him saying: what is between you and us, Jesus Son of God. Have you come before the time to grieve us and to destroy us? (Mark 5:8 ‖ Luke 8:29) Then Jesus said to them: come out from there evil host. . . . (Matt 8:31) So the demons entreated him: since we have to go out from here, grant us authority to go into these swine. (Matt 8:32a) Then he said to them: go, (Luke 8:33) and the demons went out from the men and entered the swine (Matt 8:33b) and all the herd went in sudden haste, slipped off into the sea | and cried out with a loud voice and said, What have we to do with thee, Jesus Son of the most high God. I adjure thee by God torment me not. And Jesus commanded the unclean spirit to come out of the man. . . . and those devils besought him to give them leave to enter the swine; and he gave them leave. And the devils went out of the man and entered into the swine. And that herd hastened to the summit and fell down into the midst of the sea, about two thousand, |
| and died in the water. | and they were choked in the water. |

Two other very lengthy examples will be lumped together here without reproducing their texts. The first is the account of the transfiguration in Matt 17:1-5. Both in Shem-Tob and the Arabic Diatessaron (24.2-12) the account is a mixture of Matthew and Luke 9:28-35. The overlaps between Tatian's harmony and the text of Shem-Tob are striking. The second is Matt 17:17 and 19 between which is sandwiched Mark 9:20-28. This is also the case for the Arabic Diatessaron (24.35-46).

The relationship between Shem-Tob and Tatian is not entirely clear. Although it is similar to that between the Old Syriac and the Diatessaron, and between the Old Latin and the Diatessaron, it differs sometimes from them by containing very lengthy insertions from parallel accounts in agreement with Tatian. The relationship of Shem-Tob to Tatian goes beyond the numerous short Tatianic readings in the Syriac and Latin. In some passages it apears to be an actual reproduction of the Tatianic text itself.

These passages are, of course, limited in number and are quite sporadic, involving perhaps only ten percent of the entire text or less.

Two explanations are apropos to this situation. First, in some cases it is possible that the Old Latin, the Old Syriac, and the text of Shem-Tob reflect an ancient form of the separate gospels in which the synoptic texts were closer together in wording than they appear in the modern editions of the Greek New Testament.[28] Second, it is hard to escape the conclusion that several lengthy passages in Shem-Tob corresponding to parallel synoptic accounts and in agreement with the Diatessaron are due to the direct influence of the Diatessaron on the transmission of the text of Shem-Tob. If the Hebrew Matthew contained in the *Even Bohan* predates Shem-Tob and was used by Jews in anti-Christian polemics, as the evidence suggests, it may be that some Tatianic readings, especially the longer passages, were interpolated into the Hebrew text at an early time in order to provide a basis for debate for Jews who lived in areas where the Diatessaron was in use. The fact that they were inserted sporadically points to the selectiveness with which the contestants chose scripture for purposes of debate. If this is the case, the text of Shem-Tob in the relevant passages becomes a valuable Hebrew witness to the Diatessaron.

## Puns, Word Connections, and Alliteration

A major characteristic of Shem-Tob's Hebrew Matthew is the use of puns, word connections, and alliteration. Readings portraying these literary devices are numerous and belong to the very structure of the Matthean Gospel. Sometimes such elements can be reproduced in translation but only with great difficulty and usually only by one who is interested in preserving or enhancing the integrity and literary beauty of the base text. There are two reasons to suspect these literary elements here belong to the old substratum to Shem-Tob's Matthew and are the product of an original Hebrew composition, not a translation: (1) The text is so saturated with them (far beyond what appears in the Greek) it does not seem reasonable that any translator, regardless of his motives, would have created them. (2) The polemical nature of the *Even Bohan* proscribes any reasonable suspicion that a fourteenth-century rabbi would have gone out of his way to

---

[28]George Howard, "Harmonistic Readings in the Old Syriac Gospels," *HTR* 73 (1980): 485.

beautify and otherwise enhance the text of the Gospel of Matthew. The following are examples from each of the three categories listed above.

### Puns

Many of the sayings of Jesus and even narratives about him according to Shem-Tob are constructed around puns and wordplays. Matt 7:6 reads: "do not throw your pearls before swine, lest they trample them under foot and turn to attack you." In Shem-Tob the words for "swine" and "turn" are alike, being *ḥazir* (חזיר) and *yaḥᵃzor* (יחזר) respectively. Matt 10:25 reads: "If they have called the master of the house Beelzebul." In Shem-Tob "master of the house" and "Beelzebul" are *baal habayit* (בעל הבית) and *baal zᵉvuv* (בעל זבוב) respectively. Matt 10:36 reads: "and a man's foes will be those of his own household." In place of this, Shem-Tob reads: "The enemy will be loved ones," which makes a wordplay on "the enemy" *ha'oyᵉvim* (האויבים) and "loved ones" *'ahuvim* (אהובים). In Matt 17:22 the text in part reads: "The Son of Man is to be delivered into the hands of men." For "Son of Man" Shem-Tob reads *ben ha'adam* (בן האדם) and for "men" *bᵉne ha'adam* (בני האדם). Matt 18:27 reads: "And out of pity for him the lord of that servant released him and forgave him the debt." In place of this, Shem-Tob reads the pithy saying: "Then his master had pity on him and forgave him everything." This is a play on the words "to pity" from the root *ḥamal* (חמל) and "to forgive" from the root *maḥal* (מחל). Matt 21:19 reads: "And seeing a fig tree by the wayside he went to it and found nothing on it but leaves only. And he said to it, 'May no fruit ever come from you again'." Shem-Tob in part reads: "he found nothing on it except leaves . . . may fruit not come forth from you for ever." Two wordplays in Hebrew form the structure of this statement as the following diagram shows:

מצא בה רק העלים
יצא ממך פרי לעולם

The wordplays are made by the combination of *matsa'* (מצא) "found" / *yetse'* (יצא) "come forth" and *ha'alim* (העלים) "leaves" / *lᵉolam* (לעולם) "for ever." Matt 23:27-28 reads in part: "[27]for you are like whitewashed tombs, which outwardly appear beautiful, but within they are full of dead men's bones and all uncleanness. [28]So you also outwardly appear righteous to men, but within you are full of hypocrisy and iniquity." The saying in Shem-Tob contains a play on the words "tombs" from the root *qever* (קבר) and "within" (vs. 28) from the root *qerev* (קרב). Matt 23:29, 31 reads in part: "[29]for you build the tombs of the prophets . . . [31]Thus you witness against yourselves, that you are sons of those who murdered the prophets." For "build" Shem-Tob reads the root *banah* (בנה) and for "sons" the root *ben* (בן).

A rather lengthy passage involving a pun is Matt 16:9-11. It reads: "[9]Do you not yet perceive? Do you not remember the five loaves of the five thousand, and how many baskets you gathered? [10]Or the seven loaves of the four thousand, and how many baskets you gathered? [11]How is it that you fail to perceive that I did not speak about bread? Beware of the leaven of the Pharisees and Sadducees." Shem-Tob's text is much shorter, lacking all of vs. 10, and contains a different wording. Of primary importance is the fact that in vs. 9 it reads "were left over" *niš<sup>a</sup>ru* (נשארו) in place of the Greek "gathered" (ἐλάβετε). This is similar to the word "beware" (vs. 11) which according to the reading of mss ABDEFG of Shem-Tob is *tišm<sup>e</sup>ru* (תשמרו). At this point the British Library ms, accompanied by ms C, reads תשארו which appears to be a visual mistake for the similarly looking reading in the majority text of Shem-Tob. This mistake was perhaps made by a scribe whose eye jumped prematurely to the next word *š<sup>e</sup>'or* (שאר) "leaven" which though lacking in Shem-Tob's text is represented in Greek by ζύμης[29] and appears to have been a part of the original pericope. We conjecture, then, that a pun on the words שאר "left over," שמר "beware," and שאר "leaven" stood in the original discourse and that the last word was lost in Hebrew during transmission of the text.

The most famous pun in Greek Matthew occurs at 16:18 where the text reads: "You are Peter (Πέτρος) and on this rock (πέτρα) I will build my church." Because of the wordplay in Greek August Dell argued that this saying originally circulated in Greek and originated not in Jesus but in the Greek-speaking segment of the church.[30] Although Dell's argument has some logic, another pun exists in the Hebrew text of Shem-Tob that militates against his conclusion. The Hebrew reads: "You are a *stone* (אבן) and upon you *I will build* (אבנה) my house of prayer." The pun, *even* ("stone")—*evneh* ("I will build"), forms the very structure of the saying

---

[29]Shem-Tob uses שאר opposite ζύμη in Matt 13:13.

[30]August Dell, "Matthäus 16, 17-19," *ZNW* 15 (1914): 1-49; "Zur Erklärung von Matthäus 16:17-19," *ZNW* 17 (1916): 27-32 See Klijn's objections in A. F. J. Klijn, "die Wörter 'Stein' und 'Felsen' in der syrischen Übersetzung des Neuen Testaments," *ZNW* 50 (1959): 99-105.

in Shem-Tob. The authenticity of the Hebrew wordplay is suggested by the appearance of the same words in Matt 21:42 which is a quotation of messianic flavor from Ps 118:22: "The very *stone* which the *builders* rejected has become the head of the corner." Shem-Tob's text, which equals the Masoretic Text of Ps 118:22, again includes the בנה/אבן combination.

## Word Connections

The text of Shem-Tob is replete with word connections that give structure to individual sayings and pericopes and that tie separate sayings and pericopes together. An interesting case is Matt 4:21-23 which in the Hebrew text unites the pericopes on the calling of James and John and the early preaching of Jesus in Galilee. According to the Greek, the brothers, James and John, are sons of Zebedee (Ζεβεδαῖος). Beyond the mention of this fact the name "Zebedee" plays no further role in the immediate context. In the Hebrew text the matter is different. Matt 4:21 reads: "He turned from there and saw two other brothers, James and John, brothers who were sons of Zebedeel (זבדיאל)." The name "Zebedeel" (made up of זבדי and אל) means "gifts of God."

The next pericope begins with vs. 23. In Hebrew it reads: "Then Jesus went around the land of Galilee teaching their assemblies and was preaching to them the good gift (זבד) . . . of the kingdom of heaven." The connection is clear. The two pericopes, that is, the calling of James and John and the early preaching of Jesus in Galilee, are held together by the catchword "gift." The catchword fails to appear in the Greek or Latin although the name Zebedee ( = זבדי), meaning "my gift(s)," represents a remnant of the situation.

The sequence of the Matthean pericopes is thus clearly built upon the catchword situation of זבד "gift" although it appears only in the Hebrew. It is highly unlikely that a Jewish polemist of the fourteenth century (or any century), trying to disprove the validity of the Gospel of Matthew, would have created this word connection *ex nihilo*. This means that in all probability the sequence of these pericopes goes back to a Hebrew, not to a Greek or Latin, *Vorlage*.

The following is a list of similar connections that occur in the Hebrew text but *not* in the Greek or Latin. The Hebrew words/roots involved will be placed at the end of each example.

⁹Blessed are those who *pursue* (רודפי) peace for they shall be called the sons of God.

**5:9-10**  ¹⁰Blessed are those who are *persecuted* (הנרדפים) for righteousness for theirs is the kingdom of heaven.

רדף "to pursue" / רדף "to persecute"

¹⁴A city built upon a hill cannot be *hidden* (להסתר).

**5:14-15**  ¹⁵They do not light a lamp to place it in a *hidden* (נסתר) place.

סתר "to hide"

²⁸There *met him* (ויפגעו בו) two demon-possessed men.

**8:28, 31**  ³¹Then the demons *entreated him* (ויפגעו בו).

פגע "to meet" / פגע "to entreat"

³⁶The enemy will be *loved* ones (אהובים).

³⁷He who *loves* (האוהב) his father and mother more than me . . .

**10:36, 37, 39**  ³⁸[omitted in Shem-Tob]

³⁹He who *loves* (האוהב) his life will lose it.

אהב "to love"

⁸Those who wear noble garments are in the houses of *kings* (המלכים)

**11:8, 10**  ¹⁰This is he about whom it is written: behold, I am sending *my messenger* (מלאכי).

מלך "king" / מלאך "messenger"

¹³Then he said to the man: *stretch out* (נטה) your hand and he *stretched out* (ויט) his hand and it returned as the other.

**12:13, 15**  ¹⁵It came to pass after this Jesus knew and *turned aside* (ויט) from there.

נטה "to stretch out" / נטה "to turn aside"

³⁵They brought to him all those who were *sick* (החולים) with various kinds of diseases.

**14:35, 36**  ³⁶*They implored* (ויחלו) him. . . .

חָלָה "to be sick" / חָלָה "to implore"

³⁴They answered: *seven* (שבעה) and a few fish.

³⁵So Jesus commanded the people to sit upon the grass.

³⁶Then he took the *seven* (השבעה) loaves and broke them and gave

**15:34-37**  them to his disciples and they gave to the people.

³⁷All of them ate and were *satisfied* (וישבעו) and from that which was remaining they filled *seven* (שבעה) seahs.

שבעה "seven" / שבע "to be satisfied"

¹⁶If he does not listen to you, reprove him before another; if by every oath he does not listen to you add *still* (עוד) one or two in order

**18:16**  that your words might be before two or three *witnesses* (עדים) because by two or three *witnesses* (עדים) a word will be established.

עוד "still" / עד "witness"

|  |  |
|---|---|
| 18:23-35 | ²³At that time Jesus said to his disciples: the kingdom of heaven is like a certain king who sat to make a reckoning with his servants and ministers.<br>²⁴As he began to reckon, one came who owed about ten thousand pieces of gold.<br>²⁵But he had nothing to give and his master commanded to sell him and his children and all that was his *to repay* (לשלם) the value.<br>²⁶The servant fell before his master and implored him to have pity on him and to be patient with him because he would *repay* (ישלם) everything.<br>²⁷Then his master had pity on him and forgave him everything.<br>²⁸But that servant went out and found one of his comrades who owed him a hundred pieces of money and he grasped him and struck him saying. . . .<br>²⁹Trust me and be patient with me and I will *repay* (אשלם) everything.<br>³⁰But he was not willing to listen to him; so they brought him to the prison until he *repaid* (שלם) him everything.<br>³¹The servants of the king saw that which he did and were very angry and went and told their master.<br>³²Then his master called him and said to him: cursed servant, did I not forgive you all your (debt) when you placated me.<br>³³So why did you not forgive your servant when he supplicated you as I forgave you?<br>³⁴His master was angry with him and commanded to afflict him until he should *repay* (ישלם) him all the debt.<br>³⁵Thus will my Father who is in heaven do to you if you do not forgive each man his brother with a *perfect* (שלם) heart.<br>שלם "to repay" / שלם "perfect" |
| 19:9, 13 | ⁹He who takes her who has been *divorced* (הגרושה) commits adultery.<br>¹³Then they brought children to him that he might lay his hand on them and pray for them, but his disciples were *driving* (מגרשים) them away.<br>גרש "to divorce" / גרש "to drive away" |
| 21:37-38, 46 | ³⁷Finally, he sent them his son saying: perhaps they will *honor* (יראו) my son.<br>³⁸The workers *saw* (ויראו) his son and said to one another: this is the heir. Come, let us kill him and we will inherit his estate.<br>⁴⁶Then they sought to kill him but they *feared* (ויראו) the crowds to whom he was a prophet.<br>ירא "to honor/fear" / ראה "to see" |

<sup>9</sup>It would have been possible to have sold it for a great price and to have given it to the *poor* (לעניים).

26:9-11   <sup>10</sup>But Jesus who knows everything in regard to any *matter* (ענין) done, said to them: . . .

<sup>11</sup>Because the *poor* (העניים) will be with you always.

עני "poor" / ענין "matter"

<sup>28</sup>This is my blood of the new covenant which was poured out for many for the *atonement* (לכפרת) of sins.

<sup>34</sup>Jesus said: truly I say to you, this night before the cock-crow you will *deny* (תכפור) me three times.

26:28, 34-36   <sup>35</sup>Peter said to him: if it is possible for me to die with you, I will not *deny* (אכפור) you. . . .

<sup>36</sup>Then Jesus came with them to the *village* (לכפר) of Geshemonim and said: sit now until I go there and pray.

כפרה "atonement" / כפר "to deny" / כפר "village"

## Alliteration

In the following passages alliteration of various kinds occurs. The relevant words in Hebrew will be placed in parentheses, pointed, and transliterated.

4:12   It came to pass in those days Jesus heard that John *had been delivered up* (נִמְטַר, nimsar) *into prison* (בְּמַאֲסָר, b<sup>e</sup>ma'asar).

4:21   He turned from there and saw two *other brothers* (אָחִים אֲחֵרִים, 'ahim 'aherim).

5:23   If you should *offer your gift* (תַּקְרִיב קָרְבָּנְךָ, taqriv qarbankha) at the altar and remember that you have a quarrel with *your companion* (חֲבֵרְךָ, h<sup>a</sup>verkha).<sup>31</sup>

7:2   With what judgment you judge and with what measure you measure it will be measured to you (בְּאֵיזֶה דִין תִּדוֹנוּ וּבְאֵיזֶה מִדָּה תָּמוֹדוּ יְמוֹדֵד לָכֶם, b<sup>e</sup>'ezeh din tidonu uv'eze midah tamodu y<sup>e</sup>moded lakhem).

9:8   The crowds *saw* (וַיִּרְאוּ, vayir'u) and *feared* (וַיִּרְאוּ, vayir'u).<sup>32</sup>

11:6   Blessed is the one who (וְאַשְׁרֵי אֲשֶׁר, v<sup>e</sup>'ašre 'ašer).

11:29   Take my *yoke upon you* (עוּלִי עֲלֵיכֶם, 'uli <sup>a</sup>lekhem) and learn of me and know that *I am meek* (עָנִי אָנִי, 'ani '<sup>a</sup>ni).

---

<sup>31</sup>See also 8:4. Cf. Jean Carmignac, "Studies in the Hebrew Background of the Synoptic Gospels," *ASTI* 7 (1970): 72.

<sup>32</sup>Carmignac spotted this wordplay without benefit of the Shem-Tob text. See ibid.

| 12:15 | Many *sick* (חוֹלִים, *ḥolim*) followed him and he healed *all of them* (כּוּלָם, *kulam*). |
|-------|----------------------------------------------------------------------------|

| 12:24 | This one does not cast out demons except by *Beelzebub* (בְּבַעַל זְבוּב, *b°va'al zivuv*) *the lord of demons* (בַּעַל הַשֵּׁדִים, *ba'al hašedim*). |
|-------|----------------------------------------------------------------------------|

| 14:32 | When they went up into a boat *the wind settled down* (נָח הָרוּחַ, *naḥ haruaḥ*). |
|-------|----------------------------------------------------------------------------|

| 18:9 | If your eye causes you to *stumble* (תַּכְשִׁילֶךְ, *takhšilekha*) . . . *cast* (תַּשְׁלִיכֶהָ, *tašlikheha*) it from you. |
|------|----------------------------------------------------------------------------|

## The Divine Name

A set of interesting readings in the Hebrew Matthew of Shem-Tob is a series of passages incorporating the Divine Name symbolized by ה״ (apparently a circumlocution for השם, "The Name"). This occurs some nineteen times. (Fully written השם occurs at 28:9 and is included in the nineteen.) Usually the Divine Name appears where the Greek reads κύριος, twice (21:12 mss, 22:31) where the Greek reads θεός, and twice where it occurs alone (22:32; 27:9). (1) It regularly appears in quotations from the Hebrew Bible where the MT contains the Tetragrammaton. (2) It occurs in introductions to quotations as, for example, at 1:22, "All this was to complete what was written by the prophet according to the LORD"; and at 22:31, "Have you not read concerning the resurrection of the dead that the LORD spoke to you saying." (3) In narratives apart from quotations it occurs in such phrases as "angel of the LORD" or "house of the LORD." Thus, 2:13, "As they were going, behold, the angel of the LORD appeared unto Joseph saying"; 2:19, "It came to pass when King Herod died the angel of the LORD appeared in a dream to Joseph in Egypt"; 21:12, "Then Jesus entered the house of the LORD"; 28:2, "Then the earth was shaken because the angel of the LORD descended from heaven to the tomb, overturned the stone, and stood still."

The reading of the Divine Name in a Christian document quoted by a Jewish polemist is remarkable. If this were a Hebrew translation of a Greek or Latin Christian document, one would expect to find *adonai* in the text, not a symbol for the ineffable divine name YHWH. Furthermore, for Shem-Tob the Gospel of Matthew was an object of attack, a heretical writing that needed to be exposed for its fallacies. For him to have added the ineffable name is inexplicable. The evidence strongly suggests that Shem-Tob received his Matthew with the Divine Name already within the text and that he probably preserved it rather than run the risk of being guilty of removing it.[33]

The evidence from Shem-Tob's Matthew coincides with the present writer's earlier stated conclusions about the use of the Tetragrammaton in the Septuagint and the Greek New Testament.[34] The extant pre-Christian copies of the Septuagint that include passages incorporating the Divine Name preserve the Divine Name in the Greek text. These are (1) P. Fuad 266 (= Rahlfs 848), 50 BCE, contains the Tetragrammaton in Aramaic letters;[35] (2) a fragmentary scroll of the Twelve Prophets in Greek from Wadi Khabra (= W. Khabra XII καίγε), 50 BCE–50 CE, contains the Tetragrammaton in paleo-Hebrew letters;[36] (3) 4QLXX^Levb (= Rahlfs 802), first century BCE, contains the Tetragrammaton in the form of ΙΑΩ.[37] From these examples it may be concluded that the New Testament writers had access to copies of LXX that contained the Hebrew Divine Name. Those who used such copies of LXX for their quotations of the Old Testament probably

---

[33]Cf. the famous rabbinic passage, t. Šabb. 13.5: "The margins and books of the minim do not save." The debate that follows about what is to be done with heretical books concerns the issue of the divine names, אזכרות, in them. R. José suggests the divine name should be cut out and the rest of the document burned. R. Tarphon and R. Ishmael say the books in their entirety, including the divine name, should be destroyed. See Herford, *Christianity in Talmud and Midrash*, 155-57. By incorporating the Hebrew Matthew into his *Even Bohan*, Shem-Tob apparently felt compelled to preserve the Divine Name along with the rest of the text. ה" in Shem-Tob's Matthew should not be viewed as a symbol for both Adonai and the Tetragrammaton as was customary for Hebrew documents copied during the Middle Ages. The author of the Hebrew Matthew uses Adonai and ה" discriminately. He uses Adonai in reference to Jesus and ה" only in reference to God. Since אדוני (often itself abbreviated as אד') refers to Jesus, not God, throughout the text, the author's use of ה" is a symbol only for the Tetragrammaton and in all probability stands for the circumlocution השם, "The Name."

[34]See George Howard, "The Tetragram and the New Testament," *JBL* 96 (1977): 63-83; idem, "The Name of God in the New Testament," *Biblical Archaeology Review* 4 (1978): 12-14, 56.

[35]Françoise Dunand, *Etudes de Papyrologie* (Cairo, 1971). W. G. Waddell, "The Tetragrammaton in the LXX," *JTS* 45 (1944): 158-61. George Howard, "The Oldest Greek Text of Deuteronomy," *HUCA* 42 (1971): 125-31.

[36]D. Barthélemy, "Redécouverte d'un chaînon manquant de l'histoire de la Septante," *Revue Biblique* 60 (1953): 18-29; idem, *Les devanciers d'Aquila: Première publication intégrale du text des fragments du Dodecaprophéton*, VTSup 10 (Leiden: Brill, 1963).

[37]P. W. Skehan, "The Qumran Manuscripts and Textual Criticism," *Volume du Congrès, Strasbourg 1956*, VTSup 4 (Leiden: Brill, 1957) 148-60.

preserved the Tetragrammaton in the quotations incorporated into their texts.[38]

Although written in Hebrew, Shem-Tob's Matthew further testifies to the use of the Divine Name in the New Testament. Its conservative use of the Divine Name, which occurs only in quotations from the Hebrew Bible, introductions to the quotations, or in biblical phrases such as "angel of the LORD," and "house of the LORD," corresponds closely to the use of the Tetragrammaton in the Hebrew documents from among the Dead Sea Scrolls. As was concluded in 1977, "In the Hebrew documents from the Judean Desert the Tetragram appears in copies of the Bible, in quotations of the Bible, and in biblical-type passages such as *florilegia* and biblical paraphrases. Occasionally, it appears in non-biblical material; but this is not often and the material is Bible-like in nature."[39]

## Theological Tendencies in Shem-Tob's Matthew

In some instances the Hebrew Matthew of Shem-Tob shows theological tendencies not found in the Greek. It is unlikely these variances were introduced by a medieval Jewish translator, especially someone who was engaged in polemical disputation with Christians, because they either portray Christianity more, not less, attractively or fail to enhance the Jewish polemic against Christianity. Instead, they appear to belong to a more primitive form of the Matthean tradition than the Greek Matthew. During the early Christian centuries the disparity between Judaism and Christianity gradually increased. But the theological variances in Shem-Tob's Hebrew text often reflect a lesser disparity between the two religions than does the Greek text. An example is Jesus' attitude toward the law, a subject treated in Matthew 5. Matt 5:17-19 gives Jesus' statement about the perdurability of the law:

> Think not that I have come to abolish the law and the prophets; I have come not to abolish them but to fulfil them. For truly, I say to you, till heaven and earth pass away, not an iota, not a dot, will pass from the law until all

---

[38]See further Patrick W. Skehan, "The Divine Name at Qumran, in the Masada Scroll, and in the Septuagint," *BIOSCS* 13 (1980): 14-44; A. Pietersma, "Kyrios or Tetragram: A Renewed Quest for the Original Septuagint," in *De Septuaginta. Studies in Honour of John William Wevers on His Sixty-Fifth Birthday,* ed. A. Pietersma and C. Cox (Toronto: Benben Publications, 1984) 85-101.

[39]Howard, "The Tetragram and the New Testament," 71.

is accomplished. Whoever then relaxes one of the least of these commandments and teaches men so, shall be called least in the kingdom of heaven; but he who does them and teaches them shall be called great in the kingdom of heaven.

There follows in Matt 5:21-48 the so-called antitheses.[40] Each antithesis first quotes from the law (except the last one) and then gives Jesus' extension or comment on the law. The form is basically the same in each antithesis: "You have heard that it was said. . . . But I say to you. . . . " The subjects are killing, adultery, divorce, false swearing, the *lex talionis*, and hating your enemies.

In the Greek text of Matthew, Jesus' comment on some of the antitheses—like killing and adultery—seems to radicalize and internalize the law without, however, revoking it. In other antitheses—divorce and false swearing—Jesus' comment seems to revoke and annul the letter of the law. At least this is true in the Greek Matthew. But in Shem-Tob's Hebrew Matthew that is not the case with respect to divorce and false swearing. Instead, in these instances, Jesus' comment in the antitheses suggests he is radicalizing and internalizing the law but not revoking it. It may well be that here the Greek Matthew represents a later corrective to the more ancient statements in the Hebrew, made only after the disparity between Church and Synagogue grew. Compare the Greek Matthew and Shem-Tob's Hebrew Matthew on divorce and false swearing:

### Divorce (Matt 5:31-32)

| [Greek] | [Hebrew] |
|---|---|
| It was also said, "Whoever divorces his wife, let him give her a certificate of divorce." But I say to you that every one who divorces his wife, except on the ground of unchastity, makes her an adulteress. . . .                    (RSV) | Again Jesus said to his disciples: "You have heard what was said to those of long ago that everyone who leaves his wife and divorces [her] is to give her a bill of divorce. . . . And I say to you that everyone who leaves his wife *is to give her a bill of divorce*. But concerning adultery, he is the one who commits adultery. . . . " |

---

[40]For an excellent discussion of the issue see John P. Meier, *Law and History in Matthew's Gospel* (Rome: Biblical Institute Press, 1976).

## False Swearing (Matt 5:33-37)

| [Greek] | [Hebrew] |
|---|---|
| Again you have heard that it was said to the men of old, "You shall not swear falsely, but shall perform to the Lord what you have sworn." But I say to you, do not swear *at all,* either by heaven, for it is the throne of God. . . . (RSV) | Again you have heard what was said to those of long ago: you shall not swear *by my name* falsely, but you shall return to the Lord your oath. But I say to you not to swear *in vain by anything,* either by heaven because it is the throne of God. . . . |

The differences between the Greek and Hebrew are striking. In the Greek Jesus seems to revoke the law. In the Hebrew, he internalizes and radicalizes it, but does not revoke it.

Another difference between the Greek and Hebrew Matthew is in the character of John the Baptist. We know from other sources that there was a John the Baptist sect that existed from early times and continued perhaps for centuries.[41] In Shem-Tob's Hebrew Matthew John the Baptist emerges as a much more important figure than in the Greek Matthew. The Greek Matthew may well represent a later corrective to the more primitive statements made about John the Baptist in Hebrew Matthew before the followers of John the Baptist were seen as a threat to trunkline Christianity. Here are some of the differences between the Hebrew and Greek texts in the portrayal of John the Baptist.

## Matthew 11:11

| [Greek] | [Hebrew] |
|---|---|
| Truly, I say to you, among those born of women there has risen no one greater than John the Baptist: *yet he who is least in the kingdom of heaven is greater than he.* (RSV) | Truly I say to you, among all those born of women none has arisen greater than John the Baptizer. [The last phrase in Greek is lacking in Shem-Tob's Hebrew text.] |

## Matthew 11:13

| [Greek] | [Hebrew] |
|---|---|
| For all the prophets and the law prophesied *until* John. (RSV) | For all the prophets and the law spoke *concerning* John. |

---

[41]Cf. Acts 18:5–19:7; Justin, *Trypho* 80; *Pseudo-Clementine Recognitions* 1.54.60. Cf. C. K. Barrett, *The Gospel according to St. John* (London: S.P.C.K., 1962) 142; Raymond E. Brown, *The Gospel according to John,* Anchor Bible 29A, 29B (Garden City NY: Doubleday, 1966) A:lxvii-lxx.

Matthew 17:11

[Greek]                                        [Hebrew]
Elijah does come, and he is *to restore*       Indeed Elijah will come and *will save*
*all things.*                      (RSV)       *all the world.*
[Vs 13 tells us that "the disciples
understood that (Jesus) was speaking to
them of John the Baptist." (RSV)]

In Matt 21:31-32 Jesus speaks harsh words to those who failed to heed the warnings of John the Baptist: "Truly, I say to you, the tax collectors and the harlots go into the kingdom of God before you. For John came to you in the way of righteousness, and you did not believe him, but the tax collectors and the harlots believed him; and even when you saw it, you did not afterward repent and believe him" (RSV). In the Greek Matthew these harsh words are said to the chief priests and the elders of the people (vs 23), but in Shem-Tob's Hebrew Matthew these harsh words are spoken to Jesus' own disciples (vs 28) and the following comment, lacking in the Greek text, appears: "He who has ears to hear let him hear in disgrace."

This series of readings can hardly be taken lightly. They point to an ancient tradition in which John the Baptist was even more important than the portrayal of him given in the Greek text of Matthew.

## Different Interpretations in Shem-Tob's Matthew

There are several passages in the Hebrew Matthew that differ in meaning from the Greek Matthew. Occasionally the Hebrew appears to be more primitive than the Greek. A few instances will be noted.

In the Beelzebul (Hebrew: Beelzebub) controversy, recorded in Matt 12:24-28, the Greek version reads as follows:

> [24]But when the Pharisees heard it they said, "It is only by Beelzebul, the prince of demons, that this man casts out demons." [25]Knowing their thoughts, he said to them, "Every kingdom divided against itself is laid waste, and no city or house divided against itself will stand; [26]and if Satan casts out Satan, he is divided against himself; how then will his kingdom stand? [27]And if I cast out demons by Beelzebul, by whom do your sons cast them out? Therefore they shall be your judge. [28]But if it is by the Spirit of God that I cast out demons, then the kingdom of God has come upon you." (RSV)

A common understanding of this passage is: (1) Jesus rejects the Beelzebul charge as totally inappropriate.[42] (2) Verse 27 is taken to refer to Jewish exorcisms with the meaning that if Jesus casts out demons by the power of Satan the same is true of the Pharisees' own disciples, an argument designed to turn the tables against the opponents.[43] (3) Verse 28 concludes that if Jesus casts out demons by the Spirit of God, in some sense the kingdom of God has already come.

In the Hebrew text the matter is different. Most of the wording is basically the same with two exceptions: (1) Verse 27 reads: "If I cast out demons by Beelzebub why do your sons *not* cast them out?" This is the opposite of what is implied by the Greek, namely, that Jewish exorcists are casting out demons.[44] (2) In verse 28, instead of "then the kingdom of God has come upon you," the Hebrew reads "truly the end of the [his—G.H.] kingdom has come." In regard to the Hebrew text the following points should be made. First, although the case is different with him, Jesus does not reject as inappropriate the exorcising of demons by the power of Satan. He even queries why the sons of the Pharisees do not avail themselves of this means of bringing Satan's kingdom to an end. After all, a kingdom divided against itself cannot stand, so the turning of Satan against himself is a sure way of destroying Satan. Second, the fact is Jesus casts out demons, not by Beelzebub, but by the Spirit of God. This elicits the conclusion "*truly* the end of the kingdom is come." The reading in the Hebrew Matthew of "the kingdom" instead of the Greek "the kingdom of God" appears to refer to the kingdom of Satan rather than to the kingdom of God with the meaning that if Jesus casts out demons not by Beelzebub, which

---

[42]Cf. H. B. Green, *The Gospel according to Matthew* (Oxford: Oxford University Press, 1975) 127: "If Jesus' exorcisms show him to be in league with the devil, he is using Satan's power against Satan's own agents, and this is a situation that cannot continue."

[43]Cf. David Hill, *The Gospel of Matthew* (London: Oliphants, 1972) 216: "The sons of the Pharisees (i.e., their disciples or pupils) would be the first to condemn the intransigent attitude shown to Jesus because it implied that they were in league with Satan."

[44]This reading may be related to the targumic device of converse translation. See Michael L. Klein, "Converse Translations: A Targumic Technique," *Biblica* 57 (1976): 515-37. Here, so as not to prejudice the case, it should be understood as a converse construction, and not a converse translation. For other examples see εἰ at Mark 8:12 and parallels, εἰ μή at Mark 8:14 and parallels, ὄπισθεν/ἔμπροσθεν at Matt 15:23, οὐκ (Codex B) at Matt 12:32, and the absence of οὐκ in P[66] at John 9:27. For further examples in Shem-Tob vis-à-vis the Greek see 10:17 and 19:22.

itself would bring Satan's kingdom to an end, so much the more will he
destroy Satan's kingdom by casting out demons by the Spirit of God.

There appears to be a progression of thought here. The Hebrew text
portrays Jesus as deeming appropriate the exorcising of demons by the
power of Beelzebub, even though he himself performs exorcisms by a more
effective means, the power of the Holy Spirit. The Greek, on the other hand,
rejects with revulsion the very idea of casting out demons by the power of
Beelzebub. Should we not regard the Greek's rejection of any amicable
relationship between Jesus and Satan, even to the extent of Jesus using Satan to destroy Satan, as a later reflection of an increasing disparity between
Judaism and the new Christian religion in which Christ was accused of being
possessed by demons?

The pericope on the Canaanite woman, found in Matt 15:21-38, presents the reader with two difficulties. The most notable is the harshness
with which Jesus addresses the desperate mother who pleads for mercy for
her demon-possessed daughter. Verse 26 records his answer: "It is not fair
to take the children's bread and throw it to the dogs." Beare remarks: "The
harshness of the saying of Jesus . . . still puzzles the Christian reader, who
finds it impossible to imagine Jesus addressing a distraught mother in such
terms. . . . Dare we see in all this a reflection of the reluctance with which
the primitive Church embarked upon the Gentile mission?"[45]

A second problem is the inappropriateness of Jesus' answer to his disciples who ask him to send the woman away. Jesus responds: "I was sent
only to the lost sheep of the house of Israel" (vs. 24). But this is a reason
for sending her away, not for allowing her to stay. It thus fails to explain
his actions.

In the Hebrew text the inappropriateness of this answer disappears because the question of the disciples is different. According to the Hebrew,
verse 23 reads: "Our master, why do you leave this woman alone who is
crying out after us?" The implication appears to be: Why do you not deal
with this woman by healing her daughter? After all, she is crying out for
help. Jesus' answer in verse 24 is now appropriate: "they did not send me
except to the lost sheep from the house of Israel." The meaning is that Jesus does not wish to heal this woman's daughter because she does not belong to Israel.

---

[45]Francis W. Beare, *The Earliest Records of Jesus* (Nashville: Abingdon Press, 1962)
132-33.

The first problem regarding the harshness of Jesus' response to the woman, however, remains in the Hebrew text. Some attempt has been made to soften Jesus' words by combining several verses in Matthew in such a way as to show a progression of thought. Matt 15:24, ''I was sent only to the lost sheep of the house of Israel,'' is combined with Matt 10:5-6, ''Go nowhere among the Gentiles, and enter no town of the Samaritans, but go rather to the lost sheep of the house of Israel,'' in order to show that during his earthly ministry Jesus confined his efforts to Israel alone. These passages are then contrasted with the conclusion of the Gospel, Matt 28:19-20, which reads ''Go therefore and make disciples of all nations, baptizing them in the name of the Father and of the Son and of the Holy Spirit, teaching them to observe all that I have commanded you. . . . '' Here the risen Christ is shown to extend his ministry to include all nations. This contrast suggests that Matthew's Gospel presents a kind of salvation-history schema wherein Jesus' restricted earthly ministry is expanded in the postresurrection period to include the Gentiles. Meier writes: ''This same Jesus who, during his earthly ministry, forbids the Twelve a mission among the Gentiles and Samaritans is also the Jesus who, as the exalted Son of Man, commands the Eleven to make disciples of *panta ta ethnē.*''[46]

This solution is impossible from the standpoint of the Hebrew text. Although Matt 10:5-6 and 15:24 in Hebrew correspond in meaning to the Greek, Matt 28:19-20 does not. In Hebrew these last two verses read simply: ''Go and teach them to carry out all the things that I have commanded you forever.'' No mention is made of Gentiles or all nations and no salvation-history schema is possible.

Again a progression of thought is apparent. The Hebrew Matthew portrays Jesus the Jew holding to the very end the traditional position of Israel's supremacy. The Greek Matthew, without rejecting the idea of Israel's supremacy for Jesus during his lifetime, redeems the situation by having the risen Christ extend his power to include all nations into the kingdom of God.

There are a number of such passages in the Hebrew Matthew that differ from the Greek. A listing of several other examples follows.

---

[46]Meier, *Law and History in Matthew's Gospel,* 27.

| 19:6 | Greek | What therefore God has joined together, let not man put asunder. |
| | Hebrew | Whatever the creator has joined together man is *unable* to separate. |
| 19:22 | Greek | When the young man heard this he went away sorrowful; for he had great possessions. |
| | Hebrew | It came to pass when the young man heard he went away (angry) because he did *not* have much property. |
| 19:29 | Greek | And everyone who has left houses or brothers or sisters or fathers or mothers or children or lands, for my name's sake, will receive a hundredfold, and inherit eternal life. |
| | Hebrew | Everyone who leaves his house (and his brothers), also his sisters, his father, his mother, *his wife,* and his children for my name will receive (a hundred) like them and will inherit the kingdom of heaven. |
| 26:13 | Greek | Truly, I say to you, wherever this gospel is preached in the whole world, what she has done will be told in memory of her. |
| | Hebrew | Truly, I say to you, everywhere this gospel . . . is proclaimed in all the world, that which this one has done will be said in reference to *my* memory. |
| 28:6 | Greek | Come, see the place where he lay. |
| | Hebrew | Come, therefore, and see the place where the Lord *arose.* |

## Passages Suggesting
## a Variant Hebrew Substratum for the Greek

Assuming that Shem-Tob's Hebrew Matthew represents Hebrew composition (even though corrupted by medieval Jewish scribes), it is interesting to note that some differences between the Hebrew and Greek Matthew are similar to those between the Masoretic Text of the Hebrew Bible and the Greek translation of it. The following discussion demonstrates this point.

A number of differences in the Hebrew and Greek texts of the Jewish Bible go back to different vocalizations of Hebrew words or to similar-looking Hebrew words. Here are some typical examples:

| Amos 1:6 | MT | גָּלוּת שְׁלֵמָה | entire exile |
| | LXX | αἰχμαλωσίαν τοῦ Σαλωμων | captivity of Solomon |

The Greek apparently stands for שְׁלֹמֹ'ה, a different vocalization for the same consonantal text as read by MT.

| Amos 3:15 | MT | וספו | and will come to an end |
|-----------|-----|------|-------------------------|
|           | LXX | καὶ προστεθήσονται | and will be added |

The Greek text apparently stands for ונוספו, a form close in appearance to MT, and may represent a variant Hebrew *Vorlage* which LXX translated. We, of course, do not possess a Hebrew text of Amos that reads ונוספו, so in this case the theory of a variant *Vorlage* cannot be tested. The next example, however, provides us the data needed to test the theory.

|        | MT | אביך | your father |
|--------|-----|------|-------------|
| Ex 3:6 | SamPent | אבתיך | your fathers |
|        | Acts 7:32 | τῶν πατέρων σου | your fathers |

The statement in Acts is a quotation from Exodus 3:6 that according to MT reads the singular for "father." Since Acts reads the plural one could argue that it reflects a variant Hebrew *Vorlage* which contained the plural form אבתיך. The certainty of this can be demonstrated by the fact that the Samaritan Pentateuch reads this exact form. The difference in the two Hebrew forms is, of course, an addition of only one letter.

Variations like these often form the difference between Shem-Tob's Hebrew Matthew and the Greek Matthew. An example is Matt 8:21. Here the Greek reads "*Another* (ἕτερος) of his disciples"; the Hebrew reads "*One* (אחד) of his disciples." Although we are without data to prove what word actually stood in a theoretical Hebrew substratum to the Greek, a strong case can be made for the word אחר which is often rendered by ἕτερος in LXX (cf. Gen 4:25, 8:10, and so forth). Furthermore, confusion between ר and ד is one of the most common causes for variation in ancient Hebrew documents due to the fact that these letters are so similar in appearance. It could be conjectured, then, that the difference in Shem-Tob's text and the Greek go back to different Hebrew texts which read אחד and אחר respectively.

Another example is Matt 11:5. The Greek reads "and the poor have the *good news preached* (εὐαγγελίζονται) to them." The Hebrew reads "and the poor are *acquitted* (מתפשרים)." In LXX the word εὐαγγελίζειν consistently stands for the root בשר (cf. 1 Kings 31:9, 2 Kings 1:20, 18:31, and so forth). One can argue, then, that this root stood here in a Hebrew substratum to the Greek text. If so, the appropriate form would be מתבשרים which is similar in appearance to מתפשרים. It is interesting that mss EF of Shem-Tob actually read the conjectural form, and in all prob-

ability represent a later revision designed to bring the Hebrew into correspondence with the canonical Greek/Latin text.[47]

We append here a list of several other examples.

<table>
<tr><td rowspan="4">3:11</td><td>I baptize you with water (ἐν ὕδατι) unto repentance.</td></tr>
<tr><td>I baptize you in the days of (בימי) repentance.</td></tr>
<tr><td>Greek: with water = במים</td></tr>
<tr><td>Shem-Tob: in the days of = בימי</td></tr>
</table>

|      | |
|------|-|
| 3:11 | I baptize you *with water* (ἐν ὕδατι) unto repentance. <br> I baptize you *in the days of* (בימי) repentance. <br> Greek: with water = במים <br> Shem-Tob: in the days of = בימי |
| 5:4 | Blessed are those who *mourn* (οἱ πενθοῦντες). <br> Blessed are those who *wait* (החוכים). <br> Greek: mourn = הבוכים[48] <br> Shem-Tob: wait = החוכים |
| 7:4 | *Allow* (ἄφες) me to cast the mote out. <br> *Wait* (כתר) for me . . . and I will cast the straw out. <br> Greek: allow = התר <br> Shem-Tob: wait = כתר |
| 7:6 | Do not give *that which is holy* (τὸ ἅγιον) to the dogs. <br> Do not give *holy flesh* (בשר קדש) to the dogs. <br> Greek: that which is holy = אשר קדש <br> Shem-Tob: holy flesh = בשר קדש |
| 7:11 | If you being evil *know* (οἴδατε) to give good gifts. <br> If you being evil *come* (תבואו) to give good gifts. <br> Greek: know = תבינו <br> Shem-Tob: come = תבואו[49] |
| 7:29 | For he was teaching them as one having authority <br> and not *as* (ὡς) their scribes. <br> For he was preaching to them with great power, <br> not *as the rest* (כשאר) of the sages. <br> Greek: as = כאשר <br> Shem-Tob: as the rest = כשאר |
| 8:26 | Why are you *fearful* (δειλοί)? <br> Why do you *look* (תראו)? <br> Greek: fearful = תיראו <br> Shem-Tob: look = תראו |

---

[47]Lachs conjectured that the original Hebrew read "the poor are made rich" (מתעשרים).
See Samuel Tobias Lachs, "Hebrew Elements in the Gospels and Acts," *JQR* 71 (1980):
38-39.

[48]For πενθεῖν = בכה see Gen 23:2.

[49]Mss DE read תביאו.

9:34

By the *prince* (ἄρχοντι) of demons he cast out demons.
By the *name of* (בשם) demons he cast out demons.
Greek: by the prince = בשר
Shem-Tob: by the name of = בשם

11:8

What did you go out to see?
A man clothed in *soft* (μαλακοῖς) clothing?
What did you go out to see?
. . . a man clothed in *noble* (רבים) garments?
Greek: soft = רכים
Shem-Tob: noble = רבים[50]

13:48

When it was full, they drew it up *on the shore* (ἐπὶ τὸν αἰγιαλόν).
When it is full they draw it *out* (לחוץ).
Greek: on the shore = לחוף
Shem-Tob: out = לחוץ

18:30

But going he *cast* (ἔβαλεν) him into prison.
So he *brought him* (ויוליכהו, mss ABDEFG) to prison.
Greek: cast him = וישליכהו
Shem-Tob: brought him = ויוליכהו

21:23

The chief priests *and the elders of the people*
(καὶ οἱ πρεσβύτεροι τοῦ λαοῦ).
The priests *and the rulers of the people* (וקציני העם).
Greek: and the elders of the people = וזקני העם
Shem-Tob: and the rulers of the people = וקציני העם

22:23

On that day the Sadducees *came to* (προσῆλθον) him.
On that day the Sadducees *met* (קראו) him.
Greek: came to = קרבו
Shem-Tob: met = קראו

23:37

Jerusalem, Jerusalem, who kills the prophets
and *stones* (λιθοβολοῦσα) those sent to her.
Jerusalem, who kills the prophets
and *removes* (ומסלקת) those who are sent.
Greek: stones = ומסקלת
Shem-Tob: removes = ומסלקת

24:6

See that you are not *alarmed* (θροεῖσθε).
Beware lest you become *foolish* (תהבלו).
Greek: alarmed = תבהלו
Shem-Tob: foolish = תהבלו

---

[50]See Luke 7:25: ἐνδόξῳ = רבים (?).

|        | He who has dipped his hand in the dish with me |
|--------|---|
|        | *will betray me* (με παραδώσει). |
| 26:23  | He who dips his hand with me in the dish *will sell me* (ימכרני). |
|        | Greek: will betray me = ימסרני |
|        | Shem-Tob: will sell me = ימכרני |

|        | *And they sang a hymn* (καὶ ὑμνήσαντες) |
|--------|---|
|        | and went out to the Mount of Olives. |
| 26:30  | *And they returned* (וישבו, mss ABEF) |
|        | and went out to the Mount of Olives. |
|        | Greek: and they sang a hymn = וישרו |
|        | Shem-Tob: and they returned = וישבו |

|        | Do you think that I am not able |
|--------|---|
|        | *to entreat my Father* (παρακαλέσαι τὸν πετέρα μου)? |
| 26:53  | Do you not understand that I am able |
|        | *to meet my enemies* (לפגוע באויבי)? |
|        | Greek: to entreat my father = לפגוע באבי |
|        | Shem-Tob: to meet my enemies = לפגוע באויבי |

|        | Come see the place where the Lord *lay* (ἔκειτο). |
|--------|---|
|        | Come, therefore, and see the place where the Lord *arose* (עמד). |
| 28:6   | Greek: lay = מֻעָד[51] |
|        | Shem-Tob: arose = עמד |

## Shem-Tob's Text and Synoptic Variation

Assuming that Shem-Tob's Hebrew Matthew represents Hebrew composition (even though corrupted by medieval Jewish scribes) it is interesting to note that sometimes it provides suggestions for the cause of variation in parallel passages in the Greek synoptic gospels. In these instances it resembles the Masoretic Text (MT) which explains differences in parallel passages in the Septuagint. Two examples from the Hebrew Bible will be followed by several examples from Matthew.

| 1 Kings 8:16 | שבטי ישראל ] σκήπτρῳ ᾽Ισραήλ |
|--------------|---|
| 2 Chronicles 6:5 | שבטי ישראל ] φυλῶν ᾽Ισραήλ |

In this set of synoptic passages שבט is translated ''scepter'' by LXX in 1 Kings and ''tribes'' in 2 Chronicles. The word שבט is a polysemous word which can mean either. The synoptic variation, therefore, simply reflects different renditions of the same Hebrew *Vorlage*.

---

[51]In Jer 24:1 κειμένους renders מוּעָדִים.

| 2 Samuel 10:8 | השער [ πύλης |
|---|---|
| 1 Chronicles 19:9 | העיר [ πόλεως |

This set of synoptic parallels presents an example of variation due to different though similar-appearing *Vorlagen*. It is well known that the author of Chronicles used a copy of Samuel that sometimes varied from the MT of Samuel.[52] In the present case MT of Samuel reads השער "the gate" while the copy of Samuel used by the Chronicler apparently read העיר "the city." In each instance LXX gives the appropriate translation.

Similarly, the text of Shem-Tob provides clues to some variant readings in the synoptic gospel parallels. It either reads one word with two or more meanings (often based on differing vocalizations), each of which is now reflected in Greek synoptic parallels, or one word that is visually similar to another that theoretically stood in a variant Hebrew substratum to a synoptic parallel. An example of a single Hebrew word differently vocalized may be the following.

| Matt 12:50 | μου ἀδελφός |
|---|---|
| Mark 3:35 | ἀδελφός μου |
| Luke 8:21 | ἀδελφοί μου |
| Shem-Tob | אחי |

The Greek texts of Matthew and Mark read "my brother." Luke differs by reading "my brothers." The text of Shem-Tob can be either singular or plural depending on its vocalization, whether אָחִי "my brother" or אַחַי "my brothers." It thus suggests the possibility that the synoptic variants were caused by different vocalizations of the same Hebrew word.

The next example of synoptic variation may have been caused by one Hebrew consonantal text that theoretically can reflect different Hebrew roots.

| Matt 23:31 | ὅτι υἱοί ἐστε |
|---|---|
| Luke 11:48 | ὑμεῖς δὲ οἰκοδομεῖτε |
| Shem-Tob | שבנים אתם |

These Greek phrases occupy corresponding parts in a saying against the scribes and Pharisees. According to Black (following Torrey) υἱοί ἐστε

---

[52]A number of students of Frank Cross have written on this subject. Among them see J. D. Shenkel, "A Comparative Study of the Synoptic Parallels in I Paraleipomena and I-II Reigns," *HTR* 62 (1969): 63-85; Eugene C. Ulrich, Jr., *The Qumran Text of Samuel and Josephus* (Missoula MT: Scholars Press, 1978).

("you are sons") and ὑμεῖς δὲ οἰκοδομεῖτε ("you build") may go back to Aramaic אתון בנין אתון (understanding בְּנִין and בָּנַיִן respectively).[53] A similar explanation based on a Hebrew substratum is supplied by the reading in Shem-Tob: בָּנִים אתם "you are sons." If the text is vocalized בֹּנִים אתם the translation is "you build."[54] The word בָּנִים is plural of בן "son"; בֹּ'נִים is plural masculine participle of בנה "to build."

It is noteworthy that these two roots alternate elsewhere in Hebrew literature. A Midrash (Bab. Tal. Berakot 64 a) based on Isaiah 54:13 containing an 'al tiqre[55] reading is:

> The disciples of the wise increase peace in the world, as it says, "And all your children shall be taught of the Lord, and great shall be the peace of your children." Read not "your children" (בניך) but "your builders" (בוניך).

The antiquity of this particular alternation of words is demonstrated by the appearance of both in 1QIsaᵃ 54:13.

The remaining examples consist of readings in Shem-Tob containing a word or a phrase similar in appearance to another word or phrase that theoretically could have served as a Hebrew substratum to a Greek synoptic parallel.

| | |
|---|---|
| Matt 15:17 | ἐκβάλλεται |
| Mark 7:19 | ἐκπορεύεται |
| Shem-Tob | הולך |

Matthew reads "is cast out"; Mark reads "goes out." Some Markan witnesses read variously ἐκβάλλεται, ἐξέρχεται, or χωρεῖ, but these appear to be secondary. The difference in "cast out" and "goes out" may be explained by Shem-Tob's הולך, qal participle of הלך "to go," and the similar-appearing הושלך or מושלך, hophal perfect (with *waw* consecutive

---

[53]Black, *An Aramaic Approach to the Gospels and Acts,* 12-13; C. C. Torrey, *Our Translated Gospels* (New York: Harper, 1936) 104.

[54]For the pronoun following the participle see 18:10, 23, etc.

[55]See אל תקרי in *Encyclopedia Talmudica,* ed. Meyer Berlin and Shlomo J. Zevin (Jerusalem: Talmudic Encyclopedia Institute, 1974) 2:258-60; I. L. Seeligmann, "Voraussetzungen der Midraschexegese," in *Congress Volume Copenhagen,* SVT 1 (Leiden: Brill 1953) 160; S. Talmon, "Aspects of the Textual Transmission of the Bible in the Light of Qumran Manuscripts," *Textus* 4 (1964): 125-32 (also published in *Qumran and the History of the Biblical Text,* ed. F. M. Cross and S. Talmon [Cambridge: Cambridge University Press, 1975] 256-63).

understood) or hophal participle, both from שלך "to cast." In LXX ἐκβάλλειν translates שלך in a number of instances: Lev 1:16, 14:40, Deut
29:38, Ecc. 3:6, Isa 2:20, Jer 22:28. In the last instance the hophal וְהֻשְׁלְכוּ
is rendered by ἐξεβλήθη. Similarly Shem-Tob at times reads שלך where
the Greek Matthew employs ἐκβάλλειν: 8:12[mss], 22:13, 25:30. The theoretical Hebrew variants behind these readings thus may have been:

הולך   Shem-Tob, Mark

הושלך   Matthew.

| Matt 18:6 | καταποντισθῇ |
| Mark 9:42 | βέβληται |
| Luke 17:2 | ἔρριπται |
| Shem-Tob | ויוטל |

Matthew reads "sunk"; Mark and Luke read "cast." Shem-Tob reads יוטל
(hophal imperfect of טול) "thrown" in basic agreement with Mark and
Luke against Matthew. The Matthean variant καταποντισθῇ possibly
goes back to the Hebrew root טבל "to dip/sink" which in the hophal imperfect would be יוטבל, a word differing from Shem-Tob's reading only
by the addition of one letter. The theoretical Hebrew variants behind the
synoptic readings may be diagramed as:

ויוטל   Shem-Tob, Mark, Luke

ויוטבל   Matthew.

| Matt 8:28 | ἐκ τῶν μνημείων |
| Mark 5:2 | ἐκ τῶν μνημείων |
| Luke 8:27 | ἐκ τῆς πόλεως |
| Shem-Tob | מהקברים |

In the pericope on the Gerasene/Gadarene demoniac(s) Matthew and Mark
read "from the tombs" where Luke reads "from the city." An explanation for the variation is suggested by the reading of Shem-Tob, מהקברים,
which corresponds to the Greek of Matthew. "From the city," on the other
hand, reflects מהקריה, a word that closely resembles the text of Shem-
Tob.

| Matt 20:32 | ἐφώνησεν αὐτούς |
| Mark 10:49 | φωνήσατε αὐτόν |
| Luke 18:40 | ἀχθῆναι πρὸς αὐτόν |
| Shem-Tob | ויקראם |

In the pericope on the healing of the blind man Bartimaeus (named only in
Mark) or, in Matthew in the pericope on the healing of two blind men,

Matthew reads "and Jesus having arisen *called them.*" This is supported by Mark's text: "and Jesus having arisen said *call him.*" Luke, on the other hand, says "and Jesus having arisen commanded him *to be brought to him.*" The difference in the accounts "called" versus "brought" can be traced to the Hebrew root קרא "to call" read by Shem-Tob and the similar root קרב "to bring."

| Matt 21:12 | ἐξέβαλεν |
|---|---|
| Mark 11:15 | ἐκβάλλειν |
| Luke 19:45 | ἐκβάλλειν |
| John 2:14-15 | εὗρεν . . . ἐξέβαλεν |
| Shem-Tob | וימצא |

These gospel parallels come from the pericope on cleansing the temple. The three synoptics read "cast out," Shem-Tob reads "found," while John reads both "found" and "cast out," giving the appearance of conflation. The variant forms can be explained on the basis of similar Hebrew words. Several times ἐκβάλλειν in LXX translates the hiphil of יצא: 2 Chron 23:14, 29:5, 16. In Shem-Tob the hiphil of this root frequently occurs where ἐκβάλλειν appears in the Greek text: at 7:4, 5, 22, 9:25, and so forth. Thus the variants may go back to:

וימצא "found"      Shem-Tob, John[a]
ויוצא "cast out"   Matt, Mark, Luke, John[b].[56]

| Matt 7:14 | οἱ εὑρίσκοντες αὐτήν |
|---|---|
| Luke 13:24 | ἰσχύσουσιν |
| Shem-Tob | המוצאים אותה |

In the saying on the two ways Matthew reads "few are those who *find* it." Luke reads "many will seek to enter and will not *be strong/prevail/be able.*" The primary meaning of the verb ἰσχύω is "to be strong/to prevail" and only by extension does it come to mean "to be able." Several times in LXX ἰσχύω is used to render אמץ "to be strong" (cf. Deut 31:6, 7, 23; Josh 10:25; 1 Chron 22:13). One can explain the variation in Matthew and Luke, then, on the basis of different Hebrew substrata, one of which reads the root מצא "to find," now reflected in Shem-Tob and Greek Matthew, and the other of which reads the similar-appearing root אמץ "to be strong," reflected by ἰσχύω in Luke.

---

[56] For the apocopated hiphil form, ויצא, see Gen 15:5; Deut 4:20.

These forms are confused elsewhere in the Bible. In Amos 2:16 LXX[B] reads καὶ ὁ κραταιὸς οὐ μὴ εὑρήσει τὴν καρδίαν αὐτοῦ "and the strong will not find his heart." This stands for ואמיץ לבו "and the strong of heart" in MT. The Greek apparently equals ולא ימצא אמיץ (את) לבו, a doublet based on the similarity of מצא and אמיץ. The reading in ms W, καὶ εὑρύσει τὴν καρδίαν αὐτοῦ equals ומצא (את) לבו; that in OC', καὶ εὑρήθη ἡ καρδία αὐτοῦ equals וימצא לבו; that in V, καὶ ὁ κραταιὸς εὑρήσει τὴν καρδίαν αὐτοῦ equals ומצא אמיץ (את) לבו. These variants reflect visually similar readings in Hebrew and may be diagramed as:

ומצא (את)

לבו

ואמיץ[57]

| Matt 25:24 | θερίζων ὅπου οὐκ ἔσπειρας |
| Luke 19:21 | θερίζεις ὃ οὐκ ἔσπερας |
| Shem-Tob | ותקצור אשר לא זרעת |

In the parable of the talents Matthew reads "reaping *where* (ὅπου) you did not sow." Luke reads "you reap *what* (ὃ) you did not sow." The difference in these passages may be explained by Shem-Tob's אשר which can mean "which/what" or in the form of באשר or שם . . . אשר can mean "where."

| Matt 7:11 | δόματα ἀγαθά . . . ἀγαθά |
| Luke 11:13 | δόματα ἀγαθά . . . πνεῦμα ἅγιον |
| Shem-Tob | מתנות טובות . . . רוחו הטוב |

The Greek text of Matthew reads "If, therefore, you being evil know how to give *good gifts* (δόματα ἀγαθά) to your children, how much more will your Father who is in heaven give *good things* (ἀγαθά) to those who ask him." Luke and Shem-Tob read basically the same except in the second

---

[57]The variants in Matt 7:14 and Luke 13:24 may also be explained on the basis of the Aramaic root שכח which means both "to find" and "to be able." It has been argued that this root means "to find" but not "to be able" in Palestinian Aramaic. See Black, *An Aramaic Approach to the Gospels and Acts*, 133-34. The word, however, has now been found with the meaning "to be able" in Palestinian Aramaic, i.e., in 1QapGen 21, 13, and is noted by Fitzmyer and Harrington in their collection of Palestinian Aramaic texts. See Joseph A. Fitzmyer and Daniel J. Harrington, *A Manual of Palestinian Aramaic Texts* (Rome: Biblical Institute Press, 1978) 339. For a discussion and bibliography see J. A. Fitzmyer, *The Genesis Apocryphon of Qumran Cave 1. A Commentary*, 2nd ed. (Rome: Biblical Institute Press, 1971) 150.

position Luke (according to the majority reading) has "Holy Spirit" and Shem-Tob has "his good spirit." At this point several variants occur in Luke. The Western text, represented by D it, reads "good gift" (ἀγαθὸν δόμα) followed by Θ's plural (δόματα ἀγαθά). P⁴⁵ L *pc* aur vg read "good spirit" (πνεῦμα ἀγαθόν) and Syˢ arm read "good things" ( = ἀγαθά). Two basic forms appear to be represented: (1) δόμα(τα) ἀγαθόν(-ά) (ἀγαθά being an abbreviation of this); and (2) πνεῦμα ἀγαθόν (πνεῦμα ἅγιον being a secondary modification into more common terminology). These forms may be explained by variant Hebrew phrases, one represented by Shem-Tob, the other by a misreading of the phrase, thus: Shem-Tob = רוחו הטוב and the misreading = מתן הטוב. מתן הטוב, itself an incorrect grammatical form (not unusual in Shem-Tob),[58] may have occurred by a compression of *resh* and *waw* in the Herodian script and a confusion of *heth/tav* and *waw/final-nun*. In the Herodian script when *resh* is immediately joined by the short stroke of the *waw* the result is remarkably similar in appearance to *mem*.[59] *Heth/tav* and *waw/final-nun* are naturally close in appearance and require no special explanation for their confusion.

## Other Interesting Readings in Shem-Tob's Matthew

For a conclusion to this profile of Shem-Tob's text of Matthew there is appended here a number of other interesting readings. These, contrasted with the Greek, will give further indication of the differences that exist between the two text forms.

| 3:11 | Greek | He will baptize you with the Holy Spirit and with fire. |
| | Shem-Tob | He will baptize you with *the fire of the Holy Spirit*. |
| 8:20 | Greek | And Jesus said to him: Foxes have holes and birds of the air have nests; but the Son of Man has nowhere to lay his head. |
| | Shem-Tob | Jesus answered him: the foxes have holes and the birds have nests; but the Son of Man, *the Son of the virgin*, has no place to enter his head. |

---

[58]Cf. 7:18 ועץ הטוב; 12:41 זה הדור; 13:38 ופרי הטוב; 15:15 זאת החדה.

[59]See F. M. Cross, Jr., "The Development of Jewish Scripts," in *The Bible and the Ancient Near East*, ed. G. E. Wright (Garden City NY: Doubleday, 1961). On pp. 138-39 several examples of Herodian script are presented.

| 13:23 | Shem-Tob | [At the end of the parable of the sower the following plus reading appears.] As for the hundred, this is the one purified of heart and sanctified of body. As for the sixty, this is the one separated from women. As for the thirty, this is the one sanctified in matrimony, in body, and in heart. |
|---|---|---|
| 19:12 | Greek | For there are eunuchs who have been so from birth, and there are eunuchs who have been made eunuchs by men, and there are eunuchs who have made themselves eunuchs for the sake of the kingdom of heaven. |
|  | Shem-Tob | Because there are eunuchs from their birth; *these are those who have not sinned.* There are eunuchs made by man and there are self-made eunuchs *who subdue their desire* for the sake of the kingdom of heaven; *these are those who enter into great prominence.* |
| 23:33 | Greek | You serpents, you brood of vipers, how are you to escape being sentenced to Gehenna? |
|  | Shem-Tob | Serpents, seed of vipers, how will you escape the judgment of Gehenna *if you do not turn in repentance?* |
| 24:40 | Greek | Then two men will be in the field; one is taken and one is left. |
|  | Shem-Tob | Then if there shall be two ploughing in a field, *one righteous and the other evil,* the one will be taken and the other left. |
| 24:41 | Shem-Tob | [At the end of this verse the following plus reading appears.] This is because the angels at the end of the world will remove the stumbling blocks from the world and will separate the good from the evil. |
| 25:13 | Greek [Mss] | Watch therefore, for you know neither the day nor the hour in which the Son of Man comes. |
|  | Shem-Tob | Be careful, therefore, because you do not know the day or the hour when the *bridegroom* will come. |
| 26:23 | Greek | He answered, "He who has dipped his hand in the dish with me, will betray me." |
|  | Shem-Tob | He answered them: "He who dips his hand with me in the dish will sell me." All of them were eating from one dish. Therefore, they did not recognize him; because if they had recognized him they would have destroyed him. |

# Summary and Conclusion

A remarkable Hebrew text of the Gospel of Matthew appears in the fourteenth-century Jewish polemical treatise entitled *Even Bohan,* authored by Shem-Tob ben-Isaac ben-Shaprut. An investigation into this text leads to the conclusion that an old substratum to the Hebrew Matthew in Shem-Tob is a prior composition, not a translation. The old substratum, however, has been exposed to a series of revisions so that the present text of Shem-Tob represents the original only in an impure form. A prefourteenth-century date for the old substratum is established by its unique textual links with a number of earlier anti-Christian quotations of Matthew in Hebrew. An interesting scenario emerges when these quotations are arranged in chronological sequence and followed by the corresponding readings from Shem-Tob and du Tillet. When these texts are so arranged it becomes clear that a gradual evolution in the Hebrew tradition has taken place beginning with the earliest quotations, running through Shem-Tob's Matthew, and ending with du Tillet. The evolution involves two kinds of changes: (1) stylistic modification consisting primarily of improvements in grammar and the substitution of synonymous words and phrases; and (2) revisions designed to bring the Hebrew into closer harmony with the Greek and Latin texts. A conjecture for these latter revisions is that they were for the purpose of establishing a common textual base for discussion and debate between Jews and Christians in the Middle Ages. Two of Shem-Tob's comments on the text also imply he is transcribing an already existing Hebrew Matthew for his polemical treatise, not creating a fresh translation.

Finally, the compositional nature of the old substratum to Shem-Tob's Hebrew Matthew is supported by a literary profile of the text. It is replete with literary devices characteristic of composition, such as puns, word connections, and alliteration, and with passages that reflect variant Hebrew substrata to the Greek or that give a Hebrew basis for synoptic variation. The text also is written in a kind of Hebrew one would expect for a document composed in the first century but preserved in late rabbinic manuscripts. It is basically composed in biblical Hebrew with a healthy mixture of Mishnaic Hebrew and later rabbinic vocabulary and idiom. In this respect it is analogous to the Masada Scroll of Ben Sira when compared to the late fragments of this same document from the Cairo Geniza. Ben Sira was clearly written in biblical Hebrew, influenced by Mishnaic Hebrew and contemporary Aramaic. The medieval fragments from the Cairo Geniza, like the late manuscripts of Shem-Tob's Hebrew Matthew, show numerous changes due to the corrections of medieval scribes designed to bring the text into a more contemporary form in regard to spelling, vocabulary, and other linguistic phenomena.

Once the revisionary nature of the present text of Shem-Tob's Hebrew Matthew is recognized one is able to recapture much of the old unrevised substratum by comparing the manuscripts of Shem-Tob with each other and with the Greek and Latin texts of Matthew. Those Hebrew readings that are farthest from the Greek and Latin and less polished in style should be considered as belonging to the oldest layer of the text. Those that are closest to the Greek and Latin and are polished in style, especially when portraying a later rabbinic hand, should be considered as later revisions.

Other points of interest in regard to Shem-Tob's Hebrew Matthew are:

1. The Hebrew text of Matthew in the *Even Bohan* is not to be equated with those printed in the later revisions of Münster and du Tillet. Previous neglect of Shem-Tob's text is probably due to its mistaken identity with these other texts. Although the texts of Münster and du Tillet have an occasional link with Shem-Tob they in fact represent late revisions of the Shem-Tob-type text, corrected more or less consistently in order to conform more closely to the medieval Greek and Latin texts of the First Gospel. They are the end result of an evolutionary process of the Hebrew Matthew that began in primitive times and underwent a series of stylistic and textual changes throughout the early and late medieval periods.

2. The relationship between Shem-Tob's Matthew and other textual traditions is difficult to assess due to the fact that Shem-Tob basically represents a unique text type. Nevertheless, some affinity exists between Shem-Tob, the Old Latin, the Old Syriac, and the Diatessaron of Tatian. Of considerable interest is Shem-Tob's several readings that agree with the Coptic Gospel of Thomas.

3. The evidence for a relationship between Shem-Tob's Matthew and the Hebrew gospels referred to by early Gentile Christian writers is almost totally negative. With a few minor exceptions none of the quotations from the Hebrew gospels quoted in early Gentile Christian literature corre-

sponds to Shem-Tob. It may be concluded with considerable finality that Shem-Tob's Hebrew Matthew is unrelated to the various apocryphal Hebrew gospels alluded to by early Gentile Christians. Shem-Tob's Matthew was preserved by Jews and perhaps by Jewish Christians, but not by Gentile Christians, and was only quoted sporadically by Jewish writers until it reemerged *in toto* in the *Even Bohan*.

If the conclusion to this study is correct, namely, that the old substratum to the Hebrew Matthew found in the *Even Bohan* is an original Hebrew composition, the question of the relationship of this old Hebrew substratum to the canonical Greek text is of great importance. As stated before, three basic possibilities exist: (1) The old substratum to Shem-Tob's text is a translation of the Greek Matthew. The conclusion stated above, in the judgment of this writer, rules out this possibility. (2) The Greek Matthew is a translation of the old Hebrew substratum. This likewise does not appear to be a possibility. Although the two texts are accounts of the same events basically in the same order, careful analysis of their lexical and grammatical correspondences fails to support the Greek as a translation. (3) Both the old Hebrew substratum and the Greek Matthew represent compositions in their own respective languages. This latter appears to be the best explanation of the evidence. It implies that the two texts are two editions in different languages of the same traditional material with neither being a translation of the other.

There is evidence from ancient times that this sometimes occurred. Josephus tells us that his work, *The Jewish War* (75-79 CE), was first written in Aramaic or Hebrew and then translated into Greek (Josephus, *War* 1.3). The evidence suggests, however, that Josephus did not actually translate, in a literal sense, the Semitic original but in fact virtually rewrote the whole account.[1] The Aramaic/Hebrew original apparently served only as a model for the Greek version to follow.

In regard to the Hebrew and Greek Matthew, their similarity in arrangement and wording suggests that one, as in the case with Josephus, served as a model for the other. It might appear from the linguistic and sociological background to early Christianity and the nature of some theological tendencies in Shem-Tob's Matthew that the Hebrew text served as a model for the Greek. The present writer is, in fact, inclined to that po-

---

[1]See H. St. J. Thackeray, *The Jewish War I-III,* Loeb Classical Library (Cambridge: Cambridge University Press, 1961) ix-xi.

sition. The relationship of the Greek Matthew, however, to the other two synoptics strongly suggests an interaction among them on a Greek level. This brings forth the synoptic problem with all its complexities, a problem the present study does not propose to address. In view of this, any conclusion in regard to the priority of the Hebrew Matthew vis-à-vis the Greek, or vice versa, must not be hastily drawn. Which one came first will be determined conclusively only after much further study and accumulation of evidence.

# Index
## of Names and Subjects